Lawlessness and Reform
The FBI in Transition

Tony G. Poveda
State University of New York at Plattsburgh

Brooks/Cole Publishing Company
Pacific Grove, California

Consulting Editor: *Roy R. Roberg, San Jose State University*

Brooks/Cole Publishing Company
A Division of Wadsworth, Inc.

Printed in the United States of America
10   9   8   7   6   5   4   3   2   1

Library of Congress Cataloging-in-Publication Data
Poveda, Tony G.
    Lawlessness and reform : the FBI in transition / Tony G. Poveda.
      p.   cm. — (Contemporary issues in crime and justice series)
    Includes bibliographical references.
    ISBN 0-534-12882-3
    1. United States. Federal Bureau of Investigation.   I. Title.
  II. Series
  HV8141.P65   1989
  353.0074 — dc20   89–23963
                                      CIP

Sponsoring Editor: *Cynthia C. Stormer*
Editorial Assistant: *Cathleen Sue Collins*
Production and Design Coordination: *Marlene Thom*
Manuscript Editor: *Evelyn M. Ward*
Permissions Editor: *Carline Haga*
Cover Design: *Roy R. Neuhaus*
Art Coordinator: *Lisa Torri*
Printing and Binding: *Malloy Lithographing, Inc., Ann Arbor, Michigan*

CREDITS
Thanks are due to the following authors, publishers, and publications, for permission to use the material indicated.
    Segments of Chapter 4 have been revised from "The Rise and Fall of FBI Domestic Intelligence Operations," by Tony Poveda, *Contemporary Crises: Crime, Law, and Social Policy*, 1982, Elsevier Science Publishers.
    Segments in Part Two, Scandal and Reform, from Tony Poveda (1985), "The Effects of Scandal on Organizational Deviance: The Case of the FBI," *Justice Quarterly*, 2(2): 237–258. Reprinted with permission of the Academy of Criminal Justice Sciences.
    Scattered quotations throughout Chapters 5, 6, 7, and 8 from the *New York Times.* Copyright © 1971, 1973, 1976, and 1988 by The New York Times Company. Reprinted by permission.
    Page 108, excerpts from *Theft of the Nation* by Donald R. Cressey. Copyright © 1969 by Donald R. Cressey. Reprinted by permission of Harper & Row, Publishers, Inc.

To My Mom and Dad

FOREWORD

Through the Contemporary Issues in Crime and Justice Series, students are introduced to important topics that until now have been neglected or inadequately covered and that are relevant to criminal justice, criminology, law, political science, psychology, and sociology. The authors address philosophical and theoretical issues and analyze the most recent research findings and their implications for practice. Consequently, each volume will stimulate further thinking and debate on the topics it covers, in addition to providing direction for the development and implementation of policy.

Lawlessness and Reform is an original and thought-provoking work that provides a wealth of information with respect to the rise and fall of the "old" Hoover FBI and the continual development and transformation of the "new" FBI. The author has extensively surveyed the literature, including documents obtained through the Freedom of Information Act, congressional records, and current research, to piece together a fascinating and intriguing account of personal power and control by one man of our nation's leading law enforcement organization. How did such total dominance of the FBI develop, and why was it allowed to continue for such a long period of time? And perhaps just as important, what types of policies and procedures are being followed in the contemporary, or "new," FBI? Have the excesses of the past against individual freedoms been curtailed, or have more sophisticated policies and operational strategies simply been substituted for the old ways?

Although it would be an understatement to say that much has been written on the Hoover FBI, Poveda's account adds new insights into the social, political, and organizational processes surrounding the "building" of the FBI by its director into one of the most powerful organizations in the free world. Additionally, by examining the impact of this history on the current FBI, there is much to be gleaned regarding policy development, reform, and control of the nation's leading law enforcement organization. Hopefully, this original work will be read not only by researchers and students interested in the subject matter but also by lawmakers and public policy advocates concerned with law enforcement reform and the protection of individual liberties in a democratic society.

Roy Roberg

PREFACE

Much has been written about J. Edgar Hoover and the Hoover FBI, but surprisingly little has been said of the contemporary FBI. On occasion we catch glimpses of the "new" FBI when an undercover operation, such as ABSCAM, surfaces or when an espionage case breaks, or, on the negative side, when questionable investigations are publicly disclosed, as in the CISPES case or the Library Awareness Program. This book is a critical inquiry into the FBI that emerged in the aftermath of Watergate, the so-called "new" FBI. This inquiry attempts to discern what is new and distinctive about the post-Hoover FBI. But it is intended to be more than a descriptive account. The major organizing theme is, as the title suggests, lawlessness and reform. How did lawlessness become institutionalized in the Hoover FBI? Did the FBI scandal in the wake of Watergate produce enduring substantive reforms? Have the abuses of the past been eliminated? Did the Reagan administration unleash the FBI? These are some of the questions that are addressed as this book traces the roots of lawlessness in the Hoover FBI, attempts to understand the scandal and apparent reform of the 1970s, and assesses the impact of the Reagan years on the FBI of the 1980s. The answers to these questions raise important policy considerations for control of the contemporary bureau.

Lawlessness and Reform is organized into four parts. Part One focuses on the Hoover FBI, tracing the emergence of the Hoover FBI in the context of the New Deal expansion of federal authority and examining the eventual role of domestic intelligence in the organizational power of the FBI. FBI lawlessness is understood in relation to the characteristics of the Hoover FBI as well as the broader political and social milieu of the bureau. Part Two analyzes the scandal and reform events of the 1970s and considers how the abuses of the Hoover era were finally publicly disclosed, how they led to a major scandal, and the immediate impact of these disclosures on the post-Watergate FBI. Part Three examines the "new" FBI, tracing the development of the new investigative priorities in the postscandal bureau and attempting to understand why organized crime and white-collar crime were neglected in the "old" FBI. It also considers the influence of the Reagan administration on these priorities, particularly in regard to the resurgence of domestic intelligence during the 1980s in the form of terrorism investigations. This part also examines the computerization of the FBI and the advent of proactive investigative methods, especially undercover operations. Part Four takes stock of what we have learned in the preceding chapters and arrives at an assessment of how the Hoover FBI was transformed, also raising questions about the dangers (potential and actual) of this transformed bureau.

I have tried to write a book that is readable and understandable to a broad audience. As a college text, this book is most appropriate as a supplementary reading at either the undergraduate or graduate level. Since the story of the FBI intersects with numerous disciplines, this book could be used not only in an array of criminal justice courses but also in courses in public administration, public policy, sociology of the police, organizational behavior, and history courses with a focus on contemporary U.S. history. Furthermore, I would hope that *Lawlessness and Reform* would be of interest to policymakers and practitioners who are concerned with criminal justice and with issues relating to the control of law enforcement in contemporary society.

Acknowledgments

The research, writing, and publication of a book require the efforts of many people beyond the labor of the author. In the course of the approximately nine years that this book was in the making, I have incurred a debt of gratitude to many. First and foremost, I must thank my department secretary, Rita Latour, for typing the entire manuscript; her word processing skills and great willingness to tolerate my endless corrections and revisions made this part of the manuscript preparation effortless for me. I am indebted to my colleagues at SUNY–Plattsburgh for their support and constructive comment on my work, particularly Robert Weiss, Paul Clare, and Edward Schaffer. The documents librarian at Plattsburgh, Joseph Swinyer, also went out of his way to obtain materials for me and to help me locate critical documents. I must also thank the administration at Plattsburgh State for supporting me in two sabbatical leaves during this period, which made possible much of the research and writing of this book.

I am grateful to Ann Marie Buitrago at the Center for Constitutional Rights, who generously shared with me documents pertaining to the CISPES case, which the center obtained through the Freedom of Information Act.

Various publishers have kindly allowed me to reprint revised versions of articles that I have previously published:

1. Parts of chapters 5 and 6 were drawn from my article "The Effects of Scandal on Organizational Deviance: The Case of the FBI," *Justice Quarterly* 2 (June, 1985): 237–258. Reprint permission was granted by the Academy of Criminal Justice Sciences.
2. Parts of chapter 4 were drawn from my article "The Rise and Fall of FBI Domestic Intelligence Operations," *Contemporary Crises: Crime, Law and Social Policy* 6 (1982): 103–118. Reprint permission was granted by Elsevier Science Publishers.
3. Parts of chapter 3 were drawn from my article "The FBI and Domestic Intelligence: Technocratic or Public Relations Triumph," *Crime and Delinquency* 28 (Apr., 1982): 194–211. My thanks to Sage Publications.
4. Parts of chapters 5 and 6 were drawn from my chapter "Scandal and Reform in the FBI," in *Contemporary Issues in Law Enforcement,* James J. Fyfe (ed.), Sage Research Progress Series in Criminology, vol. 20 (Oct., 1981): 82–103. Again, my thanks to Sage Publications.

Additionally, the *New York Times* granted permission to reprint material from the following six articles:

1. "FBI Reports Office Raid," the *New York Times* (Mar. 10, 1971): 7.
2. "Mitchell Issues Plea on FBI Files," the *New York Times* (Mar. 24, 1971): 24.
3. Wicker, Tom (1973) "A Battle Congress Could Win," the *New York Times* (Apr. 5): 45.
4. Crewdson, John (1973) "Burglaries Laid to Agents of FBI in 30-year Period," the *New York Times* (Aug. 24): 1.
5. Crewdson, John (1976) "FBI Chief Curbs Intelligence Arm," the *New York Times* (Aug. 12): 1.
6. "FBI Out of Control," the *New York Times* Editorial (Aug. 12, 1976): 30.

Harper and Row also granted me permission to paraphrase Cressey's "five interlocking hypotheses" from *Theft of the Nation* by Donald R. Cressey, Harper and Row Publishers, 1969.

I am further indebted to all the fine people at Brooks/Cole who made this publication experience a pleasant one—to Claire Verduin, managing editor, and Roy Roberg, series editor, for their encouragement and recognition of the merit in my work; to Cindy Stormer, for her astute management of this project; and to Marlene Thom, for guiding the manuscript through the intricacies of the production process. I also would like to acknowledge the constructive comments of the following reviewers: Lawrence Travis, University of Cincinnati; Peter Unsinger, San Jose State University; and Samuel Walker, University of Nebraska–Omaha. Their comments served to help me refine my manuscript into this final product.

Finally, I am grateful to my family for their support and patience with the long hours I have spent in the study and library while working on this project. *Lawlessness and Reform* is the product of those labors along with the efforts of the many people I have acknowledged and probably a few whom I have forgotten, but I take responsibility for the final synthesis. I hope this work will contribute to a better FBI, one that is accountable to the public and under the rule of law.

Tony G. Poveda

Contents

Part Four   Assessment of Reform   165

Lawlessness and Reform
The FBI in Transition

Chapter 1

AN OVERVIEW

At the time of his death in 1972, J. Edgar Hoover had spent a lifetime creating the most powerful law enforcement agency in the United States. The Federal Bureau of Investigation enjoyed one of the most favorable images of any federal agency. Not only had it been relatively immune from public criticism for nearly five decades, but it had also been insulated from any meaningful legislative oversight and had carved out a semiautonomous status within the U.S. Justice Department. The bureau's decade-old multimillion-dollar Washington headquarters, which overshadows the Department of Justice building, is symbolic of this Hoover legacy.

Much has been written about J. Edgar Hoover and the Hoover FBI, but surprisingly little attention has been given to the nature and character of the FBI that emerged in the post-Hoover era, the so-called new FBI. This book is a critical inquiry into the transformation of the Hoover FBI and addresses a series of questions related to this transformation: How and why did lawlessness become institutionalized in the Hoover FBI? How were the secrets of the Hoover FBI finally revealed? Have the abuses of the past been eliminated? Did the FBI scandal of the 1970s produce enduring reforms? Did the Reagan administration unleash the FBI in the 1980s? What is new and distinctive about the post-Hoover FBI? More than fifteen years since the Watergate scandal of the Nixon administration[1] and Hoover's death before that, it is time to take stock of such questions. These questions are of both scholarly and policy import and are the central focus and theme of this volume.

FBI Lawlessness

In early 1988 documents released through the Freedom of Information Act (FOIA) disclosed extensive FBI surveillance in the early 1980s of U.S. citizens and groups opposed to the Reagan administration's policies in Central America (Shenon, 1988b). The group that was originally targeted, the Committee in Solidarity with the People of El Salvador (CISPES), was investigated under allegations that it was an "agent of a foreign power" and later as an "international terrorist" organization. Although these allegations were never established and the investigation was terminated in 1985, the CISPES investigation produced 178 spin-off investigations, including nine other groups and 169 individuals (Shenon, 1988a). Although six FBI supervisors were disciplined by FBI Director William Sessions, this episode raises questions about the permanence of the reform measures of the 1970s and the character of the "new" FBI.

These recent disclosures of FBI political surveillance are reminiscent of the widespread domestic intelligence operations of the Hoover FBI where communists, communist-influenced groups, and other subversives were carefully surveilled (Halperin et al., 1976; Theoharis, 1978; Donner, 1980). It was the disclosure of abuses associated with the bureau's domestic intelligence function that ultimately led to the FBI scandal of the mid-1970s (Elliff, 1979). It was revealed, for example, that the FBI had established a series of counterintelligence programs (COINTELPRO) from 1956 through 1971 aimed at "disrupting and neutralizing" domestic political groups. Some of these operations were later found by a Justice Department committee to have exceeded the bureau's authority and to be "abhorrent in a free society" (U.S. Senate, 1976b: 3–76). It was also disclosed in the early 1970s that the FBI had conducted illegal burglaries in the past ("black bag" jobs, or surreptitious entries) and that such burglaries were "an old, established investigative technique" (U.S. Senate, 1976b: 353–371). The Hoover FBI's vendetta against Martin Luther King, Jr., has also been well documented (Halperin et al., 1976: 61–89; Garrow, 1981). It is important to emphasize that these and numerous other lawless activities of the Hoover FBI represented ongoing organizational practices, not isolated episodes or the misconduct of individual agents.

Some critics of the post-Hoover FBI fear that the revelations of bureau surveillance of dissident groups in the early 1980s signal the revival of "old" priorities, and that a Hoover-style agency will re-emerge, especially in the area of domestic intelligence. Although there is some basis for this concern, to some extent this misses the essence of the contemporary FBI, which has developed its own organizational style and distinctive investigative methods.

A crucial element of FBI reform in the aftermath of Watergate was the erosion of the FBI's internal security apparatus, which had been the postwar basis of bureau organizational power. Domestic intelligence operations were dramatically reduced in the immediate post-Watergate period (U.S. Comptroller General, 1976, 1977) and remained at a comparatively low level through fiscal year 1982. In the early 1980s, domestic intelligence did make a comeback in terms of FBI priorities and resources, as terrorism was elevated to top priority status in October 1982, along with organized crime, white-collar crime, and foreign counterintelligence (U.S. House, Appropriations Hearing, 1985: 999). In addition, the authority for conducting domestic intelligence was expanded by Reagan's executive order on intelligence in 1981 and the revision of the Levi Guidelines on domestic security in 1983. However, in spite of this resurgence in domestic intelligence in the form of terrorism investigations, the resources appropriated to the Terrorism Program are well below that expended on its other top priority programs. Moreover, the Webster FBI in the early 1980s actually had a calming influence in regard to the terrorism alarm (U.S. House, 1987b: 171), unlike the Hoover FBI in previous periods of internal security panic.

Again, this preoccupation with the ghost of J. Edgar Hoover has skewed our perceptions away from those characteristics that are distinctive about the contemporary FBI. Clearly, in the aftermath of the FBI scandal of the mid-1970s, there was a reordering of top investigative priorities with white-collar crime, organized crime, and foreign counterintelligence occupying center stage. It is important to recognize that these priorities are not only different from those of the Hoover FBI but that they also reflect a very different political and administrative context of bureau operations. In the autonomy of the Hoover FBI, bureau priorities often reflected the idiosyncratic concerns of its director. In the contemporary FBI, priorities are much more in concert with the political and ideological persuasions of the governing administration. In many ways, this integration of the FBI into the executive branch and the intelligence community represents one of the most significant changes in the post-Hoover FBI.

Finally, it is important to recognize that the FBI of the late 1970s and 1980s has been refashioned into a high-tech, proactive law enforcement agency. Undercover operations and the application of computer technology are at the "cutting edge" of the contemporary bureau. They are also at the core of the new FBI mystique. With the collapse of the G-man myth in the 1970s (Powers, 1983), this emerging high-tech mystique provides a new basis for FBI organizational power and legitimacy. Although the computerization of the FBI certainly enhances administrative efficiency and aids investigations in a variety of ways, and undercover operations surely enable the bureau to investigate previously undetectable crimes, these developments are not without their problems. The proactive targeting of potential offenders and a national databank of computerized criminal history records (Burnham, 1983, 1984; Laudon, 1986) are among those practices that pose potential dangers to civil liberties. These high-tech, proactive developments raise important issues relating to privacy, entrapment, discriminatory law enforcement, and equal protection of the law. But perhaps most important, they raise questions about the control of law enforcement itself and what system of external checks and balances should be in place in order to ensure a fair balance of crime control and due process values (Packer, 1968). FBI reform needs to be concerned with these issues and questions as well as with the older ones relating to eliminating the lawless aspects of the Hoover FBI, most notably the widespread political surveillance of U.S. citizens.

In this introductory chapter, I will provide an overview of the events that led to the FBI scandal of the 1970s, the reform of the Hoover FBI, and the emergence of a "new" FBI. I will also sketch the theoretical framework that will provide a basis for understanding these events.

The Scandal

Where did the cracks first begin to appear on the Hoover FBI armor? Although there had been criticisms of the bureau before 1970, they were few and far between. Most notably, Martin Luther King, Jr., had criticized the FBI in the early 1960s for its failure to protect civil rights workers in the South (Garrow, 1981; O'Reilly, 1988). On occasion, a former agent would question Hoover's authoritarian rule of the bureau. By the late 1960s, however, there was a growing chorus of politicians calling for Hoover's resignation (Keller, 1989: 134–150). Yet none of this did much to tarnish the FBI's image.

It took a series of massive public disclosures during the 1970s coupled with the broader government scandal of Watergate to unleash the forces of reform. Among the significant events in this process of unveiling the secrets of the FBI's past were the following:

1. *Citizens break into the FBI's Media office in March 1971.* A group calling itself the Citizens' Commission to Investigate the FBI broke into an FBI office in Media, Pennsylvania, just outside of Philadelphia. This was one of the most serious breaches of FBI security in its history. Raw FBI files were stolen and disseminated to the press. They revealed that the FBI was involved in the political surveillance of U.S. citizens to a much greater extent than had been previously suspected (Perkus, 1975).

Perhaps more significant, documents obtained in the Media break-in opened an FBI Pandora's box, including the use of the Freedom of Information Act to secure additional documents, as NBC correspondent Carl Stern did with regard to COINTELPRO. Some of the documents obtained in the break-in had made reference to COINTELPRO, the FBI's previously secret counterintelligence program. The Media break-in also gave rise to civil suits as those targeted for political surveillance became aware of their victimization, such as in the *Kenyatta* v. *Hoover* and *Socialist Workers Party (SWP)* v. *Attorney General* cases, among others. These civil suits in turn produced further disclosures.

2. *President Nixon discloses FBI burglaries in August 1973.* At a San Clemente news conference, in response to a question about the legality of the 1971 break-in of Daniel Ellsberg's psychiatrist's office, President Nixon revealed that FBI burglaries had taken place "on a very large scale" during the administrations of Presidents Kennedy and Johnson. Nixon's statement was confirmed on the following day by the Justice Department, which indicated that such burglaries had been "an old, established investigative technique" for more than thirty years but

had been discontinued in 1966. The Department of Justice sources also volunteered that these "illegal and unlawful" burglaries by FBI agents had never been approved by any authority higher than Hoover (Crewdson, 1973a: 1).

3. *Attorney General Levi reveals the scope of Hoover's secret files in February 1975.* Although it had long been rumored and suspected that Hoover maintained secret files on public officials and others who simply opposed him, Attorney General Levi's testimony before a U.S. House subcommittee represented the first actual documentation of the existence of such files. Hoover's "personal and confidential" files were destroyed shortly after his death; however, most of the "official and confidential" files survived. Levi's testimony pertained only to some of those secret files that had survived (U.S. House, 1975a: 7–13).

4. *Suit of Socialist Workers Party (SWP) discloses in July 1976 that FBI burglaries had occurred more recently than 1966.* The Socialist Workers Party suit, initiated in 1973, revealed that FBI burglaries had continued after 1966, the year the Department of Justice claimed this practice had ended. It was also disclosed that information about these later burglaries had been withheld from FBI Director Kelley (Crewdson, 1976a: 1). These disclosures resulted in the prosecution of the top FBI officials who had authorized them. W. Mark Felt, the FBI's number two man during the early 1970s, and Edward Miller, head of FBI domestic intelligence, were ultimately convicted for approving the break-ins (*San Francisco Chronicle,* Nov. 7, 1980: 1), but they were pardoned by President Reagan in 1981.

Clearly, these events are only part of the story that put the FBI on the road to scandal. Even such a partial chronology would be remiss, however, if it did not mention the role of the U.S. Senate and House Select Committees on Intelligence (the Church and Pike committees, respectively) in bringing public attention to the lawlessness of the intelligence agencies, including the FBI. These activities were detailed in the committee hearings (1975) and final reports (1976).

For the most part, the public disclosures that plagued the FBI in the early 1970s remained isolated episodes that involved allegations of individual misconduct, some of which focused on the deceased Hoover, others of which centered on Acting Director Patrick Gray. Gray eventually withdrew his nomination for FBI director and resigned as acting director in April 1973, when it was revealed in his confirmation hearings that he had destroyed documents pertinent to the Watergate investigation. This focus on individual misconduct and the political misuse of the FBI actually contained, at least temporarily, the broader scandal that could have developed. In fact, writing in the *New York Times* at this time, Tom Wicker (1973: 45) complained of the missed opportunities by the Senate in the Gray confirmation hearings in asking basic questions about the role of the FBI and in conducting a broader investigation of the FBI.

It was left unwittingly to President Nixon's San Clemente disclosure of FBI burglaries as part of his Watergate defense to, in effect, broaden the scandal. The significance of Nixon's statement is that the organizational nature of FBI deviance had been revealed. The FBI itself had been labeled a deviant organization. This was perhaps a subtle shift in the scandal process, but it marked the turning point from a "little scandal," involving the misconduct of individuals, to a "big scandal," where lawlessness is linked to institutionalized organizational practices

(Sherman, 1978: 66). There was a growing perception that the FBI was out of control, as acknowledged in a *New York Times* editorial at the height of the scandal (Aug. 12, 1976: 30).

Reform and the "New" FBI

The three-year period from 1974 through 1976 constitutes the period of the FBI big scandal. It was the consequence of an avalanche of disclosures about FBI misconduct that culminated in the Church and Pike committees' hearings and final reports. Most of the measures to reform the Hoover FBI were taken at this time. The reform of FBI domestic intelligence was at the top of the agenda. These operations, which were at the center of many of the Hoover-era abuses, were dramatically reduced. FBI Director Kelley reorganized the intelligence division, Attorney General Levi issued guidelines on domestic security investigations, permanent intelligence committees were established to provide better legislative oversight, and there was an expectation that future hearings would produce a legislative charter for the FBI (Elliff, 1979).

After 1976 there were no new major disclosures of FBI lawlessness. The problems of past disclosures remained, however, in the form of disciplining agents and officials who were still caught up in cases involving past abuses. By the late 1970s the media had begun to recognize the existence of a "new" FBI. All major news magazines carried feature stories on the "new" bureau. *U.S. News and World Report* (Jan. 29, 1979) interviewed Director Webster on the FBI's new course. *Newsweek* (Feb. 25, 1980) noted how a "new FBI is watching." *Time* (Feb. 18, 1980) had a cover story on Operation ABSCAM. It was the publicity surrounding the FBI's undercover Operation ABSCAM, which resulted in the conviction of several congressmen and public officials, that most dramatically brought public attention to this "new" FBI. Most emphasized in the media coverage were the bureau's proactive sting methods and its new investigative priorities: white-collar crime and public corruption, organized crime, and foreign counterintelligence.

Although we catch a glimpse of the "new" FBI from media coverage of events, such as ABSCAM or the CISPES investigation, or the occasional congressional hearing, there is surprisingly little systematic study of the contemporary FBI. To understand the transformation of the Hoover FBI into the "new" FBI of the 1980s, we must have an appreciation for the organizational dynamics of the Hoover FBI, the scandal and reforms of the 1970s, and a better sense of what is new and distinctive about the post-Hoover FBI. That remains the task of this inquiry.

Toward a Theory of FBI Organizational Behavior

It has been commonplace to portray the FBI, especially the Hoover FBI, as a direct outgrowth of the personality of the bureau's director. For example, two recent biographies of J. Edgar Hoover (Powers, 1987; Theoharis and Cox, 1988), although they differ in their treatment of Hoover and the emphasis they give to the underlying motivations of the former director, do seem to be in agreement that Hoover constructed the FBI in his own image and that he was a master bureaucrat. Although there is no denying the uniqueness and idiosyncracies of Hoover and his impact on the bureau after forty-eight years as its director, this traditional emphasis has the disadvantage of obscuring the broader historical and social forces that have also shaped the bureau. In this sense, the Hoover FBI is not simply an aberration of Hoover's character but is also the product of specific historical eras as well as wider trends and social forces affecting the United States in the FBI's formative years. This is equally true of changes in the contemporary bureau. The recognition of how FBI organizational behavior intersects with history and social structure is the basis for the theoretical approach of this book and is crucial to addressing the questions that we have delineated for this inquiry.

First, it is important to recognize the link between the growth in the powers of the Hoover FBI and the New Deal expansion of federal authority in the 1930s (Walker, 1977: 151ff.; O'Reilly, 1982; Powers, 1983: 33ff.). The Roosevelt administration played a critical role in the creation of the "war on crime" and the notorious gangsters of the Depression era as well as the G-men who would gain fame from doing battle with them. Although Hoover, the shrewd bureaucrat, certainly exploited the public relations potential created by this 1930s war on crime, it was the Roosevelt administration and its New Deal policies that provided the wider context for this expansion of federal authority, initially in the economic realm but later in the law enforcement arena as well.

It is also important to acknowledge the influence of the police professionalism movement, only in its early stages in the 1920s, on the evolution of the Hoover FBI (Walker, 1977: 70; Kelling and Moore, 1988: 4–5). The autonomy that the Hoover FBI ultimately achieved within the Justice Department and the executive branch was a direct outgrowth of the emerging professionalization of the police. The advocates of police professionalism had sought to establish the independence of the police from political influence. The police of this reform era would be highly efficient, using impersonal management techniques, and authority would be highly centralized within the department, with a strong police executive to create a buffer from partisan politics. It was also important to the professionalism movement that the standards and procedures in recruitment be rationalized so as to raise the quality of police personnel (Walker, 1977: 53–54, 67–68). This police reform program, as we shall see, was virtually identical to Hoover's agenda for reshaping the bureau of the 1920s and 1930s.

The German sociologist and one of the foremost scholars of bureaucracy Max Weber provides a still wider intellectual orientation for grasping the evolution of the FBI as an organization. For Weber, the rationalization of modern life was one of the distinctive features of contemporary societies. *Rationalization* refers to the increased planning, efficiency, coordination, and application of scientific technology and the corresponding decline in the magical elements of thought in modern life; Weber calls this process "the disenchantment of the world" (Gerth and Mills, 1958: 51–52, 139). The primary vehicle for rationalizing modern life was the growth of bureaucracy, which became the dominant mode for achieving administrative efficiency and coordination in the twentieth century. In addition, Weber saw the most serious challenge facing modern societies in the need to control expanding state bureaucracies. The shift in power from "political master" to bureaucracy rested with the increased expertise and secrecy that has become lodged in the bureaucracies of government (Gerth and Mills, 1958: 232ff.; Scott, 1987: 306–307). The Hoover FBI's expertise in domestic intelligence as well as the secrecy of its operations were anticipated in Weber's writings.

These converging social, political, and historical forces provide the broad contours for the formation and development of the FBI. What we still need to incorporate in our theoretical framework, however, is the organizational dynamics that will capture the vicissitudes of lawlessness and reform in different historical eras. For this perspective, we shall draw on organizational theory to understand the interplay between a focal organization, the FBI, and its environment (Scott, 1987: 120). The concept of *organizational pathology* is of particular relevance. Moreover, two types of pathologies are of special concern in our analysis: the problem of overconformity and the problem of unresponsiveness (Scott, 1987: 301–315). These pathologies address ways in which the power of organizations can be misused or displaced. In the case of overconformity, the organizational participants become so preoccupied with rules and regulations that the very procedures designed to increase efficiency in actuality produce inefficiency. The rules that were set up to be simply means to ends become the ends in themselves, and the participants become engaged in what Merton (1938) called ritualism. The second pathology relates to how all organizations must provide benefits to some external publics for their continued existence and how those benefits may get skewed in certain directions, responding more to special interests than to the public welfare (Scott, 1987: 306–312). These organizational pathologies become more manifest in some historical eras than others, and therein lies the connection to our lawlessness and reform theme. We shall develop this idea in a moment, but we must first introduce some additional concepts.

About twenty years ago Herbert Packer distinguished between the crime control and due process models of criminal justice. The *crime control model* emphasizes the apprehension, conviction, and punishment of criminals as the most important function of the criminal justice system. The *due process model* emphasizes the constitutional procedures, rights of defendants, and the adversary nature of the justice system as its central features (Packer, 1968: 153–165). Although there is some common ground in these two models, there is a basic tension that exists between crime control and due process. This tension reflects the basic dilemma of the role of the police in a democratic society: how to maximize police efficiency in catching criminals and enforcing the law and yet stay within the rule of law (Skolnick, 1966). This dilemma is played out in different historical periods, with the crime control model sometimes asserting its dominance—as in the 1930s, what Walker (1977) called the "law and order" decade—and at other times due process values becoming more prominent—as in the 1960s with the Warren Court due process revolution in criminal procedure. The decade of the 1980s, with the expansion of prison populations, the concern with closing the loopholes in the justice system, and the persistent crime problem dramatized by the "war on drugs," must be characterized as an era in which crime control values are resurgent and due process values are in retreat.

More specifically, we are concerned with explaining the rise and fall of FBI lawlessness relative to its domestic intelligence activities, linking this lawlessness to the ups and downs in crime control and due process values, and showing how these trends become manifest in organizational pathologies. Later chapters will elaborate, but suffice it for now to simply assert that FBI lawlessness with respect to its domestic intelligence operations was most extensive in three historical eras: the Red Scare[2] that culminated in the Palmer raids of 1919–1920 (Murray, 1955; Preston, 1963); the McCarthy era[3] of the early 1950s, when communists were believed to have infiltrated major social institutions (Theoharis, 1971); and the law-and-order crisis of the 1960s, in which social order was disrupted by black militants, student riots, and antiwar demonstrations (Skolnick, 1969). Each of these eras may be characterized as a period of alarm, indeed one of public hysteria, over the threat to law and order posed by radicals, aliens, and dissenters in the United States. In each of these periods of alarm, crime control values were clearly dominant. Due process values were subordinated to the internal security concerns of the historical moment. In the climate of each of these historical eras, there were enormous environmental pressures on the bureau to deal with the internal security threat. Indeed, the bureau itself played a role in reinforcing the sense of crisis and alarm (Murray, 1955: 194; Belknap, 1977a: 152; Halperin et al., 1976: 103ff.; Sullivan with Brown, 1979a: 88ff.). The combination of the external conditions of public alarm and crime control in each of these periods along with the internal organizational conditions of autonomy, centralization of the intelligence function, and executive secrecy all facilitated the potential for organizational pathologies. Wilensky (1967: 113) has observed how these conditions may even contribute to intelligence failures because they distort the information received externally by the organization as well as affect the internal flow of information.

In the circumstances described, organizational participants are so focused on a limited set of goals—in the case of the bureau, the pursuit of radicals, aliens, or dissenters—that other goals, particularly those relating to due process and the rule of law, are decidedly subordinated to them. The situation is analogous to a corporation in which there are strong pressures to produce a product according to certain specifications and deadlines. These corporate pressures produce a kind of "cost-benefit morality" in which other considerations, such as safety, are downplayed. Otherwise "normal" organizational conditions, such as the limited information and narrow responsibilities of individual participants, may in fact facilitate such an outcome: the manufacture of an unsafe product. This appeared to be the case with the Ford Pinto, with its faulty gas tank location, and the Chevrolet Corvair, with its numerous design flaws (Scott, 1987: 317; Ermann and Lundman, 1987: 8–11; Wright, 1979: 63–68).

Although FBI lawlessness, in terms of its domestic intelligence operations, may have its origins during periods of alarm over internal security, such activities, once institutionalized in ongoing organizational practices, may take on a life of their own. Since such practices are normally secret, termination of questionable activities is not likely unless there is public disclosure, and even then termination or reform may not occur, depending on how these activities are presented and defined to the public—what Ermann and Lundman (1987: 13–27) have called "the organizational deviance-defining process."

In this overview, I have attempted to sketch this book's theoretical framework, which will be elaborated in the following chapters, as we struggle to grasp the changes that the post-Hoover FBI has experienced. It is important again to stress that FBI organizational behavior is understandable in terms of social and historical patterns and regularities and not simply as an aberration of J. Edgar Hoover's, or some other director's, personality.

A Note on Methodology

Much of what the FBI does is not easily observable. It is only in recent years that information about FBI operations has begun to reach the public domain. For the first time, scholars and the public alike are in a position to assess the FBI's carefully constructed and maintained public image. The Pike and Church committees' hearings in 1975 and subsequent congressional oversight and charter legislation hearings have produced an abundance of information and documents for the public record. The General Accounting Office, as the investigative arm of Congress, conducted its own review of FBI domestic intelligence. In addition, Freedom of Information Act requests by scholars, journalists, and others, along with numerous court cases, have been instrumental in freeing documents highly revealing of FBI activities. The writings of former agents and bureau officials have also shed light on internal bureau operations. These sources have informed much of this book.

In the early 1980s Director Webster testified before Congress on the adverse effect of the Freedom of Information Act on FBI operations (U.S. House, 1985: 814, 836ff.). In particular, he was concerned about the use of the FOIA by criminals, especially organized crime figures, to identify informants and sources—some 15 percent of FBI FOIA requests are from criminals in prison. To the extent that use of the FOIA by criminals is successful, this could have a deleterious effect on criminal informant cooperation with the bureau because of fear of disclosure.

If Director Webster is correct and criminals are this astute in the use of the FOIA, surely scholars, who are trained observers and skilled in the use of documents, can be no less adept at using files obtained through the FOIA and other government documents for their research purposes. The wealth of information to be found in such materials might well suprise the novice. Although the reams and reams of government documents might appear intimidating, the researcher must have a guiding theoretical framework to assist in the gathering and sorting of all these undigested data. The careful piecing together of information from disparate sources can sometimes lead to the discovery that there are patterns and regularities in the real world after all. I trust that what I have found in this process of discovery has some correspondence to the world "out there."

NOTES

1. The Watergate scandal encompasses a variety of illegal activities carried out by officials of the Nixon administration, including the break-in of the Democratic National Committee headquarters at the Watergate office building in Washington, D.C., in June 1972. Although the break-in was initially characterized by Nixon's press secretary as a "third-rate burglary attempt," the burglars were linked to the Committee to Re-elect the President (CRP). The second element of the

scandal involved the cover-up by top Nixon White House officials to dissociate the administration from the break-in. The cover-up scheme included efforts to interfere with the FBI investigation of Watergate.

Watergate in its broader sense also relates to a number of covert, and sometimes illegal, activities carried out by a secret unit in the Nixon White House called "the plumbers." These questionable operations were typically justified in the name of national security. The break-in of Daniel Ellsberg's psychiatrist's office by the plumbers was one of these illegal activities. Ellsberg had been targeted because he had leaked the secret "Pentagon Papers" to the *New York Times* in 1971.

In 1973, a select Senate Watergate Committee, headed by Sam Ervin, was established to hold hearings. The following year the House Judiciary Committee conducted the impeachment proceedings that eventually forced President Nixon's resignation in August 1974.

In addition to the conviction of the five Watergate burglars, a number of top Nixon administration officials were convicted of various crimes spawned from Watergate, including John Ehrlichman, domestic affairs adviser; H. R. Haldeman, White House Chief of Staff; John Mitchell, former Attorney General and chair of CRP; and John Dean, White House Counsel (*Congressional Quarterly,* 1975).

2. In the aftermath of the Bolshevik Revolution in Russia in 1917, a growing sense of alarm developed in the United States that a similar revolution might occur here. This alarm, or Red Scare, reached a climax in 1919–1920. There were a number of events in 1919 that some believed to be a forerunner of revolution in the United States. There was considerable labor unrest: there was a general strike in Seattle, a police strike in Boston, and a nationwide steel and coal workers' strike; bomb explosions occurred in eight cities, including at the home of Attorney General A. Mitchell Palmer; and riots from May Day celebrations broke out in several cities. The press and some public officials, like Palmer, seized on these events as evidence for the Red threat and the impending revolution. The culmination of the Red Scare was a series of raids in 1919 and 1920 (Palmer raids) conducted under the auspices of the Justice Department in which several thousand radicals and aliens were rounded up in thirty-three major cities (Murray, 1955).

3. The McCarthy era refers to the alarm over communism that developed in the United States in the aftermath of World War II, which reached its height in the early 1950s. Initially, the communist concern was viewed in terms of the foreign policy threat posed by the Soviet occupation of Eastern Europe after the war. In the late 1940s, the focus shifted to internal security matters, with particular concern over the issue of communists in government. The era takes its name from Senator Joseph McCarthy of Wisconsin, who on numerous occasions claimed to have in his possession the names of communists in the State Department. As chair of a congressional subcommittee, McCarthy used its hearings as a forum for sounding the internal security alarm and raising the loyalty issue. His popularity peaked in 1953, and he was eventually censured by the Senate in 1954 as his demagoguery was finally exposed (Theoharis, 1971; Belknap, 1977a).

Part One
THE HOOVER FBI

Chapter 2

THE MAKING OF THE HOOVER FBI

Mr. J. Edgar Hoover and the FBI had developed into an extraordinarily independent agency within our Government. It is hard to exaggerate that. Mr. Hoover, in effect, took orders only from himself, sometimes from an Attorney General, usually a President, and that was it. He had created a kind of kingdom of which he was very jealous.

    Mr. Hoover built a position which I think is almost unparalleled in the administrative branch of our Government, a combination of professional performance on the job, some element of fear, very astute relations with Congress, and very effective public relations (U.S. Senate, 1976b: 469–470).

In his above testimony before the Senate Foreign Relations Committee in 1974, former Secretary of State Dean Rusk's observations on the Hoover FBI were neither particularly surprising nor even revealing to those familiar with bureau operations in the early 1970s. What is perhaps more mysterious and not so clearly understood is how J. Edgar Hoover and the FBI achieved this unique accumulation of bureaucratic power over several decades.

The main task of Part One of this book is to develop an understanding of the organizational dynamics of the Hoover FBI, an appreciation for its unique source of bureaucratic power in its domestic intelligence operations, as well as an insight into the broader social and historical forces that shaped the bureau in its formative years. The next three chapters will serve as a useful baseline for discerning the changes that occurred in the post-Hoover FBI, the central concern of the remainder of the book.

This chapter focuses on the roots of the Hoover FBI and considers how the FBI emerged from a relatively obscure federal agency in the 1920s to a superpolice agency in the 1930s, when the bureau's image became that of G-men doing battle with the crime menaces of the Depression era—kidnappers, gangsters, and bank robbers. The transformation of the bureau during the New Deal provides insight into patterns and characteristics that would be elaborated in subsequent decades. This is the formative period of the Hoover FBI, which would ultimately reach an unparalleled place both in the federal government as well as in the public consciousness before Hoover's death in 1972. To appreciate the events of the post-Watergate period, when Hoover's bureaucratic edifice began unravelling, we must first understand the nature and character of the FBI Hoover had taken forty-eight years to build.

The Beginnings

When J. Edgar Hoover was first appointed director of the Bureau of Investigation[1] in 1924, the bureau was a scandal-ridden agency. Its chief had been ousted, and the attorney general of the United States had been forced to resign. Attorney General Harry Daugherty had resigned in the wake of charges that his Justice Department had failed to prosecute war contractors' frauds against the government, and bureau Chief William Burns, also head of the famous private detective agency, was removed for using his official position to aid his company in a campaign against labor unions (Lowenthal, 1950; Belknap, 1977b). Burns also admitted before a congressional subcommittee that he had sent three agents to Montana to build a case against Senator Wheeler, who had just begun his inquiry into Daugherty and the Justice Department (Cook, 1958: 238). Even prior to this scandal in the Harding/Coolidge administration, the bureau had been subject to criticism of its conduct in the dragnet raids of draft dodgers during World War I[2] and the subsequent roundup of radicals and aliens in 1919 and 1920 known as the Palmer raids. It took, however, the broader governmental scandal of Teapot Dome[3] before the seamy side of Justice Department and bureau activities were brought under serious public scrutiny.

So the bureau that Hoover inherited had fallen into disrepute in its early years.[4] It should be pointed out, however, that Hoover was not blameless in regard to these early activities. Hoover was head of the General Intelligence Division (GID), which was responsible for coordinating the Palmer raids, and he was assistant to the chief under Burns. During the ensuing scandal, Hoover's career barely escaped disaster. His survival of the fallout from the Palmer Raids and Teapot Dome scandal was itself a considerable bureaucratic and political achievement. From this brush with scandal, Hoover learned many lessons that would influence his stewardship of the bureau. He learned that his own position was dependent not just on the political support of his superiors but also on his own independent power base in Congress and with the public (Powers, 1987: 112). He emerged from these early years in the Justice Department with keen political skills, including a knowledge of the importance of building alliances, an appreciation for strong organization and discipline in public administration, and a driving personal ambition, which was now tempered by the caution of potential failure (Powers, 1987: 128–129). Nevertheless, in spite of Hoover's role in the Red Scare, the newly appointed and reform-minded Attorney General Harlan Fiske Stone was sufficiently impressed with Hoover's performance as acting director that he made his appointment permanent on December 10, 1924 (Belknap, 1977b).

In the first decade of Hoover's administration of the bureau, the agency maintained a low profile. Stone's 1924 reforms had eliminated some of the more notorious and controversial activities. The GID was abolished, and the bureau was told to limit its investigations to violations of federal law.[5] Hoover was further instructed to remove incompetent agents and eliminate the practice of politically appointing agents (Whitehead, 1956; Cook, 1958; U.S. Senate, 1976b). During this period, the bureau's authority was relatively narrow, being limited to violations of federal law not assigned to other government investigative agencies. The bureau's constancy in its responsibilities is reflected in its expenditures for this period, which reflected little growth between 1923 and 1932.[6] The low profile of the early Hoover bureau is underscored by a 1928 incident in which Hoover was mistaken by one member of a congressional subcommittee as the head of the Secret Service (Alexander, 1937). Such a mistake would not have been made just ten years later.

During the 1924–1933 period, Hoover quietly went about reforming the bureau along some of the lines laid out by Stone and also took direction from the program of the emerging police professionalism movement (Walker, 1977: 70; Kelling and Moore, 1988: 4–5). Hoover was an advocate of a police professionalism that would insulate police work from political influence and favored strong police executive leadership to provide a buffer from partisan politics. Hoover also advocated the upgrading of police training and qualifications along with the elimination of politically appointed agents and officers. The bureau, of course, was to become a model of professionalism for all of law enforcement.

Related to Hoover's advocacy of professionalism was his emphasis on scientific law enforcement. His preoccupation with fingerprints as a method of identification became well known. Ironically, before 1923 the Bureau of Criminal Identification was administered at Leavenworth Prison and operated with the aid of convict labor (Lowenthal, 1950). It was in that year that the approximately one million fingerprint files were transferred to Washington, D.C. In 1930 Hoover achieved bureaucratic control over all federal files, and he subsequently campaigned to expand the number of files, both criminal and civil (Walker, 1980). Also prominent among his accomplishments during this early period was the establishment of the bureau's crime laboratory in 1932.

Such was the state of the bureau after Hoover's first decade of administration. While professionalizing the scandal-ridden agency, he had kept a low profile; in fact, other federal investigative agencies were better known to the public than the bureau. Furthermore, its investigative authority had remained both narrow and constant; there were fewer than 300 bureau agents in 1933. Hoover had transformed the bureau from an old-style detective agency to a nonpolitical scientific law enforcement organization that was firmly under his control.

The New Deal Expansion of Federal Authority

The advent of the Depression and the New Deal would change the obscurity of both Hoover and his bureau. Roosevelt's New Deal was a major ideological shift in response to the economic crisis posed by the Depression of the 1930s, representing a reversal of the principle that the best government is that which governs least. President Herbert Hoover had been reluctant to use federal resources as a response to social and economic problems. In the Roosevelt administration, the federal government assumed "the role of a beneficent friend, a mighty arm against insecurity and an employer to serve" (Wecter, 1971: 81). Roosevelt's predecessor, Herbert Hoover, had clung to the traditional faith that local agencies and private efforts would lead to recovery along with the strategy of bolstering financial institutions rather than direct aid to individuals (Wecter, 1971). Three years into the Depression, with mass unemployment, riots, hunger, marches, and even starvation, the traditional faith in local relief and recovery had been severely tested. The New Deal offered an alternative platform for economic recovery, which entailed the unprecedented assertion of the national government into social and economic affairs.

It is in this context that we must understand the making of the Hoover FBI. While the economic crisis was the central concern of the Roosevelt administration, the crime wave of the 1930s began to take on a symbolic importance during this era of breakdown and crisis. The solution to the crime problem of the 1930s was along the same ideological lines as Roosevelt's New Deal for economic recovery and relief: the expansion of federal authority and the mobilization of grass-roots support for federal programs.

The 73rd Congress added more provisions to the federal criminal code than all of the previous congresses (Seagle, 1934). Practically all of Roosevelt's and Attorney General Cummings's Twelve-Point Crime Program was enacted into law in 1934, extending the list of crimes that became federalized—bank robbery, interstate flight of felons, murder or assault of federal officials, kidnapping, racketeering, extortion, obscenity, and so on. Congress offered three kinds of justifications and arguments for this expansion of federal authority: (1) Prohibition had developed criminal gangs that operated on an interstate basis; (2) the automobile and airplane had given criminals mobility and the advantage over local police; and (3) local law enforcement and the administration of justice were incompetent, corrupt, or both (Mayer, 1935: 144).

This expansion of federal authority was not without its critics. William Seagle, writing in *Harpers Magazine* in 1934, states the opposition arguments: "In fact the whole program of federal crime control is reactionary. The circumstances of its origins, the character of its sponsorship, its support in the remote reactionary parts of the country, the haste with which it was adopted . . . all are grounds of suspicion and alarm" (Seagle, 1934: 760).

He also points to the "sorry record" of the Justice Department in the Palmer era and of Treasury agents during the Prohibition era. Seagle traces Roosevelt's interest in crime control to the formation in 1925 of the National Crime Commission, a private group of prominent businessmen and statesmen interested in combating crime. Roosevelt was one of the members of the executive committee of this commission, which advocated "get tough" measures in dealing with crime. Among its accomplishments were the Baumes Law in New York, which required a mandatory life sentence for four felony convictions (Seagle, 1934: 753).

A critical condition for the credibility of New Deal crime policy was the demonstration to the public that there was a crime wave and that there were dangerous criminals worthy of attention by the federal government. As we shall see, the Roosevelt Justice Department assumed a leadership role in the anticrime crusade of the 1930s. We shall consider next the anticrime hysteria of the 1930s and its relevance for the Hoover FBI.

Public Enemies and G-Men

The Hoover bureau's rise from its relative obscurity during the 1924–1933 period is linked to this expansion of federal authority in the New Deal era. It is also tied to the manufacture of a crime wave in the 1930s and the personification of the crime menace in the form of public enemies—gangsters such as Al Capone and John Dillinger. Furthermore, the transformation of bureau agents into G-men heroes in this war on crime is rooted in the economic crisis of the Depression.

Mayer (1935: 145) argues that the underlying dynamic in the creation of the G-man myth was four years of national panic and the "public's desperate need for a bogeyman." He further argues that just as the Jews had become scapegoats in Europe, public enemies had become their symbolic equivalents in Depression-era America. Similarly, Powers (1983: 3) notes, "The G-Man was the country's solution to a crisis in American popular culture produced by the Depression, aided and abetted by Prohibition. The public enemy . . . was the symbol of this crisis."

The task of New Deal programs, including its crime policy, was not only to provide substantive solutions to particular problems but also to restore the national confidence and solidarity that had been lost in the early Depression years. The gangsters of the 1930s provided a unique symbolic focus for the Depression, pitting, as they did, the forces of the underworld against those of organized society and provided the cultural material from which the legitimacy crisis of the 1930s could be played out. Again, as Powers (1983: xiv ff.) argues, the "war" between gangsters and G-men could have been a script out of popular culture's action detective story.

Let us consider more carefully how these 1930s gangsters became public enemies and how bureau agents became G-men heroes. In order to accomplish this feat, the American public had to be convinced first that there was a crime wave. Actually, this crime wave can be broken down into a series of successive crime menaces. It began with the kidnapping menace, which gave way to the bank robbery menace, and, by the end of the decade, the sabotage and espionage menace (Cook, 1958).

The initial alarm for the crime wave was sounded by the kidnapping of the Lindbergh baby on March 1, 1932. National horror and outrage were generated by media coverage that disclosed that the infant of a famous American had been taken from his home in the middle of the night while the family slept. Public opinion was mobilized, and the upshot of the alarm over kidnapping was the passage of a federal law against kidnapping at the close of Herbert Hoover's administration

(Cook, 1958: 243). One of the implications of this in the public mind was that local law enforcement had somehow been derelict in its duty.

Whether there was a kidnapping wave or not is difficult to determine, since no national statistics on kidnapping were kept prior to 1934 (Mayer, 1935). A 1932 national survey on kidnapping by the St. Louis police department reported 285 kidnappings in 502 cities (Seagle, 1934: 756), not an alarming figure in itself. Furthermore, the Wickersham Commission, which had been created by President Hoover to study law and order on a national scale, released its final report in 1931, one year before the Lindbergh kidnapping, and did not even mention kidnapping (Alexander, 1937).

In his critical assessment of the G-man myth, Mayer denies that a crime wave existed, even during Prohibition, and he cites President Hoover's own Committee on Social Trends, which found "no support for the belief that an immense crime wave has engulfed the United States" (Mayer, 1935: 146). In a more recent appraisal of crime during the Depression, Currie (1985: 123ff.) argues that the evidence is mixed. Serious crime, homicide in particular, rose in the early years of the Depression, but by the mid-1930s, it unexpectedly leveled off or, as in the case of homicide, declined. Wilson's (1983b: 237) assessment of the evidence also supports the view that the economic dislocations of the Depression did not produce a crime wave and, in fact, seemed to result in a decline in some forms of crime. Currie further notes that there was a widespread public expectation in the early years of the Depression that massive unemployment and economic hardship would unleash an enormous crime wave. That this crime wave did not materialize, except briefly in the early 1930s, only became apparent in hindsight.

This expectation of a crime wave was seized on by the Roosevelt Justice Department and exploited for policy objectives. At the center of the anticrime crusade in the early New Deal era was Roosevelt's first attorney general, Homer Cummings.[7] From 1933 through 1935, Cummings was the most conspicuous figure in this crusade, and owing to his efforts, a federal role was carved out in the crime wave of the 1930s (Powers, 1983). In fact, Milton Mayer, writing in *Forum* in 1935, refers to the panic over the crime problem as "Mr. Cummings's crime wave" and to his speeches and publicity on crime as stirring the public into a "vigilante frenzy" (Mayer, 1935: 145). For example, in a September 1933 speech Cummings asserted that "organized crime is an open challenge to our civilization" and spoke of the threat of an "armed underworld" and how the country must "arm" itself against the "racketeers" (Powers, 1983: 40–41). Cummings was also an advocate of the "shoot to kill" doctrine, popular at the time as a way of dealing immediate justice to the criminals of the 1930s (McLellan, 1936). For Cummings and the New Deal Justice Department, the basic strategy in the war on crime was the mobilization of public opinion to support the police; corollary to this was the building of public respect for the law. Cummings convening of a major conference on crime in Washington, D.C., in December 1934 was aimed at the development of such "a national movement to meet the menace of lawlessness" (U.S. Attorney General, 1935: 1).

Besides generating anticrime hysteria and successfully promoting the New Deal crime policy, which was reflected in the passage of the crime control legislation of 1934, Cummings also advocated the idea of a superpolice force at the national level. Since local law enforcement had fallen into disrepute in the

Prohibition era, the idea of such a force had considerable appeal. On June 10, 1933, President Roosevelt issued an executive order that the Prohibition Bureau and Bureau of Investigation be merged into a Division of Investigation within the Justice Department. This new bureau would facilitate the federal government's war on kidnappers and racketeers. Hoover, however, was "appalled by the idea of any consolidation." He felt that any merger of his 326 well-trained, incorruptible, and efficient agents with the 1,200 Prohibition agents of questionable training and honesty would only serve to undermine the integrity and identity of the bureau he had worked so hard to create (Whitehead, 1956: 91). According to Whitehead, in his sympathetic treatment of FBI history, Hoover took his opposition to Cummings and won his argument.[8] The FBI remained a separate entity from the Prohibition Bureau, and any prohibition matters uncovered by FBI agents continued to be referred to the Prohibition unit, which had been separately administered in the Justice Department since 1930.[9]

Powers (1983: 41) argues that this proposed administrative reorganization and the Cummings anticrime crusade were nothing more than symbolic crime fighting on the part of the Roosevelt administration. However, the 1934 crime control legislation significantly enlarged the bureau's investigative responsibilities and was more than just symbolic. The transfer of resources to the FBI of the mid-1930s was very real indeed. Between 1932 and 1935, FBI appropriations increased by 72 percent and, furthermore, the FBI's share of the total Justice Department budget also increased from about 9 to 14 percent (U.S. Attorney General, 1935: 142, 178; Cook, 1958: 264). J. Edgar Hoover had become the unwitting beneficiary of this reorganization of bureaucratic power within the Justice Department, and the seeds of the modern Hoover FBI had been sown.

It was not until 1935 that the forces of law and order gained the upper hand in the public relations war with the gangsters of the Depression era. Up to that point, gangster movies, such as *Little Caesar* (1930) and *Public Enemy* (1931), turned gangsters like Al Capone into folk heroes. There was a fascination with these public enemies; the media, in fact, took great delight in the ineptitude of the police in bringing these celebrity criminals to justice.

> And it was the era of the anti-hero, an era when the hokey biographies of badmen filled the 10-cent movie houses. The fantasy of the "good crook" even afflicted some solid citizens. After the FBI ambushed John Dillinger, a Virginia newspaper editor called it a dastardly deed. "Any brave man," he wrote, "would have walked down the aisle and arrested Dillinger [in the movie house]. . . . Why were there so many cowards afraid of this one man? The answer is that the federal agents are mostly cowards" (Sherrill, 1973: 25–26).

This folk hero status of the gangsters of the 1930s was itself symptomatic of America's crisis of confidence in its values and institutions. The hard times of the Depression generated sympathy for those who opposed the established order, even if they were violent criminals.

Cummings's anticrime crusade successfully reversed the tide of public opinion by 1935, when the media and Hollywood started to take a more pro–law enforcement view. In 1935 Hollywood adopted its own censorship code on movies and actually banned gangster movies, with a few exceptions, such as *G-Men* (1935), which glorified the FBI (Powers, 1983). Under the new movie code, crime could no longer be portrayed as paying and criminals as heroes.

In fact, the manufacture of public enemies as folk heroes and the glorification of the FBI as superpolice went hand in hand. The myth of the FBI (and of G-men) could not have been created without the corresponding transformation of ordinary criminals into public enemies.[10] The myth of the invincible FBI was made possible by the legend of Dillinger and other public enemies. If one considers John Dillinger's criminal career, the inflation of his status to a national public enemy becomes more apparent. When he was shot and killed in front of the Biograph Theater in Chicago on July 22, 1934, the most serious federal charges against him were violations of the Dyer Act—that is, auto theft (Mayer, 1935: 145). Dillinger was also wanted on numerous other charges, including bank robbery and the killing of a Chicago policeman, but these were not federal offenses at the time. Dillinger's criminal career had started rather inauspiciously with the robbery of a grocery store, from which he came away empty handed and for which he served nine years in prison (Powers, 1983: 115–117). In prison, Dillinger met the members of his future gang that would embark on a pattern of bank robberies and killings in 1933 until his death the following year. Ironically, he was not even the leader of this gang. In spite of this rather ordinary criminal career, Cummings issued an order to the bureau in 1934 to shoot Dillinger on sight (Mayer, 1935: 145). McLellan (1936: 238) claims that Dillinger had not even been accused of any killings prior to this order, and points out that no such order had been given to kill Capone on sight even though he was suspected of no less than 127 murders.

What was it in Dillinger's career that turned him into the celebrity criminal of the 1930s? To begin with, his criminal career became interwoven with the politics of the 1934 crime control acts. Cummings and Roosevelt needed to make an example of Dillinger to marshal support for their Twelve-Point Crime Program (Powers, 1983: 45). In addition, the media treated the Dillinger story as a kind of Keystone Cops comedy, with the police bungling various phases of Dillinger's career of crimes, which included his escape from a jail in Indiana and, even more embarrassing to the bureau, the Dillinger gang's escape from a country place in Little Bohemia, Wisconsin. Hoover had prematurely announced the gang's capture to the press and was humiliated when it escaped, tipped off by dogs barking at the approaching agents (Powers, 1983: 120–121). This was a major public relations triumph for Dillinger, the public enemy, over the bungling G-men. The eventual shooting and killing of Dillinger provided a symbolic triumph for the forces of law and order over those of the armed underworld.

Hoover and the Triumph of the FBI Myth

In the early 1930s and first couple of years of the New Deal, the public enemies appeared to have a public relations edge over law enforcement, as reflected in the media and popular culture. The indignities that law enforcement suffered in media coverage of the criminal careers of the various public enemies and the folk hero status accorded to these crime figures were a source of considerable irritation to law enforcement officials. In his profile of Hoover in 1937, Jack Alexander maintains that the Kansas City massacre was the turning point for Hoover in his attitude toward the media. On June 17, 1933, "Pretty Boy" Floyd and two others attempted to free Frank Nash from police and FBI custody. In their failed attempt, one FBI agent and three policemen were killed, and two other FBI agents were wounded. Nash was also killed in the shoot-out (Cook, 1958: 245). When "Pretty Boy" Floyd was shot by FBI agents the following year, Hoover remarked that he was "just a yellow rat who needed extermination" and then announced that "Baby Face" Nelson was "next in line" (Crawford, 1937b: 264).

In response to the arrogance displayed by gangsters in this incident and the embarrassment for law enforcement and, in particular, the bureau, Hoover became convinced that an anticrime crusade was needed (Alexander, 1937). Furthermore, Hoover began to see the importance of public relations to the work of the bureau. Prior to this, Hoover had been reluctant to engage in publicity efforts or even to cooperate with Hollywood journalists and other writers (Alexander, 1937; Sherrill, 1973).

Until 1935, Cummings and the Justice Department had been in the forefront of the anticrime movement, with Hoover continuing to maintain a low profile as he had done since 1924. Ironically, Cummings's crime wave and his widening of the federal role in crime control paved the way for Hoover's later success. In the early 1930s, Hoover not only saw his agency's appropriations more than double but the bureau's resources also increased relative to those of the Justice Department. Moreover, with Cummings as his mentor (Powers, 1983: 50), Hoover learned the wisdom of crime waves and public opinion as a method for improving the status of law enforcement, especially his own bureau.

By 1935 Hoover succeeded Cummings as leader of the national anticrime movement and emerged as the "public's favorite cop" (Powers, 1983: 51). There are several reasons for Hoover's eclipse of Cummings. Powers (1983) attributes this role reversal to the influence of Hollywood movie producers and the needs of popular culture to develop G-men heroes who are close to the action.[11] For this purpose, the attorney general—a bureaucrat sitting behind his desk in Washington—is too far removed from the crime scene. The FBI director, as head of a crime-fighting agency, fits more closely the public's conception of such a hero. However, it seems there is more to this shift in the balance of power in crime fighting than simply the influence of popular culture. By emphasizing federal authority in law enforcement and increasing the bureau's investigative responsibilities, the New Deal crime policies and Cummings's anticrime rhetoric had unwittingly concentrated a growing amount of federal resources in Hoover's hands.

These factors contributed to Hoover's increasing influence within the Justice Department and in law enforcement circles and popular culture. As resources began to shift to the FBI and the public began to adopt a more favorable view of law enforcement, Hoover quickly developed the art of cultivating the bureau's image as an invincible and infallible agency. Herein is the root of the modern myth of the FBI.

Hoover's initial efforts at FBI publicity began in his collaboration with Courtney Ryley Cooper, a free-lance writer from Kansas City who was hired in the Research Division of the bureau in 1933.[12] Between 1933 and 1940, Cooper wrote twenty-four bureau-approved articles in mass circulation magazines (Powers, 1983: 98; Alexander, 1937). The central purpose of these articles was to glorify Hoover and the FBI in their crime exploits. The Hearst press was one of Hoover's most faithful glorifiers during the 1930s and designated the FBI "the greatest detective agency in the world" (Crawford, 1937a: 232). In the war on crime of the 1930s, the official credit for any law enforcement achievement or conquest of a public enemy was given to either the organization as a whole or to the director but never to an individual agent. "Cooper's portrait of the FBI was decisive in shaping the bureau's self-image; and, in turn, that self-image determined forever after what the FBI did and how it presented itself to the public" (Powers, 1983: 108).

Hoover also collaborated with Rex Collier, a Washington journalist, who created a short-lived, bureau-authorized comic strip in 1936 called "War on Crime" (Alexander, 1937; Powers, 1983: 142). In these early publicity efforts, FBI history was rewritten to eliminate bungling, inept law enforcement and to emphasize the inevitable conquest of the forces of law over the evil criminal underworld.

In 1935 these public relations efforts were institutionalized in bureau operations in the newly formed Crime Records Division. These operations were first disclosed in 1938 by a fired New York City agent, Leon Turrou,[13] who revealed that the FBI had a staff of about six full-time agents who did nothing but prepare articles, speeches, and books under Hoover's name (Cook, 1958: 253–254).[14]

In addition to the portrait of the FBI as a highly efficient, well-trained, and scientifically run organization, criminals were depicted as a large subgroup of the U.S. population that bordered on the primitive and were armed and dangerous. Hoover was prone to exaggerate the number of criminals in the United States in the 1930s, and his estimates of the size of this group sometimes varied widely and even contradicted the bureau's own official statistics. In March 1936 Hoover claimed that the "armed forces of crime" consisted of more than 3 million active participants. Three months later, the figure was put at about 0.5 million; and six months later it was up to 3.5 million. These estimates all varied from the 1936 official statistics, which placed the number of major felonies committed in the United States at 1,334,000 (Cook, 1958: 257).[15] Alexander (1937) also provides an insightful account of the FBI tour as another element in FBI public relations. He describes how, during the thirties, visitors were shown the artifacts of famous criminals that were on display—Dillinger's death mask, the straw hat he was wearing, various submachine guns and weapons captured by FBI agents. The overall impression conveyed in these displays was that of "looking upon the rude implements and superstitious talismans of a barbarous race that is slowly perishing under the relentless impact of a superior one" (Alexander, 1937: 21).

Bureau public relations aimed at glorifying the FBI (the G-man myth) and at transforming ordinary criminals into public enemies and even into a kind of criminal underclass would provide the basic theme for Hoover's FBI for decades to come. This basic pattern was set against the backdrop of New Deal crime policy, which itself was a diversion from the pressing problems of the Great Depression. The pattern was simple enough: manufacture a crime menace and then persuade the public that the threat is being conquered by the bureau. The Depression era generated a series of crime menaces, beginning with kidnapping, then bank robbery, and, finally, espionage during the war era. The New Deal solution to these menaces was to expand federal authority in law enforcement and intelligence activities. The unintended consequence of this was to concentrate an increasing amount of federal resources in Hoover's FBI, the designated agency for dealing with these problems.

As an organization, the bureau of the Depression era was still small by contemporary standards, but its basic contours had been laid out. The reform-minded Hoover, strongly influenced by the police professionalism movement, framed the FBI's basic organizational features: independence from partisan politics, strong executive leadership, the rationalization of management and recruitment practices, and the introduction of scientific techniques in law enforcement. Moreover, the Roosevelt administration and its New Deal policies of expanding federal authority in economic and social matters provided the impetus for the growth in the FBI's resources and powers during the decade of the 1930s.

Finally, during this era the FBI developed its own distinctive bureaucratic ideology, a glorifying myth that extolled its unique assets as an organization—the G-man myth—and that placed it at the pinnacle of law enforcement agencies. As Blau and Meyer (1971: 50–55) note, such ideologies or myths function to forge a working organization out of a collectivity of individuals with separate goals. Such ideologies create "a sense of purpose among its members, strengthening their commitment and loyalty and spurring them to greater efforts in behalf of the organization" (Blau and Meyer, 1971: 51). Glorifying myths, however, also have a downside. Again, as Blau and Meyer (1971: 52) observe, "myths, by capturing the imagination of the organization members, distort their perspectives, blind them against realities, and set them on courses of action that are detrimental to the organization's objectives." This ambiguity in the role of organizational ideologies would appear to be prophetic for the FBI, especially as the G-men shifted their pursuit from gangsters and bank robbers to communists and subversives.

This, then, was the formative period of the Hoover FBI. It remained, however, for the restoration of domestic intelligence authority to the FBI at the outbreak of World War II to provide the bureau with its distinctive organizational power base. While domestic intelligence had brought the early bureau into disrepute with the "slacker" and Palmer raids, domestic intelligence in the post–World War II era would become a unique basis for accumulating bureaucratic power in the FBI. We shall turn to this part of the FBI story next.

NOTES

1. The Bureau of Investigation did not become the Federal Bureau of Investigation until 1935.

2. In New York City alone, approximately 75,000 men were arrested and jailed in these "slacker" raids (Lowenthal, 1950: 28).

3. The Teapot Dome scandal takes its name from a naval oil reserve in Wyoming. The scandal itself, at least initially, focused on the bribery of Secretary of Interior Albert Fall by two oilmen to secretly lease Teapot Dome and Elk Hills, another naval oil reserve in California. Both of these reserves had been set aside

by previous administrations for future emergency needs, particularly in case of war. While the actual lease of these reserves to the oil companies took place in 1921, public revelations about the leases did not surface until 1924. A Senate inquiry headed by Thomas Walsh gradually unraveled the bribery scheme; Fall was convicted of accepting the bribes and went to prison for a year in 1931, although, paradoxically, the two oilmen were acquitted.

The scandal widened, however, and ensnared a number of others who had been influenced by the money of large oil companies, including Attorney General Daugherty, who was rumored to be linked to a million-dollar slush fund set up by big oilmen; it was also alleged that he had failed to enforce the law in relation to the oil leases as well as in antitrust, customs, and liquor cases. Daugherty resigned under a cloud of scandal. Senator Walsh also uncovered connections between oil industry money and Republican campaign funds. The Teapot Dome scandal occurred and was disclosed during the presidential administrations of Harding and Coolidge (Solberg, 1976: 83–107).

4. The Bureau of Investigation was not established until 1908 by an executive order under Attorney General Bonaparte.

5. This meant that the bureau's investigations were restricted to criminal violations and that intelligence operations were no longer authorized.

6. In 1923 bureau expenditures were $2,166,197; in 1932, $2,689,262 (Donner, 1980: 45; Cook, 1958: 264).

7. Actually, Roosevelt's first attorney general was former U.S. Senator Walsh, who died of a heart attack before taking office on March 2, 1933. He had headed the Senate committee that investigated the Palmer raids, and it was rumored that he intended to fire J. Edgar Hoover (Powers, 1983: 34).

8. It should be noted that Hoover's attitude and conduct here are in marked contrast to his later reputation as an empire builder.

9. With the repeal of Prohibition in 1934, the Prohibition Bureau agents were transferred back to the Treasury Department, where they had been before 1930. It was only for the brief period from 1930 to 1934 that the Prohibition Bureau was part of the Justice Department.

10. Similarly, the need for a "superprison" to house the "supercriminals" was a logical development; hence, the construction of Alcatraz as a remote and secure place for the most dangerous federal criminals of the 1930s (Powers, 1983).

11. Powers (1983: 49) also mentions that Cummings's attention was diverted by other administration issues, such as the battle over the Supreme Court.

12. Cooper was actually added to the Department of Justice (DOJ) staff as an assistant to Henry Suydan, a Washington journalist who had been hired by Cummings but who left the DOJ in 1937. Their assignment was to embellish the bureau's image (O'Reilly, 1982: 644).

13. Turrou was fired by Hoover for writing his own memoirs about an espionage case (Cook, 1958: 253).

14. By 1938 even Cummings had become concerned about the extent of bureau public relations and ordered the FBI to limit its publicity activities (O'Reilly, 1982: 646).

15. The FBI statistics do not estimate the number of criminals in the United States, only the number of crimes reported to the police. Clearly, one criminal may commit more than one crime in the course of a year, and conversely, one crime may be committed by several criminals.

Chapter 3

COMING OF AGE
AS AN INTELLIGENCE AGENCY

The Depression-era banditry on which the Hoover FBI based its rise from obscurity proved to be a short-lived phenomenon. The decline of the frontier as well as the success of federal efforts to combat bank robbery undermined the basis for the bureau's new-found success as the premier G-man agency (Inciardi, 1975: 94–97). By the end of the 1930s, the crime menaces of kidnapping and bank robbery were history.

The 1938 U.S. Justice Department's *Annual Report* documents the hard times on which the bureau had fallen as the Depression-era crime menaces subsided.

> It was necessary during the fiscal year of 1938 to adopt a program of vigorous retrenchment due to a deficiency in the Bureau's appropriations, caused by unforeseen emergencies. Five of the Field Divisions of the FBI were abolished and a revision of the territorial allocations to the various Bureau offices was necessary. During a portion of the year one-half of the investigative personnel was placed on enforced leave of absence in order to conserve travel and other expenses of operation (U.S. Attorney General, 1938: 159).

Although the experience of the 1930s had established some of the distinctive patterns and characteristics of the Hoover FBI, it had also made clear how tenuous the bureau's organizational power was, which fluctuated with each successive crime menace. The restoration of domestic intelligence authority to the FBI in 1939 more firmly entrenched its bureaucratic power so that its viability did not have to rely on the existence of transient public enemies and crime menaces.

In this chapter, we trace the further transformation of the Hoover FBI into an intelligence agency and the development of the FBI's mystique as a fearless protector of American society from espionage, subversion, and communism.

The Restoration of Domestic Intelligence Authority

In the aftermath of the scandals of the Harding administration, which had ousted both Bureau Chief Burns and Attorney General Daugherty, U.S. Attorney General Harlan Stone abolished the FBI's domestic intelligence operations; in 1924 he ordered that FBI activities "be limited strictly to investigations of violations of law" (U.S. Senate, 1976b: 395). The bureau's legal authority remained limited to criminal investigations until 1939 when, on executive order, intelligence operations were restored.[1]

The most publicized aspect of FBI growth in the New Deal was in terms of its law enforcement functions, particularly its war against the gangsters of the Great Depression. But accompanying the expansion of federal authority in the law enforcement arena was the secret growth of the FBI as an intelligence agency. As early as 1934, President Roosevelt had ordered a probe of the Nazi movement in America. In 1936 he further secretly directed the bureau to develop intelligence concerning subversive activities in the United States, particularly by communists and fascists (U.S. Senate, 1976b: 392–396; O'Reilly, 1982: 646). It was not until the September 1939 presidential directive, after war broke out in Europe, that the public was informed of the FBI's restored intelligence function.[2] The directive provided that the FBI and certain military agencies have primacy in investigations related to espionage, sabotage, and counterespionage and that the FBI serves as a clearinghouse for police agencies in these matters (U.S. Comptroller General, 1976). This directive made it necessary for the bureau to establish a new General Intelligence Division.

The restoration of intelligence functions to the FBI gave it new life, as the 1938 and succeeding annual reports reveal; domestic intelligence provided the bureau with a new source of appropriations and ultimately a unique source of power within the federal government. Prior to the 1939 directive, the bureau's appropriations stood at $6,222,976 (U.S. Attorney General, 1938: 159). This represented a 14.7 percent share of the total U.S. Department of Justice budget, up only slightly from the 13.8 percent in 1934 when the Roosevelt administration dramatically expanded FBI authority (U.S. Attorney General, 1935: 142, 178). But, as already noted, fiscal year 1938 was a period of severe retrenchment for the bureau. Therefore, the impact of Roosevelt's 1939 executive order on bureau resources is of considerable interest. With its additional intelligence responsibilities, it is perhaps not surprising that bureau appropriations began to increase again. But what is surprising is the extent of the increase, particularly in relation to the Justice Department budget.

By 1940 the FBI's appropriations had increased to $8,639,541, it was opening three new field offices, the number of FBI agents had increased from 797 to 947, and the FBI's share of the total Department of Justice (DOJ) budget had risen to 20.6 percent. The DOJ appropriations actually decreased slightly between fiscal years 1938 and 1940 (U.S. Senate, 1976b: 407; U.S. Bureau of the Budget, 1940). By the end of World War II, in fiscal year 1945, the FBI's budget had increased to $44,780,000; 81 percent of this amount had been specifically ear-marked for work related to "national defense." The FBI's appropriations were now 42.9 percent of the total DOJ budget (U.S. Bureau of the Budget, 1945).

A question of critical importance to the postwar FBI was what would happen to these national defense appropriations with the termination of the war. Congress's expectation was that these were special wartime appropriations and a part of the national defense; when the national emergency ended, so would this aspect of the bureau's activities (U.S. Senate, 1976b: 407–408). The transition to peacetime was thus critical to the bureau in regard to whether its wartime gains would be maintained.

Table 3-1 shows in a quantitative way the transformation of FBI organi-zational power in the period following restoration of FBI domestic intelligence authority. If we use the relative size of the FBI allocation within the DOJ budget as a measure of FBI bureaucratic power and autonomy within the Justice Depart-ment and, by extension, within the executive branch, then it is clear that the bureau's "temporary" budgetary gains of World War II were maintained after the war—and even through 1968!

How was the FBI able to accomplish this bureaucratic coup? Its first task was to consolidate intelligence responsibilities under the bureau's authority. In 1940 President Roosevelt assigned foreign intelligence responsibilities in the Western Hemisphere to a Special Intelligence Service (SIS) of the FBI. After subsequently establishing the Office of Strategic Services in 1941 (the wartime forerunner of the CIA), Roosevelt directed that Latin America nevertheless remain under the jurisdiction of the bureau (the SIS). This foreign intelligence re-sponsibility of the FBI was, however, withdrawn in 1946, although the FBI had proposed expanding its wartime Western Hemisphere operations worldwide during the postwar period (U.S. Senate, 1976b: 424–426).[3]

However, during the Cold War era, the distinction between foreign and domestic intelligence was a subtle one. Communists were part of an international conspiracy controlled by the Kremlin. The Communist Party USA represented the extension of Soviet power and influence in the United States and thus became the major target of an expanded FBI domestic intelligence during the Cold War.

Furthermore, President Truman gave the FBI, as opposed to the Civil Service Commission, exclusive power to investigate allegedly subversive federal employees (U.S. Senate, 1976b: 434–435). By 1952, the FBI had run name checks on more than 6.6 million federal employees for possible disloyalty (Halperin et al., 1976: 110). The FBI now had undisputed and exclusive jurisdiction over domestic intelligence in the United States and had the unique power to gather intelligence

Table 3-1. FBI appropriations and relative size within Justice Department budgets (1938-1975)

Fiscal Year	FBI Appropriations (dollars)	FBI Budget as Percentage of Total DOJ Budget
1938	6,222,976	14.7
1940	8,639,541	20.6
1945	44,780,000	42.9
1950	53,530,000	39.1
1955	88,930,447	45.2
1960	116,224,408	42.7
1965	161,080,000	41.8
1968	194,895,000	44.1
1970	255,612,000	29.7
1975	428,789,000	20.2

Source: U.S. Bureau of the Budget, 1938–1975. Appropriation figures are drawn from the "Federal Program by Agency and Account" portion of the budget and reflect *actual* amounts, not estimates.

information on U.S. citizens and, by its targeting of investigations, to define who was subversive, disloyal, and dangerous to the state.

The achievement of a monopoly position in domestic intelligence was not, however, sufficient to maintain the bureau's appropriations at wartime levels. The FBI needed a mechanism to regularize its appropriations so that it would not be subject to the vicissitudes of foreign and domestic threats to the nation in any given fiscal year. The use of political intelligence became one such means for ensuring appropriations and institutionalizing power.

Bernstein (1976) has detailed the growth of FBI power since 1940 and has shown how political intelligence was a key instrument in FBI empire building in every successive presidential administration from Roosevelt to Nixon. Bernstein offers an example from the Johnson administration:

> Johnson and Hoover seem to have developed a cozy, though uneasy, relationship: two men of power courting, exploiting, and mistrusting each other. Hoover, following his earlier successful tactics with Roosevelt and Biddle, happily shared with Johnson juicy morsels about the President's political adversaries and allies. Johnson requested and secured from the Bureau what the Church Committee described as "purely political intelligence [about senators] obtained as a by-product of otherwise legitimate national security electronic surveillance of foreign intelligence targets." The President probably used some of this information against his opponents on the Hill (Bernstein, 1976: 73).

Clearly, the FBI's expanded intelligence apparatus enhanced the bureau's capacity to gather political intelligence.[4] Such information is double-edged; it can be used to court favor with those in power, or it can be a source of blackmail. Hoover's confidential files were long suspected of being used for political blackmail and intimidation. As Theoharis and Cox (1988: 309) observe, "Hoover did not have to blackmail congressmen directly; it was sufficient that they feared he could do so." The source of power was the files, and from the standpoint of the executive, such intelligence could be used for partisan or personal purposes (Bernstein, 1976: 61).

In addition to the growth of FBI power to use and misuse intelligence information within government, its exclusive jurisdiction over domestic intelligence also provided it with the unique capability of influencing public opinion on national security matters, particularly in relation to internal threats. In the postwar era, the FBI and Department of Justice played an active role in contributing to the alarm and hysteria over communism and internal security that came to be known as McCarthyism (Theoharis, 1971: 123ff.; Belknap, 1977a: 152; Sullivan with Brown, 1979a: 88ff.). Halperin and colleagues (1976: 103ff.) observed how the FBI exploited the Cold War fears of communism rather than served as a calming influence. Since the FBI had monitored the Communist Party USA and political left in the war years, it was in a position, unlike any other agency, to state the "real" danger posed by communism. Hoover, however, chose not to reveal information that could have had a calming effect: the declining membership of the Communist Party, the small number of potential underground communist government employees (fewer than one-hundred), and the fact that the FBI had very little, if any, evidence of Communist Party membership among government employees. William C. Sullivan, head of the FBI's Intelligence Division from 1961 to 1971, asserts that it was the FBI that had kept Senator McCarthy in business: "We gave McCarthy all we had, but all we had were fragments, nothing that could prove his accusations. For a while, though, the accusations were enough to keep McCarthy in the headlines" (Sullivan with Brown, 1979b: 14). Hoover's *Masters of Deceit,* published in 1958, was part of the bureau's continuing campaign of stirring up Cold War fears even after McCarthyism was on the wane (Sullivan with Brown, 1979a).[5]

As early as 1940 it became evident that the bureau was pursuing its own independent political objectives in the intelligence area. In the FBI's efforts to document the existence of communists in government, it established covert ties to congressional subcommittees such as the House Un-American Activities Committee. These committees were important sources of anticommunist propaganda (O'Reilly, 1982: 655–658). After the war, Hoover's continuing insistence on the problem of internal security eventually led to a break with the Truman administration over the employee loyalty issue. President Truman did not believe there was a loyalty problem; Hoover was equally insistent that spies and subversives were a serious problem. In 1947, in an appearance before the conservative House Un-American Activities Committee, Hoover "served notice that he had renounced his historic allegiance to the executive and was joining forces with Congress in the battle over the loyalty issue" (Powers, 1987: 286).

This unprecedented political alliance with congressional conservatives who opposed Truman's loyalty position is perhaps not as much of a paradox as it might appear. As Bernstein (1976: 62) notes, the growth of FBI power both expands and contracts with presidential power. Delegating more autonomy to the FBI may limit executive control of the bureau, but it also insulates the president from the fallout of FBI illegalities and improprieties. At the same time, FBI actions often serve the president's own purposes in "using political intelligence, blocking dissent, and thwarting dissident movements" (Bernstein, 1976: 63). Nevertheless, Hoover had begun the process of eroding presidential and Justice Department control of the FBI during the Truman administration. The internal security issue was so critical to the bureau's postwar organizational power that it meant Hoover would even have to take the risky political move of abandoning his traditional power base in the executive branch when he split with Truman on the loyalty issue (Powers, 1987: 287). In its promotion of the communist menace of the 1950s, the FBI's organizational interests ceased to coincide with those of the Truman administration, especially in relation to internal security matters.

It was thus a combination of the shrewd use of political intelligence and a massive public relations campaign to exploit Cold War fears that eased the bureau's transition from wartime to peacetime and allowed it to maintain its wartime gains and even to expand its powers. The Cold War era—with its fear of foreign threats, the expansion of presidential power, and the erosion of congressional authority—set the stage for the bureau's coming of age as an intelligence agency and its assumption of expanded powers within the federal government.

The New FBI Myth

The McCarthy era also set the stage for an elaboration of the FBI's organizational ideology pertaining to its invincibility and infallibility. This glorifying myth, which was first cultivated in the mid-1930s by portraying Depression-era gangsters as the notorious public enemies, now had to be extended to the public enemies of the Cold War, the communists and other subversives. As in the earlier era, the mystique of the FBI was enhanced by the public's perception of the dangerousness of the public enemies pursued by the bureau. Having established itself as the government agency with exclusive jurisdiction in the domestic intelligence field, this monopoly position placed the bureau in a rather unique situation regarding internal security. Without fear of being challenged in its views, the FBI had considerable discretion in defining the foreign and domestic threats to national security. This also meant that the bureau could portray itself as a defender against the enemies of the state. As Powers (1983: 235) notes, anticommunism was Hoover's religion of the 1950s and 1960s; he established the FBI as a bulwark against the atheistic communists and others who threatened traditional American values. The bureau's annual reports during this period registered the alarm posed by the communist threat.

> The FBI responsibility for protecting the internal security of the United States assumed far greater importance during the year as domestic enemies of the nation grew increasingly more bold. Encouraged by their success in hiding behind every technicality and delay which our laws allow—and heartened by the attitude of false complacency which has gripped vast segments of the population—Communist Party members and other subversive elements asserted themselves with renewed vigor (U.S. Attorney General, 1957: 198).

This same annual report goes on to depict the Communist Party U.S.A. as "an integral part of the international conspiracy against God and freedom which is under the Kremlin's leadership" (U.S. Attorney General, 1957: 200).

Hoover had learned the value of publicity and public relations from Attorney General Cummings, who had successfully mobilized the anticrime crusade of the mid-1930s. The FBI of the 1950s, as previously noted, contributed to the alarm of the McCarthy era, which, of course, served to elevate the bureau's importance as a defender against internal subversion. This view was advanced in numerous speeches, magazine articles, books, and movies. Among the articles were "Red Spy Masters in America" in the August 1952 *Reader's Digest* and "Communists Are After Our Minds" in the October 1954 *American* (Sherrill, 1973: 31). Hoover's *Masters of Deceit* (1958), which sold around 250,000 copies, was one of three books Hoover "wrote" on communism during this period. Among the movies promoting the FBI and the theme of anticommunism were *I Was a Communist for the FBI* (1951) and *Walk East on Beacon* (1952) (Sherrill, 1973: 31). Even William Sullivan, former head of the Intelligence Division, argued that the "FBI's main thrust was not investigations but public relations and propaganda to glorify Hoover" (Sullivan with Brown, 1979a: 80). He also confirmed what others have also noted, that the function of the Crime Records Division was publicity; that is, the division handles all correspondence with the public, contacts with the press, and relations with Congress. The real job of the special agent in charge of the field office was "visiting the 'right' people, those who molded public opinion in his territory" (Sullivan with Brown, 1979a: 83). With the press contacts developed by the special agent, Hoover could place "news" stories in newspapers all over the country. The network of FBI field offices performed an important public relations function for the bureau by working to shape public opinion regarding subversion and dissent as well as by constructing a favorable public image of the bureau as a protector of democracy.

Image Versus Performance

During the 1950s and through most of the 1960s, the FBI image as a bulwark against communism remained intact. But gradually, a disparity began to emerge between the bureau's public relations claims regarding the threat of communism, its own allocation of resources to domestic intelligence, and its performance in pursuing subversion.

If one examines FBI annual reports during the early 1950s, fully two-thirds of these reports were devoted to the description of the communist threat and the bureau's role in combating it; yet, as Halperin and colleagues estimate, perhaps one-third of the bureau's total investigative force was doing "security" work during the Cold War (Halperin et al., 1976: 107). It is also interesting to note that once intelligence activities were firmly established as part of bureau operations, the share of resources for intelligence was remarkably constant—about 19 percent of the bureau's investigative resources, regardless of variation in public relations concerns or actual changes in threats to national security posed by civil disorder or domestic dissent. Table 3-2 demonstrates this constancy in allocation of resources.

These data seem to support Sullivan's claim that the bureau was more concerned with public relations than with investigations. If the bureau could use

Table 3-2. Percentage breakdown of FBI investigative matters (1965-1975)[a]

Fiscal Year	Intelligence Investigative Matters	Criminal Investigative Matters	Other
1965	19	67	14
1966	19	66	15
1967	17	69	14
1968	19	68	13
1969	18	68	14
1970	16	66	18
1971	19	62	19
1972	21	63	16
1973	21	63	16
1974	21	67	12
1975	19	69	12

[a]*Investigative matters* is an administrative term used by the FBI to measure work load and should not be confused with a case or investigation; one case may entail many "investigative matters."
Source: U.S. Comptroller General, 1976: 132.

public relations to maintain and even increase its appropriations, it could then allocate those appropriations according to its own organizational priorities. Funds appropriated to the bureau came in a lump sum,[6] unlike the appropriations to other government agencies, which were assigned to specific line items. The FBI appropriations were assigned to broad categories, such as "security and criminal investigations," with the actual amount allocated to domestic intelligence remaining a secret, at least until 1975 when the United States House and Senate Committees on Intelligence obtained from FBI officials the $82 million estimate for FBI intelligence operations for fiscal year 1975. No further breakdown of the FBI intelligence budget was allowed, however, owing to "national security" reasons. This budgeting process allowed Hoover to argue for additional appropriations to address global threats and problems but then to use the appropriations in ways that would show the most concrete accomplishments for the next fiscal year's appropriations. The FBI director's testimony at appropriations hearings and the FBI annual reports are replete with statistical accomplishments of the previous fiscal year: fines, recovery of stolen goods, fugitives located, convictions. The successes were invariably accomplished at a rate higher than that of the previous year, and the average monetary return in recovered goods and items always exceeded the FBI's appropriations. Pincus comments astutely on the irony of the situation:

> Taken alone, these statistics appear ludicrous when ranged against the more serious problems that Hoover said the country faced—organized crime and espionage, for example—and which should have been a prime focus for the assets he received. Yet interviews with past and present Bureau officials confirm that a substantial amount of agent time across the country is devoted to the tasks that result in providing these statistics, rather than toward

investigations that require large numbers of agents and long periods of time and may not produce any dollar statistics at all (Pincus, 1973: 86).

It would be a mistake to conclude from this that FBI domestic intelligence activities were only a public relations ploy. It is not that FBI resources were diverted away from domestic intelligence but that the national security concerns raised by Hoover in his persistent outcry against communists and communist influence in American life were critical to the bureau's total appropriations. This was Hoover's unique way of maintaining and, indeed, expanding the bureau's organizational power. There can be little doubt that Hoover used this technique successfully. Over the last twenty years of his directorship, Hoover received all the funds he asked for and, on two occasions, even more (Pincus, 1973: 77).

There can also be little doubt that Hoover was serious about communism and domestic security; his credentials as an authority on communism go back to his early days in the Palmer Justice Department right after World War I (Powers, 1987). The bureau's restored domestic intelligence functions after 1939 were extensively put to use in surveilling U.S. citizens. By 1950, 11,930 Americans were listed on the security index; these were individuals who the FBI believed to be dangerous and in the event of a national emergency would be detained (U.S. Senate, 1976b: 441). The FBI also developed a mail opening program and a black bag, or surreptitious, entry program (that is, illegal break-in) as part of its intelligence operations. By 1960 the FBI had opened approximately 432,000 headquarters files on individuals and groups who were classified as subversive (U.S. Senate, 1976b: 451). During the 1960s the bureau initiated approximately 45,000 investigative matters a year, on average, in relation to subversive and extremist activities. At its peak in 1973, the FBI had nearly 2,000 domestic intelligence informants in well over one-hundred different targeted organizations. The broad and expansive scope of FBI domestic intelligence in the postwar period, which affected the lives of hundreds of thousands of U.S. citizens as well as hundreds of groups, has been well documented (Halperin et al., 1976; Theoharis, 1978; Donner, 1980).

While it is clear that the FBI invested substantial resources in its intelligence operations, the effectiveness and results of these activities are not so apparent. Perhaps a further paradox of the FBI's domestic intelligence operations is that the very characteristic that has been the bureau's source of power—namely, its secretiveness—constitutes a liability in the measurement of public performance. The 1957 *Annual Report* of the FBI stated the problem as follows: "The effectiveness of the FBI in combating espionage, sabotage, subversive activities and related threats to America's security cannot be measured in terms of mere arrests and convictions; nor can a public accounting be made of all accomplishments attained" (U.S. Attorney General, 1957: 199).

The FBI was unable to provide a public measure of its domestic intelligence performance. It provided instead a public image of itself as a defender of the state against communists and other subversives. If the public measures (arrests and convictions), which the bureau itself rejected as appropriate measures of intelligence activities, were used to evaluate the FBI performance in the domestic intelligence field, the bureau's track record was not very remarkable. Even in the McCarthy era, when there was considerable legislative and judicial support for prosecuting subversives, there was a total of 108 convictions of Communist Party members under the Smith Act[7] between 1949 and 1957. (And many of these convictions were reversed.) During the same period, there were nine fugitives located and twelve convictions under the espionage laws (U.S. Attorney General, 1950–1957).

Similarly, the Socialist Workers Party had been under FBI surveillance since 1940. Except for 1941, when there were eighteen prosecutions under the Smith Act, this surveillance discovered no violations of the law by SWP members (U.S. House, Appropriations Hearings, 1975: 1032). If we look at fiscal year 1975, in which we know that $82 million was allocated to FBI intelligence, what were the accomplishments in terms of these public measures? In the summary of statistics in its annual report for 1975, the FBI lists its accomplishments according to fines, convictions, fugitives located, property recovered, and so on. These statistics are broken down by crime classifications, which cover two pages. Of these numerous crime categories, only three directly relate to intelligence activities: bombing matters, espionage, and sabotage. Only "bombing matters" showed tangible results with eleven fugitives located and seventeen convictions. There were no espionage or sabotage convictions, and only one sabotage fugitive located (U.S. Attorney General, 1975: 189–190).

If we consider that domestic intelligence represented 19 percent of the FBI's investigative and budgetary resources during fiscal year 1975, these do not appear to be impressive accomplishments. It is no wonder that the bureau did not emphasize these statistics in its annual appropriation hearings; its statistics on fines and recovery of stolen goods were far more impressive.

But perhaps the bureau is correct: arrests and convictions may not be very satisfactory measures of intelligence operations, since the purpose of intelligence is not simply to gather evidence for prosecution but also to gain advance knowledge of planned subversive activities. Although the FBI never systematically evaluated its intelligence operations with regard to this measure, the General Accounting Office (GAO) has done so on two occasions. In the GAO's review of domestic intelligence in ten FBI field offices during 1974, it found, on the basis of a random sample of domestic intelligence cases (17,528 individual cases), that 3 percent (533) were referred for prosecution, 1.6 percent (281) were prosecuted, 1.3 percent (231) were convicted, and 2.7 percent (476) resulted in advance knowledge of planned activities (U.S. Comptroller General, 1976: 140–143). In its assessment, the GAO stated:

> The FBI has devoted considerable resources to domestic intelligence investigations and carried out an extensive program in terms of caseload. Few tangible results are evident. This is particularly true with respect to its stated purpose of identifying internal security violations. Few cases have produced foreknowledge of violence or other events which might represent a threat to the national security (U.S. Comptroller General, 1976: 138).

In a follow-up review, the GAO did not find more tangible results in the 319 cases it examined during 1976. In only 3.1 percent (ten) of those cases was evidence gathered that might have been useful in related criminal investigations or in providing advance knowledge of planned violent activities (U.S. Comptroller General, 1977: 41).

This is not the first time that Hoover's public relations claims for FBI effectiveness have been called into question. In the 1930s he boasted that the bureau had "the finest force of employees in any government agency in the United States" (Lowenthal, 1950: 343). About the same time, a U.S. Senate Committee hired the Brookings Institution to study the relative efficiency of seven federal law enforcement agencies for the 1935–1936 period. When Brookings ranked the seven agencies according to quality of arrest,[8] the FBI ranked next to the bottom of the list (Lowenthal, 1950: 344; Cook, 1958: 256).

Again, when John F. Kennedy was assassinated in 1963, the FBI's handling of the Lee Harvey Oswald case came under close scrutiny. Apparently, even Hoover was shocked at the bureau's poor performance. Although the FBI had opened a security file on Oswald in 1959 (and closed it in 1962), there were numerous telltale signs that Oswald was a security risk and that FBI agents had failed to follow up on these signs. Among the danger signals, two months before the assassination, Oswald met in Mexico City with a KGB agent who was part of a unit believed to be responsible for assassination and sabotage assignments. The report on Oswald's Mexico City visit had not been acted on. Perhaps even more astonishing, two weeks before the assassination, Oswald visited the Dallas FBI office and left a note threatening to blow up the FBI office and Dallas Police Department if agents did not stop bothering his wife; she had been interviewed by an agent a few days earlier. Again, this note was not acted on. Hoover was so appalled by the Oswald intelligence failure that he censured seventeen agents (including William Sullivan), against the advice of other top FBI officials. Chapter 8 of the Warren Commission Report in 1964 detailed the deficiencies in the FBI investigation of Oswald (Powers, 1987: 383–390).[9]

What is amazing is that the FBI was able to conceal this disparity between image and performance for so long and to maintain its myth of infallibility. It was finally the Nixon administration that became dissatisfied with the FBI's domestic intelligence operations. The civil disorders and antiwar protests in the late 1960s, along with the inability of the White House to anticipate the plans of domestic dissenters, led to increasing disenchantment with the bureau's intelligence efforts (U.S. Senate, 1976b: 924). Sullivan, who headed the FBI Intelligence Division at the time, admits that the New Left was unanticipated by the bureau:

> The trouble at Columbia came as a surprise to the FBI, as much of a surprise as our discovery of the true strength of the Mafia when we raided their meeting in Appalachin. Before we read the headlines and saw the pictures of Mark Rudd smoking a cigar with his feet up on Grayson Kirk's desk, we didn't know the New Left existed (Sullivan with Brown, 1979a: 147).

The dissatisfaction with FBI intelligence culminated in the celebrated Huston Plan[10] in July 1970. The Huston Plan represented an attempt to achieve more cooperation among the intelligence agencies as well as to lower the restraints on the intelligence collection techniques employed. The White House and the intelligence community were frustrated by Hoover's curtailing of certain collection techniques since the mid-1960s (surreptitious entry, electronic surveillance, no campus informants under the age of twenty-one). In March 1970 Hoover had also severed formal liaison ties with the CIA; he subsequently severed ties with the other intelligence agencies (U.S. Senate, 1976b: 924).

Hoover's preoccupation with image and the potential for certain intelligence activities to embarrass the bureau, even though those activities had been permitted regularly in the past, placed him in a paradoxical situation. At the same time that Hoover was becoming increasingly concerned that revelations of questionable activities might harm the bureau's reputation, he was faced with mounting executive pressure to gather intelligence. The wiretap hearings in 1965 and the revelations of CIA connections to the National Student Association in 1967 made the continuation of some intelligence operations more risky, from a public relations standpoint. Clearly, the "flap potential" of intelligence activities was increasing, yet the bureau had to maintain its image as a bulwark against communism and subversion. This was the bureau's basic dilemma.

The significance of the Huston Plan is that the FBI's successful concealment since the McCarthy era of the disparity between its image and performance in the domestic intelligence arena had been exposed—at least to the White House and the intelligence community. The bureau's old ruse of arguing for appropriations in terms of global threats and problems, and then spending the money in self-serving ways to produce more concrete statistical accomplishments for the next fiscal year's appropriations, was no longer credible. This awareness and dissatisfaction with FBI domestic intelligence was translated by the Nixon administration into rapidly declining FBI appropriations relative to the Justice Department budget after 1968 (see table 3-1). That statistic had been relatively constant for twenty-three years since the end of World War II. The bureau's post–World War II source of power was now being eroded.

The institutionalization of domestic intelligence in the postwar FBI not only assured it of a continuing source of appropriations but also provided the Hoover FBI with a unique source of organizational power within the federal government. Although this unique bureaucratic empire began to unravel somewhat in the late 1960s, as criticism and dissatisfaction with Hoover began to mount, the public disclosures of the Watergate era led to a wholesale reevaluation of the Hoover FBI. We turn next to an understanding of how this basic source of FBI organizational power was also the major source of organizational abuses in the Hoover FBI.

NOTES

1. Even though lacking legal authority in the 1924–1936 period, the bureau's intelligence operations did not completely cease during this period. The recent disclosure of FBI files from 1924 to 1930 shows that the bureau continued to monitor radical activities. Hoover found a way to circumvent Stone's ban by relying on private spies and informers for information, and bureau agents continued to collect radical publications and press accounts of radical activities. In Hoover's interpretation of the ban, the bureau simply could not initiate an intelligence investigation (Theoharis and Cox, 1988: 92).

It was also during this period that Hoover created an "obscene" file where agents reported on the obscene and indecent activities of public officials and bureau adversaries (Theoharis and Cox, 1988: 84).

2. The discovery of the restoration of domestic intelligence responsibilities to the FBI alarmed the political left. In a March 2, 1940, editorial, *The Nation* was highly critical of the 1939 directive and Hoover's testimony before the House Appropriations Committee, criticizing the bureau for engaging in activities for which it had no authority and objecting to the term *subversive*, which is not defined anywhere in federal law.

3. The Office of Strategic Services was abolished by President Truman after the war.

4. In practice, the distinction between political intelligence and legitimate national security or law enforcement information was difficult to maintain. This was certainly the view of the Church Committee (Bernstein, 1976).

5. Sullivan (with Brown, 1979a) notes that Hoover did not write *Masters of Deceit* in 1958 but that its writing was a task delegated to six agents including himself.

6. This was true at least until fiscal year 1975, when the Department of Justice introduced a new form of budget review (U.S. House, Appropriations Hearings, 1975: 278–279).

7. The Smith Act of 1940 provided the FBI and Justice Department with new federal laws for monitoring radical political groups, especially those associated with the various socialist parties and the Communist Party USA. Among its provisions, the Smith Act made it a federal crime "to knowingly or willfully advocate, abet, advise, or teach the duty, necessity, desirability, or propriety for overthrowing any government of the United States by force or violence" (Morgan, 1980: 34). During the McCarthy era, much of the leadership of the Communist Party USA was prosecuted and convicted under the Smith Act. In 1957 the U.S. Supreme Court in the Yates decision reversed the convictions of the second-echelon leadership of the Communist Party and held that the government must show advocacy "of action and not merely abstract doctrine" (U.S. Senate, 1976b: 428). The Yates decision effectively undermined the Smith Act, and there have been no Smith Act prosecutions since 1957.

8. The criterion for quality of arrest was percent of convictions secured in cases investigated. According to the Brookings Institution, the FBI conviction rate was 72.5 percent, although Hoover had claimed a 94 to 97 percent conviction rate (Cook, 1958: 256).

9. In his recent memoirs, Clarence Kelley, who was FBI director from 1973 to 1978, confirms these two Oswald incidents. He goes even further, however, in asserting that if the intelligence agencies had pooled their information on Oswald, John F. Kennedy would not have died in Dallas on that day (Kelley and Davis, 1987: 253–254, 280, 297).

10. The Huston Plan, named after presidential assistant Tom Charles Huston, was a set of recommendations to expand the intelligence collection techniques employed by the various intelligence agencies in monitoring domestic dissenters. The plan was derived from a report prepared by the heads of the several intelligence agencies, including the FBI and CIA, after a series of meetings in 1970. In June of

that year, President Nixon had requested a review of intelligence agency collection practices with the aim of relaxing the restraints on intelligence gathering related to domestic dissenters. The Nixon White House had become increasingly frustrated at its inability to anticipate the plans of such groups (U.S. Senate, 1976b: 923–986).

Chapter 4

THE RISE AND FALL
OF FBI LAWLESSNESS

One of the ironies of the Hoover FBI in the post–World War II era is that its unique source of organizational power, its domestic intelligence operations, also became the major source of organizational abuses. The restoration of domestic intelligence proved to be a two-edged sword for the bureau. It was one of the key instruments in the growth of FBI powers during the Cold War era, yet from this new intelligence authority there derived an expanding arena of lawless and questionable operations and programs. The very activities that contributed to the Hoover FBI's unique accumulation of bureaucratic power also paradoxically contributed to the unraveling of the Hoover empire in the 1970s.

This chapter traces the rise and fall of lawlessness in the Hoover FBI and relates it to the expansion and contraction of its intelligence operations. Developing an understanding of FBI organizational misconduct, it must be cautioned, is not simple. To do so requires more than probing inside Hoover's distinctive personality and his autocratic control of the bureau for several decades; it also requires that we go beyond the particular conditions of any one historical epoch and realize the overarching historical patterns and common conditions. FBI lawlessness must be understood in the interplay between the bureau as an organization and the changing role and function of the FBI within the executive branch during different historical periods. Additionally, the vicissitudes of crime control and due process values in different eras have an impact on organizational misconduct. This chapter attempts to capture this complex interrelationship of organizations, institutions, and history.

Domestic Intelligence and Lawlessness

While the legality of FBI domestic intelligence has been discussed at length elsewhere (U.S. Comptroller General, 1976; U.S. Senate, 1976b; Elliff, 1979; Donner, 1980), it is clear that the FBI's legal authority to conduct intelligence operations has varied over time since the bureau's creation in 1908. Such legal authority existed during and immediately after World War I until its termination by Attorney General Stone in 1924. The bureau remained strictly a law enforcement agency until President Roosevelt gradually restored its intelligence authority in the 1930s. This authority has persisted in various forms under successive presidential administrations since Roosevelt.

　　While there has been some legal authority in the form of presidential directives and specific statutes (for example, involving espionage and sabotage) for the FBI to conduct such operations, this does not mean that all of the organizational actions the FBI has carried out under this authority have, in fact, been legal. Domestic intelligence encompasses both legal and illegal FBI conduct. In referring to the scandal-ridden Bureau of Investigation of the post–World War I era, Attorney General Stone recalled that "the organization was lawless, maintaining many activities which were without any authority in federal statutes" (U.S. Senate, 1976b: 388). Similarly, in their *Report upon the Illegal Practices of the United States Department of Justice,* a panel of twelve prestigious lawyers, including Roscoe Pound and Felix Frankfurter, was highly critical of the conduct of the Justice Department for its violation of constitutional rights during the Palmer raids of the same era (Preston, 1963: 222).

　　In the more recent Watergate era, the FBI's counterintelligence program (COINTELPRO), initiated in 1956, was also discovered to be a major source of lawless activities. The Petersen Committee, an internal Justice Department inquiry in 1974, found that some COINTELPRO activities may have violated certain statutes and that in certain "isolated instances" involved practices that "can only be considered abhorrent in a free society" (U.S. Senate, 1976b: 8, 73). In an internal FBI memo (July 19, 1966) regarding procedures for authorizing black bag jobs, William Sullivan admitted the illegality of such break-ins, and writes, "Such a technique involves trespass and is clearly illegal" (Theoharis, 1982: 23). In these, and in other instances as well, the FBI exceeded its legitimate authority in the political surveillance of U.S. citizens.

　　It is also clear that in the eighty-year history of the bureau, the major scandals and disclosures of lawlessness have stemmed from its role as an intelligence agency (Powers, 1987: 112ff.; Elliff, 1979: 3). Because of this, our understanding of FBI lawlessness is closely tied to the bureau's domestic intelligence responsibilities and to variation in its authority to conduct such operations in different historical periods. It is asserted that FBI lawlessness varies directly with the expansion and contraction of domestic intelligence activities.[1] Our first task in the search for understanding FBI lawlessness is the delineation of the rise and fall of bureau domestic intelligence operations since 1908.

The overview for the major patterns of domestic intelligence was set forth by the Senate Select Committee on Intelligence (U.S. Senate, 1976b: 375–554), also known as the Church Committee. This historical view of FBI domestic intelligence is supported by data from other inquiries, historical and governmental. There are three major periods of expansion of domestic intelligence and two major periods of decline that emerge from this literature. The major periods of growth are as follows:

1. The Red Scare era (1917–1920)
2. The McCarthy era (1948–1955)
3. The law-and-order crisis of the 1960s (1967–1972)

The major periods of decline are:

1. The Teapot Dome/Attorney General Stone era (1924–1936)
2. The Watergate era (1972–1977)

A variety of scholars and journalists have documented the domestic intelligence operations and FBI lawlessness of the post–World War I period, which was highlighted by the Palmer raids of 1919 and 1920, where over 10,000 persons in thirty-three cities were rounded up because of their radical threat (Lowenthal, 1950; Murray, 1955; Whitehead, 1956; Cook, 1958; Preston, 1963; Ungar, 1975; Belknap, 1977b; Donner, 1980). The documentation of domestic intelligence operations for the two periods of expansion after World War II is more extensive than for the earlier period (Wise and Ross, 1964; Wise, 1976; Perkus, 1975; U.S. Senate, 1975, 1976b; Belknap, 1977a; Fain, 1977; Theoharis, 1978; Donner, 1980).

It is even possible to quantify the variation in domestic intelligence activities since 1950 with data that have been annually collected during this period. Both the Church Committee and the General Accounting Office employed a number of measures to operationalize the amount of domestic intelligence operations, such as the number of domestic intelligence investigative matters received by the FBI, the number of individuals on the FBI security index, the number of agents doing domestic intelligence investigations, and the number of domestic intelligence informants.[2] Figure 4-1 shows the trends in domestic intelligence operations according to the measure used—the number of domestic intelligence investigative matters received. Table 4-1 shows the percent change in domestic intelligence operations according to the major periods identified earlier for the post–World War II years.

The Periods of Expansion

The three periods of expansion have a common characteristic: each was an era of alarm, even of public hysteria, over the threat to law and order posed by radicals, aliens, and dissenters in American society. In the Red Scare of 1919–1920, the concern was with Bolsheviks — Reds, radical workers, and alien anarchists. The

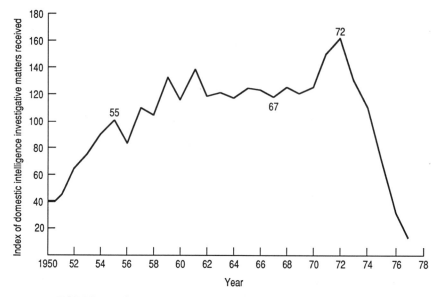

FIGURE 4-1. Changes in Domestic Intelligence Operations (1950-1977)
Source: The data for the years 1955-1975 were available from the Church Committee Hearings
(U.S. Senate, 1975: 349-350). The data for 1953-1954 were obtained from the annual reports
of the U.S. Attorney General for those years. The missing years, 1950-1952 and 1976-1977,
were estimated from other measures available for those years. A base year (1955=100) was
selected because it was an overlapping year in time series data drawn from different sources.
The scores on the vertical axis represent percentage the raw score is of the base year.

McCarthy era of the early 1950s was characterized by alarm about the growing
influence of communism in the United States, particularly communists in high
places in government. The threat of black and white radicals of the late 1960s and
early 1970s (Black Panthers, Students for a Democratic Society [SDS], the antiwar
movement, and so on) was similarly tied to their perceived potential to disrupt
social order in the United States. During each of these periods, the FBI (and its
precursor, the Bureau of Investigation) and the Justice Department (DOJ) played
an active part in the public exaggeration and magnification of internal threats to
national security. Indeed, they were at the center of federal government propaganda
activity, selectively releasing information to the media on the radical threat. The
FBI, the DOJ, and those congressional subcommittees that held hearings on internal
security threats all "educated" the public to the imminent danger posed by radicals,
aliens, and dissenters (Murray, 1955: 194; Belknap, 1977a: 152; Halperin et al.,
1976: 103ff.; Theoharis, 1971: 123ff.; Powers, 1987: 292).

      The growing crescendo of alarm over security and loyalty in each of these
periods climaxed in what Wilensky (1967) identifies as an organizational distortion
of intelligence. The intelligence distortion in each of these historical eras is also
akin to what the historian Richard Hofstadter calls the "paranoid style" of the
American political tradition, where conspiracies by radicals, aliens, and marginal
elements subvert social order and culture (Donner, 1980: 10). Hofstadter (1955:
70–73) does not deny that there are conspiracies in history, but rather asserts that
this is quite different from saying that history is a conspiracy. It is Hofstadter's

Table 4-1. Percent changes in domestic intelligence operations (1950–1977)[a]

	Period	*Percentage Change*
McCarthy era	1950–1955	+152
	1955–1967	+8
Law-and-order crisis of the 1960s	1967–1972	+57
Watergate era	1972–1977	–95

[a]Domestic intelligence is operationalized as the number of domestic intelligence investigative matters received by the FBI.

contention that Populist thought at the turn of the century was inclined toward seeing historical events in conspiratorial terms. This paranoid style also characterized each of the three periods of intelligence expansion and set the political and cultural context for FBI and DOJ behavior.

It is also characteristic of each of these historical eras that crime control values become dominant and due process concerns are subordinated. The pursuit of radicals, aliens, and dissenters becomes paramount in the organizational perspective of the FBI and DOJ. These goals become so overriding that due process goals, which might normally be taken into account, are deemphasized or even ignored. In his testimony before the Church Committee, William Sullivan similarly observed how questions of legality and ethics are seldom raised in intelligence work (Halperin et al., 1976: 226; U.S. Senate, 1976b: 7). It is in the context of these historical and organizational conditions that lawless conduct is facilitated.

Wilensky (1967: 42–61) further argues that at the organizational level certain conditions may also facilitate the distortion, and even blockage, of intelligence for interpreting events. He elaborates on the role of hierarchy, specialization, and centralization as major sources of intelligence distortion. Hierarchy is conducive to concealment and misrepresentation when subordinates may be reluctant to transmit information their superiors may not wish to hear ("bad news"). Specialization may contribute to distortion when rivalry between organizational units takes precedence over sharing information that might further the interests of a competing unit. And, finally, centralization may produce distortion by tightly controlling intelligence at the top of the organization, where it is too far removed from the day-to-day operations to be effective. Wilensky (1967: 113–119) also points to the role of executive secrecy and ethnocentrism in the production of information pathologies. These characteristics were, in various forms, manifest in the FBI and the DOJ during each of the three periods in question.

During the three periods of expansion, the FBI and the DOJ were allowed to operate with unusual autonomy and independence. During the Red Scare, DOJ autonomy was perhaps a result of default, as President Wilson had suffered a nervous breakdown and stroke in 1919 and the nation was left virtually leaderless until 1921 (Murray, 1955: 21). During the McCarthy era and the law-and-order crisis of the 1960s, FBI autonomy (including autonomy from the DOJ itself) was due to its own unique political power base in government. This organizational autonomy, coupled with its monopoly and control over information in the domestic intelligence field, allowed the FBI to define domestic threats to national security

for the executive and the American public. This particular organizational structure—autonomy, centralization of the intelligence function, and executive secrecy—strengthens the potential for "information pathologies," as Wilensky (1967:
113) calls them, and ultimately contributes to intelligence failures owing to the
distortion of information.

In spite of the anti-Red hysteria generated by the Palmer Justice Department, few tangible results were achieved by the Palmer raids. Only three pistols
that worked were seized in the raids, and a total of 591 aliens were deported from
1920 to 1921 (Murray, 1955: 249–251). During the slacker raids in New York City
in 1918, when approximately 75,000 men were arrested and jailed, 199 out of every
200 arrests were later considered to be mistakes (Lowenthal, 1950: 28). Louis Post,
who as Assistant Secretary of Labor during the Red Scare was required to sign the
deportation orders of individual aliens, probably more than anyone exposed what
he called the "deportations delirium." By insisting on evidence of personal guilt in
each case, he showed "the public the enormous discrepancy between the Justice
Department's propaganda about the Communist threat and the pathetic and harm-
less individuals Hoover had rounded up" (Powers, 1987: 115–116). The Red Scare,
in Post's view, was nothing more than a "gigantic and cruel hoax."

The box score for the McCarthy era is not much better. After all the
sensational exposés of communists in government and the alarm over the loyalty
of federal employees, only three of at least seventy-five federal employees formally
accused of communist activities were brought to trial for any crime between 1948
and 1953 (Wilensky, 1967: 135). Of the eighty-one State Department employees
Senator McCarthy publicly accused of disloyalty, one almost came to trial, but no
charges were ever formally made against the rest; Senator McCarthy insisted that
the evidence lay in secret loyalty-security files of the executive branch (Wilensky,
1967: 140). While the celebrated postwar spy cases involving Alger Hiss, the
Rosenbergs, Klaus Fuchs, and Judith Coplon lent credibility to the alarm over
internal security, these cases proved to be more symbolic than substantive. Alger
Hiss's conviction in 1950 did not establish that he was a communist or a spy but
that he had perjured himself before Congress in denying that he knew his accuser,
Whittaker Chambers (Powers, 1987: 300). While Julius and Ethel Rosenberg were
convicted and executed for espionage, there is some question as to the significance
of the information they passed to the Soviets. Although in this "crime of the
century" it was believed the Rosenbergs had passed atom bomb secrets to the
Soviets, the Rosenbergs appear instead to have passed on less significant information involving top secret military projects involving radar and aeronautics (Powers,
1987: 302–303, 557). Finally, if one considers that there were only 108 convictions
of actual Communist Party members under the Smith Act between 1949 and 1957
(U.S. Attorney General, 1950–1957), we can legitimately question, as Post did in
the earlier era, whether the "facts" of the McCarthy era justified the accompanying
panic and hysteria.

The crisis of law and order of the late 1960s and early 1970s was certainly
based on tangible events that were clearly disruptive of social order: a rising crime
rate, massive urban disorders, campus disorders, and protests and demonstrations

against the Vietnam War. Again, the issue is not the reality of these events but rather their interpretation in the paranoid style referred to by Hofstadter. In the mounting public alarm over law and order during this period, these historical events were increasingly perceived as being caused by a conspiracy of organized radicals—"outside agitators" who might even be under foreign control and influence. Both Presidents Johnson and Nixon enlisted the FBI and CIA to uncover the foreign links of the antiwar movement. The establishment of the CIA's Operation Chaos in 1967 was "predicated on the belief that the foreign connection existed, and it was just a matter of finding it" (Halperin et al., 1976: 149). The CIA conducted numerous studies assessing the foreign links of the internal security threat.

> Ironically, all these studies concluded that the domestic dissent was a product of social and political conditions in this country, and not the result of an international conspiracy. As late as 1971, when Operation Chaos had grown to grand proportions, a report was issued confirming "there is no evidence . . . that foreign governments, organizations or intelligence services control U.S. new left movements" (Halperin et al., 1976: 151).

Nevertheless, the CIA pursued the search for the illusive foreign connection, even in violation of its own charter, which prohibited its involvement in internal security matters. Operation Chaos was not discontinued until 1974, at the height of the Watergate scandal.

The Red Scare, the McCarthy era, and the law-and-order crisis of the 1960s all involved a public exaggeration and magnification of the internal threats to national security. This was further accompanied by a "distortion of intelligence"—an interpretation of historical events in the paranoid style of the American political tradition. There are, however, additional common conditions that characterize these historical eras of domestic alarm.

All of the periods of expanding domestic intelligence were preceded by a major era of social reform. The Red Scare was preceded by the Progressive era, McCarthyism by the New Deal, and the antiradicalism of the late 1960s by the civil rights movement and the Great Society programs of the Johnson administration.[3] These periods of social reform were all characterized by the ascendance of liberal thought in American life, a growth in federal government programs and activity, and the emergence or resurgence of organized radical groups as a relatively major force in American politics. In the Progressive era it was the Socialist Party and the IWW; during the New Deal, it was the resurgence of the Communist and Socialist parties, and later Wallace's Progressive Party; in the 1960s, it was the New Left (including numerous student and antiwar groups) and black nationalists groups (including Black Panthers, SNCC, SCLC, and so on).

A further condition that preceded all three periods of expansion was the existence of civil disorder in the nation, usually in the form of labor or racial strife. In the year prior to the Red Scare, which peaked in January 1920, there were a number of labor strikes that received considerable national attention: the Seattle general strike, the Boston police strike, the nationwide steel and coal strikes. In addition, there were bomb explosions in eight cities, one of them at the home of

Attorney General Palmer (Murray, 1955: 78–81, 140–158). Similarly, the years 1945 and 1946 involved an enormous upsurge in labor strikes, including major strikes in key industries (auto, steel, oil) and a number of general strikes as well (Pearce, 1981). The McCarthy years were relatively tranquil according to any conventional measure of domestic peace: number of riots, armed attacks, protest demonstrations, strikes (Taylor and Hudson, 1972). The expansion of domestic intelligence in the late 1960s was also preceded by a wave of civil disorders between 1964 and 1970. These domestic disorders, coupled with international events that were widely perceived as external threats to national security (including the Bolshevik Revolution of 1917, the Russian occupation of Eastern Europe after World War II, the Chinese Revolution in 1949, the North Korean invasion of South Korea, and finally the Vietnam War), further magnified the internal threat posed by these organized radical groups and the domestic disorders.

An apparent explanation of the growth of FBI domestic intelligence during these historical eras is that the expansion of such operations is a direct response to the increased threat posed by organized radical groups and the civil strife associated with these periods. As we have seen, this is part of the official rationale for the expansion of intelligence activities. The ostensible success of the massive federal efforts against radicalism appears to support this theory. The dramatic decline in Communist Party membership during both the Red Scare and the McCarthy era as well as the erosion of black nationalist and white radical groups in the late 1960s is certainly consistent with this explanation. However, there are data that contradict the official theory. Specifically, during each period in which domestic intelligence operations were expanded, the most dramatic increase occurred after the organized left groups had begun to decline. According to Preston (1963), the IWW and Socialist Party were at their strongest in 1912, several years before the Red Scare. Similarly, the membership of the Communist Party (CPUSA) had begun to decline sharply several years before the McCarthy era. Membership peaked in 1944, with 80,000 CPUSA members (Whitehead, 1956); in 1950, when Senator McCarthy first exploited the communist issue, membership was at 43,000; and at the end of the McCarthy era, in 1955, membership was approximately 22,000 (Belknap, 1977a: 190). The situation was no different during the expansion of domestic intelligence operations in the late 1960s and early 1970s. By the FBI's own estimates, the membership of Students for a Democratic Society, one of the more prominent white radical groups, reached a peak of approximately 40,000 in 1968 to 1969, and membership of the Black Panthers similarly peaked in 1969 (U.S. Attorney General, 1969). Campus disorders reached their highest point in 1969, and ghetto disorders peaked in 1967 (National Advisory Committee, 1976: 511ff.). As figure 4-1 clearly shows, domestic intelligence operations increased dramatically after 1969 until 1972.

These contradictory data suggest a modification to the above explanation: the changes in domestic intelligence operations are only in part a response to the activity of organized radical groups, but more so, perhaps, they are a response to domestic political divisions and policy debates which are particularly intense at these times. This interpretation is reinforced if we consider a further constellation of political factors associated with each period of expansion that also contributes to the climate of public alarm and hysteria.

Along with the decline in the political left, there is a resurgence in conservative social thought, a decline in public confidence in major social institutions, a breakdown in traditional political coalitions, and the need of policymakers to marshal support for new political and/or economic policies and to achieve a new political consensus. Let us briefly examine this constellation of political forces for each period.

The Red Scare was a conservative and nativist reaction to the disruptive political and economic changes in American society since the late nineteenth century (Theoharis, 1971). During the Progressive era, organized labor made significant gains, as evidenced in the increase in the membership of the American Federation of Labor from 500,000 in 1900 to 4,169,000 in 1919 (Murray, 1955: 8). While workers had won concessions on higher wages and shorter working hours, big business had been adamant on not capitulating on labor's right to collective bargaining. By tainting organized labor with the Bolshevik threat, the Red Scare hysteria served to undermine the position of organized labor and, in a sense, to roll back the gains of the Progressive era. While the General Intelligence Division (GID) in the bureau (formed in 1919) had been the center for government antiradical propaganda, the National Security League (supported by Rockefeller, DuPont, and Morgan), the American Defense Society, and the National Civic Federation represented the major sources of well-planned antiradical propaganda in the private sector (Murray, 1955: 85). It cannot be doubted that these groups were successful in marshaling support for their postwar programs. Although there was disagreement within the executive branch over the tactics in the Palmer raids, particularly between the Justice and Labor Departments, domestic radicalism itself was not a major campaign issue by either major party in the 1920 presidential election (Murray, 1955: 26). The legacy of the Red Scare was to strengthen the position of big business vis-à-vis organized labor; organized labor lost more than a million members in the two years following the Red Scare and did not recoup until after 1929. Indeed, the membership of the Ku Klux Klan was greater in 1924 than that of organized labor.

McCarthyism developed out of a resurgence of conservatism in the postwar Congress. Like the Red Scare, it also used antiradical and anticommunist themes as a political tactic, but this time it was to discredit the New Deal and its advocates. As Theoharis (1971) observes, the origins of McCarthyism are linked to Truman's efforts to gather support for the Marshall Plan and his containment foreign policy.[4] Congressional conservatives later exploited the anticommunist issue to magnify the internal security threat. The implication was that disloyal government employees had formulated New Deal policies: "The McCarthyites' post-1950 attack on the Truman Administration centers on the subversive character of former New Deal personnel, who used their important jobs to betray the national interest" (Theoharis, 1971: 99).

Similarly, the expansion of domestic intelligence operations after 1967 was part of a conservative backlash emphasizing the issues of law and order and the failure of Kennedy-Johnson liberalism. While Truman had attempted to fashion a new domestic political coalition for his "Cold War liberalism," Nixon likewise was fashioning an "emerging Republican majority" by combining blue-collar votes in the North with conservative votes in the South and West under a policy of rolling back the gains of the Great Society programs (Wolfe, 1979: 39).

A pattern emerges from the foregoing analysis of the three periods of expansion. Domestic intelligence operations are expanded during periods of struggle between political and economic policymakers. This struggle is typically of liberal groups in mainstream politics against conservative political forces that become politically and ideologically dominant during the period of expansion. While the impetus for this struggle may stem from organized radical groups' challenge of the power and privilege of dominant interests, the internal threat posed by the political left is exaggerated and magnified by policymakers and is used as a basis to discredit not only the radical groups but also liberal policies associated with them and to rationalize new conservative policies. The organization of the domestic intelligence function (organizational autonomy, centralization of intelligence, and executive secrecy) is structured in such a way as to facilitate this process.

How then do we explain decreases in domestic intelligence?

The Periods of Decline

We previously identified two major periods of domestic intelligence decline: the period immediately after 1924, and the Watergate era (1972–1977). The curtailment of domestic intelligence during both of these periods was part of the fallout from major government scandals: Teapot Dome in 1924 and Watergate in 1973–1974.[5] In the Teapot Dome scandal, some of the charges of corruption involved Attorney General Daugherty, which in turn brought attention to Burns, who was then director of the Bureau of Investigation and who had used his official position to aid his company (Burns International Detective Agency) in a campaign against the IWW (Belknap, 1977b). Similarly, Watergate resulted in disclosures that the Nixon administration had misused the FBI and the intelligence agencies. Yet, it was not the domestic intelligence operations themselves that became the public issues during both scandals—the Palmer raids of 1919–1920 and the FBI break-ins, mail openings, and electronic surveillance of the post–World War II period. As Chomsky has pointed out (Perkus, 1975: 10), the Watergate break-in itself was a "tea party" compared to FBI abuses against radical dissenters through its COINTELPRO and COMINFIL efforts.[6] Although COINTELPRO was publicly disclosed prior to Watergate, it was the Watergate break-in that generated public outrage, not the more severe harassment of left-wing political groups (Bernstein, 1976). The parallel to this in the 1924 reorganization of the old Bureau of Investigation was that it was the corruption of the Harding administration and the questionable practices of Burns as bureau director that led to reorganization and not the Palmer raids (Ungar, 1975). In fact, it was J. Edgar Hoover, in spite of his coordinating the raids under Palmer, who was appointed first director of the reformed bureau.

In 1924 Attorney General Stone abolished the General Intelligence Division, and the bureau's intelligence functions were accordingly terminated (Belknap, 1977b). Similarly, in the post-Watergate era, Attorney General Levi issued guidelines in 1976 governing domestic intelligence operations, and Director Kelley reorganized the bureau's domestic security operations (Elliff, 1979). The General Accounting Office (U.S. Comptroller General, 1976, 1977) review of FBI domestic intelligence indicates a rapid and continuous drop in the amount of such activities between 1972 and 1977 (see figure 4-1 and table 4-1).

What is significant about these "reforms" in both eras is that they involved voluntary restraint and self-regulation by the bureau and the DOJ and they were not reinforced by congressional legislation (for example, charter legislation) to provide legal sanctions for bureau misconduct. Furthermore, the containment of domestic intelligence occurred after the organized radical groups no longer represented a force in domestic politics, a new political consensus had been achieved, and the former political tactics of magnifying internal security threats may have begun, in fact, to threaten established institutions. Following the Red Scare, the disbarment of New York Socialists who had been legally elected to the state assembly raised widespread concern that the principle of representative government was abridged and "underscored for the entire nation the dangerous effect of continued hysterical fear" (Murray, 1955: 244). In the same way, Watergate underscored the threat to constitutional government posed by unchecked presidential power, including the use of the intelligence agencies for political purposes.

There was a parallel to this in the McCarthy era. McCarthyism was useful to the Republican Party as long as the GOP was in opposition and as long as the Communist Party was the target of the "witchhunt." After the Republican victory in 1952, and as McCarthy began to broaden his attack to encompass a wider variety of groups and institutions, he became a liability (Belknap, 1977a). The Senate censured McCarthy in 1954, and he died two years later in obscurity.

What is unique about the post-McCarthyism period is that the FBI did not curtail its domestic intelligence operations (see figure 4-1 and table 4-1), but that such activities were relatively stable over the next decade. What was curtailed was the public aspects of domestic intelligence. McCarthy's censure and the 1957 Supreme Court decision in the Yates case reflected the decline in public support for McCarthyism and the public prosecution of radicals.[7] There have been no Smith Act prosecutions since 1957. Instead, the FBI initiated its own "underground McCarthyism" in the form of such programs as COMINFIL and COINTELPRO (U.S. Senate, 1976b). Unlike the post–Red Scare and the post-Watergate periods, the FBI and the intelligence agencies were not themselves discredited as part of a broader government scandal. The FBI survived McCarthyism unscathed.

FBI Lawlessness and Social Structure

The phenomena of the Red Scare, McCarthyism, and the antiradicalism of the late 1960s must be understood in terms of the intersection of organizations, institutions, and history. These phenomena were not historical aberrations unrooted in social structure. As we have seen, there were constellations of social and political factors that were reproduced in each of these historical eras.

The FBI as an organization benefited in each era by the expansion of domestic intelligence, which provided it with a unique basis of bureaucratic power and empire building. The executive, and sometimes Congress, benefited because the intelligence provided them with a secret pool of information to discredit opponents and, by extension, their policies. Theoharis (1971) comments on the connection between McCarthyism and the desire of congressional conservatives to discredit the New Deal and its advocates. The trial and conviction of Alger Hiss were symbolic in this regard; Hiss epitomized the eastern liberal intellectual associated with New Deal reforms.[8] While the FBI and Justice Department were permitted unusual autonomy during these periods, there were nevertheless limits to this latitude. In the case of the FBI, the organization of domestic intelligence, which Hoover fashioned at his considerable discretion, was permitted as long as it furthered the public policy needs of the executive. A kind of symbiotic relationship existed between the organizational self-serving interests of Hoover and the policy needs of the executive (Bernstein, 1976). As long as both the FBI and the executive, or Congress, gained, the arrangement persisted in spite of the organizational autonomy and power it delegated to Hoover's FBI (and the Palmer Justice Department of the 1920s). However, when that organizational structure ceased to facilitate public policy goals, the executive acted to alter that structure, as it did in 1924 and, again, after Watergate.[9]

There is a final observation about these three periods of growth in domestic intelligence and FBI lawlessness. While such intelligence operations were ostensibly to undermine the effectiveness of organized radical groups and to monitor their activities, it appears that in the arena of policymaking, such operations were more useful for political purposes insofar as they advanced broader public policy objectives. This is not to deny the impact that domestic intelligence operations had on radical and subversive groups but simply to point out that there were broader public policy issues at stake. Indeed, the legacy of each of the three historical eras went well beyond the fate of the particular groups targeted. As Murray (1955: 263) notes in his historical study of the Red Scare, the legacy of the Red Scare extended at least through the 1920s, being manifested in a continuing suspicion of organized labor, hatred of Russia, intolerance toward aliens, and intense nationalism.

The Unraveling of the Hoover FBI

The post-Watergate era consisted not only in a decline in FBI domestic intelligence but also in a major reassessment of bureau investigative priorities. On the surface, the FBI scandal and reassessment appeared to be about FBI lawlessness in its intelligence operations, but more fundamentally, it was an expression of dissatisfaction with the Hoover FBI and its place in the executive and the national security apparatus. The wholesale unraveling of Hoover's FBI empire had to wait until after his death, but the process of scandal was in the works before that. The road to scandal and the dynamics of reform are the next part of the story. The Hoover FBI, which was forty-eight years in the making, was to be subject to public scrutiny and investigations perhaps unimagined by Hoover.

NOTES

1.   This is similar to Sherman's (1978: 51–52) approach to studying police corruption. Sherman argues that a useful measure of police corruption is the social organization that supports such deviance and corruption. The amount of police corruption will vary directly, according to changes in the social organization of police corruption. The social organization of corruption may refer to internal organizational controls, procedures, and structures, or it may relate to the external environment of the organization, such as tasks that facilitate corruption, like gambling and other vices.

2.   Only the first measure, investigative matters received, is available for a significant length of time, 1950 to 1977. *Investigative matters received* is an administrative term used by the FBI to measure work load and should not be confused with a case or investigation. One case may entail many investigative matters (U.S. Comptroller General, 1976: 132). The FBI's definition of the security index and other related indices (communist index, reserve index, administrative index) was constantly changing, so this presented problems in any comparison over time. The remaining measures are available for the years 1965 through 1975 and are useful to corroborate trends that appear in the first measure.

3.   *Great Society* was the term President Lyndon Johnson coined in the mid-1960s to refer to the range of domestic programs in his administration aimed at uplifting the poor and minorities and making them part of the mainstream of American life. Most notable among these programs were civil rights legislation and the war on poverty, which included Head Start, a job training program, and a short-lived community action program (Gettlemen and Mermelstein, 1967).

4.   The Marshall Plan, named after then–U.S. Secretary of State George C. Marshall, was announced in 1947 and consisted of billions of dollars in grants in aid to Western European countries to help rebuild their economies. The Soviet occupation of Eastern Europe after the war, and the devastation of the war itself, left Western Europe vulnerable to Soviet expansion. The Marshall Plan was the beginning of U.S. containment foreign policy during the Cold War years, where *containment* referred to controlling the spread of international communism (Palmer, 1962: 873; Theoharis, 1971).

5.   Refer to note 3 in chapter 2 for a description of the Teapot Dome scandal, and note 1 in chapter 1 for a brief account of the Watergate scandal.

6.   COMINFIL was an FBI intelligence program initiated during the Cold War to determine if individuals or groups were infiltrated or influenced by communists. COINTELPRO was a more aggressive FBI intelligence program aimed at disrupting or neutralizing certain targeted groups. Initially, the target was the CPUSA (1956); other groups were later focused on by this program, including the Socialist Workers Party (1961), the Ku Klux Klan (1964), black nationalists groups (1967), and the New Left (1968).

7.   In *Yates* vs. *United States,* 354 U.S. 298, 325 (1957), the U.S. Supreme Court reversed the Smith Act convictions of second-echelon Communist leaders, holding that the government must show advocacy of action and not simply belief in an abstract doctrine.

8.   In 1942 Alger Hiss, a former State Department official, was accused by Whittaker Chambers before a congressional subcommittee of being a communist. Although Hiss refuted the allegations and they initially did not appear to have much credibility, suspicion gradually mounted. By the late 1940s, Chambers's allegations carried wider implications for the credibility of the communists-in-government issue. It was never conclusively established that Hiss was a communist. However, since Hiss had denied even knowing Chambers, the issue of lying to Congress became a face-saving measure for congressional conservatives. In 1950 Alger Hiss was found guilty of perjury (Powers, 1987: 297–300; Theoharis, 1982).

9.   According to Theoharis and Cox (1988: 186, 191–192), Roosevelt was aware that FBI investigations exceeded their authority from federal statutes, but he also knew that he could use these excesses to advance his own policy interests. Ironically, Roosevelt's support of FBI intelligence expansion resulted in the surveillance of his own wife, Eleanor.

Part Two
SCANDAL
AND REFORM

Chapter 5

THE ROAD TO SCANDAL

The FBI office at Media, near here, was raided early today and Government property removed, according to an FBI spokesman. In an anonymous telephone call to a Philadelphia reporter, a group calling itself the Citizens Commission to Investigate the FBI said it had "removed all the records" (New York Times, Mar. 10, 1971: 7).

In this brief, one-paragraph article buried at the bottom of the page, the *New York Times* reported, two days after its occurrence, one of the watershed events in FBI history. The *New York Times* is not to be faulted for this apparent oversight, since the full significance of the Media break-in was not to be appreciated for several years. Two weeks later, after the perpetrators of the break-in had begun to circulate some of the stolen documents to the press and some members of Congress, Attorney General John Mitchell urged them not to publish information from the FBI files: "Disclosures of the information could endanger the lives or cause other serious harm to persons engaged in investigative activities on behalf of the United States" (*New York Times,* Mar. 24, 1971: 24).

This break-in of an FBI resident agency outside of Philadelphia proved to be one of the most serious breaches of its security in FBI history. The stolen documents, which were eventually published, revealed widespread FBI political surveillance of domestic groups, including New Left and black activist groups. According to an analysis of the documents, 40 percent of the Media files involved domestic intelligence activities (Perkus, 1975: 18). One of the congressmen who received some of the documents, Parren Mitchell of Maryland, indicated that the files showed FBI agents were engaged in illegal surveillance of groups and individuals without evidence of wrongdoing (*New York Times,* Mar. 24, 1971: 24).

The significance of the Media break-in to the Hoover FBI was both substantive and symbolic and resulted in the closing of many resident agencies[1] throughout the country and a tightening of security in all of FBI offices. Perhaps of greater importance was the formal termination of the FBI's counterintelligence programs about one month later.[2] The symbolic impact of the break-in was that the secrecy of FBI operations was now not sacrosanct. Even the Hoover FBI had to be vigilant in protecting its files and closely guarded secrets from reaching the public domain.

While the importance of a single event can be overstated, the Media break-in clearly cannot be separated from the context of the FBI in the late 1960s and early 1970s. Had such a break-in occurred during the Eisenhower years, at the peak of Hoover's powers,[3] it undoubtedly would have remained an obscure article in the *New York Times,* and there would have been little fear that such stolen documents would be published, and if they were, the flap potential would have been minimal.

But 1971 was a year in which both Hoover and the FBI were objects of mounting criticism. Senator George McGovern had urged the Justice Department to probe Hoover's persecution of agent Jack Shaw, who resigned from the bureau rather than accept a disciplinary transfer to Montana (*New York Times,* Feb. 1, 1971: 13). Shaw and fifteen other FBI agents were ordered by Hoover to withdraw from a course at John Jay College of Criminal Justice where Shaw had made confidential remarks to the instructor that were critical of the FBI. These remarks were contained in a private letter to the professor in which Shaw criticized bureau personnel practices, especially those relating to promotion and discipline, and he also questioned the kinds of investigations the FBI pursued. In the letter, Shaw cautioned that his professor maintain the confidentiality of its contents, since disclosure might result in recriminations and discipline. Little did Shaw realize that the confidentiality of the letter had been compromised when a draft of the letter was given to the typing pool in the New York City field office; it eventually found its way to Hoover in Washington, D.C. (Burnham, 1971: 27).

In addition, Senator McGovern made public an anonymous letter on FBI stationery, apparently from ten agents, charging that the FBI had lost its effectiveness because agents had to spend so much time polishing Hoover's image (*New York Times,* Mar. 1, 1971: 15). Later in the year, a two-day conference on the FBI was held at Princeton University. It was one of the few times that an independent body had dared hold a public inquiry on the bureau. Conference participants consisted of scholars, lawyers, journalists, former Justice Department officials, and former FBI agents; the conference was officially boycotted by Hoover and the FBI. The proceedings of the conference, largely critical of the FBI, were subsequently published in an edited volume, *Investigating the FBI* (Watters and Gillers, 1973).

The Media break-in may have been a necessary condition, but it was not sufficient to unlock the secrets of the Hoover FBI. In this chapter, our inquiry into the FBI focuses on the question: How were the secrets of the Hoover FBI finally revealed? Gaining an understanding of how and why the Hoover FBI began to unravel in the early 1970s is not a simple matter and requires an understanding of the nature of large organizations and bureaucratic power struggles. We must also have insight into the dynamics of scandal and the politics of public disclosure. Without this broader understanding, the FBI experiences of the 1970s will remain discrete events, unlinked to history or social institutions.

The "Invisible Government" of the FBI

There can be no doubt that the Hoover FBI had, for several decades, successfully concealed from public view important aspects of its operations that did not surface until the mid-1970s. The bureau's G-man mystique, a product of the 1930s, had obscured the seamier side of some of the agency's activities and had given it a certain immunity from public criticism. The bureau had also been insulated from any significant legislative oversight for many years. Hoover's autocratic internal control of the FBI, along with its semiautonomous status within the Justice Department, had contributed to its untouchable position as a government agency. It is of interest that Wise and Ross's 1964 book, *The Invisible Government,* which delved into the secrecy and covert actions of U.S. agencies, mainly the intelligence community, listed the FBI as one of the "lesser agencies" of this invisible government. In fact, the FBI is indexed on only eight pages in this volume. This is perhaps further testimony to Hoover's success at concealing the hidden aspects of bureau operations.

This, of course, is not to say that the FBI had completely escaped criticism and scrutiny after nearly fifty years of Hoover's tenure. Between 1939 and 1941, there was a wave of criticism centering on a series of incidents involving espionage and internal security cases that cast doubt on the FBI's effectiveness in dealing with these matters. In 1940 a U.S. Senate Committee catalogued the illegalities in one of these incidents in a manner somewhat reminiscent of the investigations of the Palmer era. And on March 13, 1940, the *New York Daily News* noted that "Mr. Hoover is widely believed nowadays to be building up a secret police organization of un-American, anti-American complexion" (Lowenthal, 1950: 328). However, given that these were war years, the espionage and sabotage menace that Hoover had been warning the public about seemed more paramount than some irregularities in the bureau's operations. Neither the Senate nor the House ordered a full-scale investigation of the FBI; instead, a more limited inquiry into wiretapping was conducted (Lowenthal, 1950: 334).

Although the FBI enjoyed a high level of public confidence since the mid-1930s,[4] the political left had always had a certain amount of skepticism and suspicion about the FBI's activities. Seagle's (1934) criticism of federal expansion into law enforcement during the Roosevelt administration, Lowenthal's (1950) documenting of bureau abuses, and Cook's (1958, 1964) appraisal of the FBI are all part of this tradition of alerting the public to the dangers of a secret police and its potential menace to democratic institutions. But until the 1970s, this clearly remained a minority perspective.

To document in a more systematic way the untouchable status of the Hoover FBI in the twenty-year period preceding the Media break-in, we have to examine public disclosures relating to questionable or illegal FBI behavior that have appeared in the national news since 1950. Figure 5-1 plots FBI public disclosures during this period based on news entries in the *New York Times Index.*[5] Public disclosures involve news events that reveal some aspect of the dark side of bureau activities. The distribution of public disclosures during this thirty-year period can be used as a measure of the FBI's ability to control information about its invisible government.

The data in table 5-1 and figure 5-1 confirm that the Eisenhower years were, indeed, the Hoover FBI's pinnacle of power, since the 1950s accounted for only 2.2 percent of public disclosures for the total thirty-year span. The data also confirm that the early 1970s was a period of massive leaks, with 44.8 percent of the total disclosures.

Powers (1983: 266–267) argues that the public's discovery of the dark side of the FBI in the 1970s had been common knowledge in some circles for many years but that the public had always ignored this bad news about the bureau. Through a process of selective perception, the public was able to maintain its G-man image until the events of the 1970s reversed this popular image. While the collapse of the G-man myth in the 1970s accurately accounts for what happened to the status of the FBI in American popular culture, it does not fully take into account the social and political forces involved in the ascendence of the FBI's "countercultural" image, to use Powers's term. It is this transformation of the FBI from G-man to villain that remains to be explained. Crucial to this explanation is accounting for how the invisible side of the FBI entered the public domain and why the series of public disclosures, which began to unfold in the early 1970s, ultimately led to a major scandal. It is necessary first to clarify some terms and concepts that are critical to the analysis.

FIGURE 5-1. FBI Public Disclosures (1950-1979)
Source: Poveda, 1981: 86.

Table 5-1. FBI public disclosures (1950-1979)

Year	Accidents[a]	Scandals[a]	Total Public Disclosures
1950–1954	0	1	1
1955–1959	2	0	2
1960–1964	10	4	14
1965–1969	11	6	17
1970–1974	39	21	60
1975–1979	6	34	40
	68	66	134

[a]Refer to note 5 on p. 71 for a definition of this term.
Source: Poveda, 1981: 87.

The Concept of Scandal

Large organizations possess the organizational power and resources to control public information about themselves. There is, of course, variation in informational control among large organizations. At one extreme the FBI, CIA, and the various intelligence agencies are statutorily entitled to maintain the secrecy of budgets, sources, methods, and agent identities. For example, a March 11, 1983, National Security Directive required that federal government employees who have access to certain classified information must submit all materials derived from such "sensitive compartmented information" to prepublication review. There is no time limitation on this directive. Anyone who signed the agreement would be bound by lifetime censorship (Ball, 1983: 16).[6] Similarly, large corporations have their "proprietary information" that they conceal from public view. At the height of the 1973 Arab oil embargo, the major oil companies resisted disclosing information about crude stocks, refining runs, and inventories, claiming this as proprietary information (Engler, 1977: 6). Former CIA director, Richard Helms, testifying before a congressional subcommittee in the early 1970s, indicated that even the CIA had trouble gathering intelligence from the oil companies (Engler, 1977: 191).

The concealment and suppression of information constitute one dimension of organizational information control. The management of public information or public relations is another dimension. In 1973, when there was considerable public skepticism about the energy crisis and gasoline shortages, the oil industry attempted to influence public opinion through a massive advertising campaign. The American Petroleum Institute and American Gas Association spent $12 million on such a campaign, while four of the major oil companies (Exxon, Shell, Texaco, and Gulf) spent $22 million on corporate image ads in addition to $115 million for product advertising (Demaris, 1974: 235).

The shaping of public information can be more subtle than this. In their history of the Royal Canadian Mounted Police (RCMP), the Browns (1973: 129) note how the RCMP, through secrecy and selective access to information, have largely written their own history. Solberg (1976: vii) makes a similar point with regard to the history of oil. The FBI has had its own officially sanctioned history, Donald Whitehead's *The FBI Story* (1956), not to mention movies, a television series, and even an officially sanctioned comic strip in 1936, the "War on Crime" (Powers, 1983). As noted earlier, most large organizations develop a glorifying myth that puts the organization in a highly favorable light, both to its members as well as to the external public (Blau and Meyer, 1971: 50–55).

The concept of scandal has at its core the idea of revelation or public disclosure. In a scandal, information about an organization is publicly disclosed that penetrates that organization's system of information control. A second element of scandal is that this information reveals embarrassing or discrediting organizational behavior, such as corruption or deviance. Molotch and Lester (1973, 1974) distinguish between two types of public disclosure—accidents and scandals—which differ in the process by which they become public. Accidents are unanticipated, unintentional occurrences that are promoted as news events—such as the Santa Barbara oil spill or Three Mile Island. Scandals are created through the intentional activity of individuals, typically inside informers, who disclose information previously not in the public domain—such as Ellsberg's release of the secret Pentagon Papers to the *New York Times* in 1971.[7] In practice, this distinction between accidents and scandals is difficult to maintain because news events often involve a combination of the two. Both accidents and scandals, however, provide insight into normally concealed organizational structures and processes. These insights or disclosures provide the basis for scandal, regardless of their etiology.

Scandal, however, is more than the disclosure of concealed organizational behavior. As Sherman (1978: 59ff.) notes, it is a process that begins with a revelation; the disclosed facts are then promoted as events by major social and political actors, the meaning and interpretation of the disclosures are publicly debated, and in a big scandal, the organization itself is publicly labeled as deviant. Sherman (1978: 66) distinguishes between a big scandal, where the organizational nature of the deviance has been disclosed, and a little scandal, where the misconduct of individuals is alleged but not linked to institutionalized organizational practices. It is in this context that we shall trace the evolution of FBI public disclosures in the early 1970s and their culmination in a big scandal in 1974.

The Major Disclosures of FBI Abuses

A cursory examination of figure 5-1 and table 5-1 reveals the early 1970s as a unique period in recent bureau history judging by the sheer volume of disclosures about the seamy side of bureau activities. Since we have taken the view that such disclosures do not just happen but rather are created through intentional activity and subsequently promoted as news by major social and political actors, a closer examination of specific disclosures should give us insight into the politics of disclosure centering on the Hoover FBI of the 1970s.

In our analysis, we shall focus on six organizational FBI practices that were revealed during the 1970s. These practices reflect institutionalized organizational behavior that appears to violate certain laws or constitutional rights. It should be emphasized that these are not isolated episodes of organizational misconduct nor are they simply the improper or illegal conduct of individual agents; rather, they are ongoing organizational practices supported by high-level administrators. These six practices are:

1. COINTELPRO—the FBI's counterintelligence program aimed at mainly domestic political groups from 1956 to 1971. The purpose was to "disrupt and neutralize" targeted groups.
2. Surreptitious entries—the use of black bag jobs, or illegal burglaries, as an investigative technique.
3. Hoover's secret files on public officials—which consisted of the personal and confidential file, some thirty-five cabinet drawers of personal correspondence that were destroyed by Hoover's secretary immediately after his death, and the official and confidential file (the OC file), which survived, although the vast majority of pages in the OC file have been withheld by the FBI as of 1988. Both of these highly sensitive files were maintained separately from the FBI's central records in Hoover's office (Elliff, 1979; Theoharis and Cox, 1988).
4. White House misuse of the FBI—the use of the FBI to gather political intelligence or to use the FBI for partisan political purposes.
5. Internal financial corruption—which included kickbacks between FBI officials and an electronics firm.
6. Informants as agent provocateurs—the use of informants to initiate violence or illegal activity, typically to maintain their cover.

An examination of the source of these disclosed organizational practices indicates that they were all initially revealed as a result of an accident or scandal news event. Not surprisingly, the FBI was not a willing source of information about its secret operations. Only one event was initially disclosed by an insider (scandal) to the executive branch. This was President Nixon's revelation at a San Clemente news conference on August 23, 1973, that FBI surreptitious entries (that is, burglaries) had occurred in previous administrations "on a very large scale." The Nixon remark was in response to a question about the 1971 burglary of Daniel Ellsberg's psychiatrist's office. On the following day, the Justice Department confirmed that it was "an old, established investigative technique" but that the practice had ended in 1966 (Crewdson, 1973a: 1).

All the other organizational practices were initially disclosed by outsiders (accidents), either as a result of the Media break-in, a Freedom of Information Act (FOIA) lawsuit/request, a civil suit, or a congressional hearing. For example, COINTELPRO was first unwittingly disclosed by the Media break-in in March 1971. It was not until months later that NBC reporter Carl Stern noticed the caption "COINTELPRO-New Left" on one of the released documents. Pursuing this clue, he filed a FOIA lawsuit to compel the bureau to produce additional COINTELPRO documents. These files were released in December 1973 and March 1974 (Perkus, 1975). Additional COINTELPRO documents were released later in the 1970s to the Church Committee (U.S. Senate, 1976a, b), and as a result of other FOIA requests, over 50,000 pages of COINTELPRO files were released in November 1977 (Ryter, 1978 a, b). The focus here, however, is on the initial disclosures.

Although it had long been suspected that Hoover maintained secret files on public officials, it was the Senate Watergate Committee in 1973 that first obtained documentation (the Sullivan memoranda)[8] that such files existed and had been misused in the past (Elliff, 1979: 56). Although the Senate Watergate Committee did not include its findings on the Sullivan memoranda in its report, the Edwards subcommittee of the House Judiciary Committee requested the Department of Justice to investigate these charges. On February 27, 1975, Attorney General Levi officially confirmed the existence of the OC files and reviewed the content of the surviving files with the Edwards subcommittee (U.S. House, 1975a). Several years later, historian Athan Theoharis, obtained the release through the FOIA of 7,000 pages of documents pertaining to Hoover's files. Theoharis's documents include accounts of the alleged sexual activities of Dwight Eisenhower, Eleanor Roosevelt, John Kennedy, and others. They also showed that Hoover supplied former Senator Joseph McCarthy with derogatory information used by McCarthy in his anticommunist attacks on individuals in the 1950s (*First Principles,* Jan./Feb. 1984: 6).

Perhaps the FBI practice that received the most attention in the early 1970s was the White House misuse of the FBI. This information first surfaced in the Gray confirmation hearings (U.S. Senate, 1973), when it was revealed that L. Patrick Gray, who was acting FBI director, had sent some FBI reports relating to the FBI's Watergate investigation to the White House and later destroyed documents that were part of the investigation. While his nomination for FBI director was withdrawn by President Nixon, the Nixon White House politicization of the FBI became a major public issue. Clearly, the Nixon administration was not unique in its political misuse of the FBI, as Nixon (1978) and his aides argued in their defense and as various scholars have since pointed out. For example, Franklin Roosevelt misused the FBI by ordering it to wiretap various associates he suspected of leaking information to the press. He also used the FBI to gather information on critics of his foreign policy. Similarly, Lyndon Johnson used the bureau during the 1964 Democratic Convention to wiretap and supply him with information on Martin Luther King and members of the Mississippi Freedom Democratic Party (Bernstein, 1976: 63, 74; Powers, 1987).

A further observation is that the initial disclosure of all but one of these organizational practices occurred in the 1970 to 1974 period. The only exception is the internal financial corruption scandal, which was revealed in the Pike Committee hearings in 1975 (U.S. House, 1975b), and then further investigated by the Department of Justice in 1976, with its final report issued in January 1978 (Marro, 1978: 8). This disclosure was exceptional, too, because it did not involve the intelligence division but involved the administrative division under John Mohr, who had retired in 1972. High-level bureau officials were found to have received kickbacks from an electronics manufacturer as a condition for selling surveillance equipment to the FBI. The DOJ report also revealed a pattern of petty corruption in which, for example, agents were used to make improvements in Hoover's home (Marro, 1978: 8).

While the use of informants by the FBI and other law enforcement agencies is widely known, their occasional role as agent provocateurs[9] is more carefully guarded information. Marx (1974) reviewed some thirty-four cases of informants whose activities received media attention during the early 1970s. Perhaps the most notorious of FBI informants was Gary Thomas Rowe, who had infiltrated the Klan in the 1960s. His testimony in 1965 against three Klansmen accused of killing Viola Luizzo, a participant in the Selma-to-Montgomery march, was largely responsible for their conviction. Thirteen years later, however, Alabama authorities, in their renewed investigation of racial killings in the 1960s, found information linking Rowe to some of these killings, including the shooting that resulted in Mrs. Luizzo's death. In the Alabama investigation, Rowe was also linked to a number of other racial killings, including the 1963 bombing of a Baptist church in Birmingham that killed four black children, and the fire bombing of the home of A. G. Gaston, a black millionaire (Raines, 1978: 1). On July 5, 1979, the family of Viola Luizzo filed a wrongful death action against the U.S. government seeking damages on the grounds that Rowe failed to prevent, and participated in, Mrs. Luizzo's murder, since he was riding in the car with the convicted Klansmen at the time of the shooting (*First Principles,* Sept. 1979: 11). Even though two Klansmen testified that Rowe admitted to the killing the day after Luizzo's death, a federal judge dismissed the suit on May 27, 1983, on the grounds that the FBI was not liable for the death, and presumably was not negligent in supervising Rowe (*First Principles,* July/Aug. 1983: 15).

The Justice Department conducted its own inquiry to determine Rowe's involvement in violent crime while an FBI informant. Although this report was completed in July 1979, the Justice Department refused to make it public and claimed that this internal report was "privileged from disclosure," especially in light of the civil action in the courts that was brought against the FBI by the family of Mrs. Luizzo. Nevertheless, seven months after its internal publication, the *New York Times* obtained a copy of the DOJ report. While the Rowe report found no conclusive evidence that he had been involved in racial killings, it did document six incidents of nonfatal violence in which Rowe had engaged. Furthermore, the internal DOJ inquiry revealed that FBI agents knew about and apparently covered up involvement by Rowe in violent attacks on blacks, civil rights activists, and journalists. As its chief paid informer in the Klan, Rowe received approximately $22,000 between 1960 and 1965. The DOJ report also revealed that Hoover had blocked prosecution of four Klansmen who had been identified by Birmingham FBI agents as the bombers of the Baptist church who killed four black children in 1963 (Raines, 1980a: 1, 16; 1980b: 1).

Analysis of the disclosure of these FBI practices in the early 1970s shows that the whistleblowers were not within the FBI but rather were people who were outsiders, not only to the FBI but usually to the executive branch as well. These practices were often disclosed gradually and sometimes under fortuitous circumstances. What is still not clear, however, is why organizational practices that had existed for years, some for decades, would be disclosed in such a massive way in the early 1970s? As we shall see, it appears that the key to unlocking these FBI secrets was tied to the politics of Watergate and the growing need of the executive for better intelligence information.

The Mobilization of Scandal

If one examines the chronology of disclosures relating to intelligence agency abuses, there were clearly revelations that occurred before the Watergate scandal of 1973–1974. In January 1970 Christopher Pyle, a former captain in Army Intelligence, revealed in an article in the *Washington Monthly* the existence of widespread Army surveillance of civilian politics (*Civil Liberties,* Apr., 1975: 5). This resulted in a class action suit against the U.S. Government (*Tatum* v. *Laird*) and Senate hearings on government surveillance, especially military spying, in March 1971. Of course, the Media break-in was in that same month, although major COINTELPRO documents were not released until the fall of 1973. While there was some basis for scandal prior to Watergate, it took the Ervin Watergate Senate hearings in 1973 and the House Judiciary Committee's impeachment hearings in 1974 to provide the forum for securing additional revelations as well as to give political meaning to the disclosures.

In an unprecedented way, the various Watergate hearings provided the political leverage for unlocking FBI secrets.[10] While the hearings endeavored to show that the Watergate abuses were uniquely tied to the Nixon White House, President Nixon and his aides used disclosures as part of their Watergate defense to show that past presidential administrations had engaged in similar practices and had misused the FBI to gather political intelligence. Nixon's disclosure of surreptitious entries and the DOJ's confirmation of these as "an old, established investigative technique" and the use of the Sullivan memoranda to reveal past misuse of the FBI by Johnson and Roosevelt were not intended to discredit the FBI but rather to bolster their own defense.

In his memoirs, Nixon recalls some of the internal debate that took place in May 1973:

> I wanted everything out on the Democrats. My staff resisted me, and for several weeks we debated back and forth about it. I felt like a fighter with one hand tied behind his back: most of my advisers argued that if I revealed the activities of previous administrations, it would look as if I were trying to divert attention from myself by smearing others. If I did not, however, I was afraid that I would remain portrayed as a willful deviant from past practice and be condemned for my legal and legitimate uses of the same tactics my predecessors had used not only more extensively but for blatantly political purposes (Nixon, 1979: 414–415).

Nevertheless, the Watergate investigators' view of the Nixon White House prevailed; the House Judiciary Committee's second article of impeachment related to the White House misuse of the FBI and the intelligence agencies. At the height of Watergate, in spite of the numerous disclosures of FBI abuses, the central public issue involving the FBI was the Nixon White House misuse of the FBI for political purposes, particularly under acting FBI Director L. Patrick Gray. It appeared for a while that a broad investigation of the FBI was going to be missed owing to the focus on White House transgressions. As early as the Gray confirmation hearings, Tom Wicker commented on the missed opportunities:

> Mr. Nixon had already missed one opportunity. When Mr. Hoover died last year and Mr. Gray was made acting director, the President could have appointed a blue-ribbon commission of law enforcement professionals, members of Congress, Government officials and public members to evaluate the FBI and to make recommendations as to how it ought to evolve in its post-Hoover phase (Wicker, 1973: 45).

Throughout the Watergate scandal, disclosures of FBI abuses were not related to FBI reform but rather to the impeachment of Richard Nixon.[11] It required still further revelations in the post-Watergate period, coupled with the growing awareness of the need for intelligence agency reform, to refocus attention on FBI abuses. These revelations were forthcoming in late 1974 with the *New York Times* publication of a front-page article exposing widespread illegal domestic spying by the CIA during the Nixon administration.[12] Attorney General Saxbe also made public a twenty-one-page Justice Department (Petersen Committee) report on COINTELPRO (*New York Times,* Nov. 16, 1974: 23), which had been prompted by earlier disclosures. While this report emphasized that many COINTELPRO activities "were entirely proper and appropriate law enforcement procedures," it also pointed out that other COINTELPRO activities had "exceeded the bureau's investigative authority" (U.S. Senate, 1976b: 73–74).

The upshot of these post-Watergate revelations was to produce new government inquiries. Unlike the Watergate investigations, which focused on wrongdoing in the Nixon administration, these post-Watergate investigations would examine lawlessness in the intelligence agencies that had encompassed several past presidential administrations. On January 4, 1975, President Ford created the Commission on CIA Activities within the United States (the Rockerfeller Commission) to investigate charges of CIA domestic spying. In the same month, the Senate established a select committee (the Church Committee) to investigate alleged illegal spying and other abuses of the CIA, FBI, and other intelligence agencies. In the following month, the House created its own select committee (the Pike Committee) to also investigate allegations of improper or illegal activities by U.S. intelligence agencies.

The mobilization of scandal beyond Watergate was necessary, because there was still more on the political agenda that had been left unfinished by the Watergate scandal. This was the matter of intelligence agency reform—and of FBI reform in particular. The Nixon White House, long before Watergate, had been disenchanted with Hoover and the FBI. From the beginning of the Nixon presidency, there had been a preoccupation with leaks in government and with securing better intelligence on domestic violence and bombings. Nixon (1978) and Ehrlichman (1982) have both written about their dissatisfaction with FBI domestic intelligence.[13] Ultimately, the Nixon administration's disenchantment with FBI domestic intelligence would be expressed in the Huston Plan in 1970.[14] In the view of the Nixon White House, Hoover's restraints on intelligence collection methods had created serious deficiencies in the administration's ability to anticipate the

plans of domestic dissenters. In 1966 Hoover had directed that his field offices discontinue the use of surreptitious entries, mail openings, and campus informants under age 21 and curtail the use of electronic surveillance. Furthermore, in 1970, Hoover severed formal liaison ties between the FBI and the CIA and later with the other intelligence agencies (U.S. Senate, 1976b: 924). The Huston Plan was essentially the White House plan to better coordinate the work of the several intelligence agencies and to relax the restrictions on intelligence collection that Hoover had apparently imposed on the FBI. Hoover's objection to the Huston Plan ultimately resulted in Nixon revoking official approval of the plan, although several of its provisions were implemented anyway.[15]

A further indication of dissatisfaction with the Hoover FBI, even preceding the period of major disclosures, was the decline after 1968 in FBI appropriations relative to the Justice Department (see table 3-1). Since the end of World War II, FBI appropriations had maintained a relatively constant proportion of the total Justice Department budget, fluctuating between 40 and 45 percent. Suddenly, after 1968, this ratio of the size of the FBI budget to the DOJ budget dropped precipitously to 29.7 percent in 1970 and to 21.4 percent in 1972[16] and remained between 20 and 22 percent throughout the 1970s. This more objective measure of FBI organizational power provides another stark glimpse of the decline in the Hoover FBI during the Nixon administration.

The organizationally weakened Hoover FBI, Hoover's death in 1972, Watergate's unlocking of FBI secrets, and, finally, the need to complete Nixon's plan to reform the intelligence agencies were all necessary conditions that led to the FBI big scandal of the mid-1970s. Forty-eight years of relative immunity from criticism and scrutiny had left the FBI with much "dirty linen." It still remains for us to discover what the outcome of this scandal was and whether FBI reform would become a reality in the 1970s.

NOTES

1.   These resident agencies are not to be confused with the FBI's field offices. Resident agencies are smaller, satellite agencies of the major FBI field offices (fifty-nine in 1971).

2.   The April 22, 1971, memo from FBI Director Hoover to the field offices terminated COINTELPRO as a program but it did not preclude counterintelligence actions on an ad hoc basis. The memo noted: "In exceptional instances where it is considered counterintelligence action is warranted, recommendations should be submitted to the bureau under the individual case caption to which it pertains. These recommendations will be considered on an individual basis" (Perkus, 1975: 27).

3.   Both Hoover's recent biographer, Richard Gid Powers (1987: 313), and Richard Nixon (1979: 71), vice-president during the Eisenhower administration, agree that J. Edgar Hoover reached the apex of power and prestige during the eight years of the Eisenhower presidency.

4.   While public opinion surveys on the FBI were not conducted before the 1960s, these more recent surveys show that there was high-level public support for the bureau in the 1960s and that this support rapidly declined in the 1970s. Gallup national surveys revealed 84 percent of the public expressed a "highly favorable"

rating of the FBI in 1966, and 71 percent did so in 1970. This popularity declined rapidly in the 1970s to 52 percent in 1973, 37 percent in 1975 (Ungar, 1975: 493, 591), and 37 percent in 1979 (Gallup, 1979).

5.   The *New York Times Index* was used as the basis for determining whether a particular event had become a national public event, since the *New York Times* is widely regarded as the newspaper of national record. Each entry in the *New York Times Index* under the subheading "Investigation, Federal Bureau of" was examined and appropriately coded using Molotch and Lester's (1973) classification of news events into routines, accidents, and scandals. Routine news entries included such events as the reporting of the number of graduates from the National Police Academy, the annual crime statistics published by the FBI in *Uniform Crime Reports,* or Hoover's annual appearance before a congressional appropriations committee. Accident news entries, which are unplanned or unanticipated events, at least from the standpoint of the FBI, consisted of events such as public criticism by the press, the 1971 Conference on the FBI at Princeton, Martin Luther King's criticism of the bureau in 1962 for its inactivity in probing civil rights violations, or the reporting of the 1973 Socialist Workers Party suit against the FBI. Scandal news entries typically involve planned events leaked by an inside informer. These included books by ex-agents that were critical of the FBI, reports that agents were disciplined, release of the DOJ report on COINTELPRO, or the results of its inquiry into FBI internal financial corruption. In both the accident and scandal news entries, embarrassing or seamy aspects of the bureau's activities are revealed or alleged.

6.   This directive, which would have applied to thousands of officials in the White House, National Security Council, State Department, Pentagon, and other agencies who have access to sensitive compartmented information, was suspended by President Reagan about a year later after encountering substantial opposition in various congressional subcommittees (*First Principles,* Mar./Apr. 1984: 10).

7.   The Pentagon Papers was a secret forty-seven-volume study of the history of U.S. involvement in Indochina and Vietnam from World War II to May 1968. The study was carried out at the request of Robert McNamara in 1967, then Secretary of Defense, and revealed, among other things, that four succeeding administrations had carried out actions and involved the United States in southeast Asia in ways that were at variance with official policy and the public statements of presidents. A Defense Department employee, Daniel Ellsberg, released most of this secret history to the *New York Times,* which began to publish it in a series of articles on June 13, 1971. The Nixon Justice Department attempted to prevent publication of the Pentagon Papers on "national security" grounds. The U.S. Supreme Court, some two weeks later, rejected the administration arguments and permitted publication (Sheehan et al., 1971: ix–xvii).

8.   William C. Sullivan, former head of the FBI Intelligence Division from 1961 to 1971, provided White House counsel John Dean with two memoranda detailing FBI abuses in past presidential administrations. These memoranda included information on Hoover's secret files. Dean subsequently provided these memoranda to the Senate Watergate Committee (Sullivan with Brown, 1979a; Elliff, 1979).

9.   The distinction between informant and agent provocateur is sometimes difficult to make. Nevertheless, the informant is one who plays an information-

gathering role, and the agent provocateur seeks to influence the actions of a group in a sometimes illegal manner (Marx, 1974: 404).

10. As Kelley (FBI director from 1973 to 1978) also subsequently pointed out, the "Watergate nightmare" made it easier for him to "initiate long overdue reforms within the organization." Without Watergate, he argues, his reforms would have taken much longer (Kelley and Davis, 1987: 152–153).

11. For example, even though the Senate Watergate Committee had obtained the Sullivan memoranda from John Dean, indicating the existence of the Hoover files and past misuse of the FBI, these findings were not included in its public report (Elliff, 1979: 56).

12. Even this story in the *New York Times* was indirectly the result of Watergate. On April 15, 1973, John Dean told federal prosecutors about the burglary of Ellsberg's psychiatrist's office and mentioned that "the plumbers" had received some CIA assistance. James Schlesinger, who was CIA director at the time, was upset at this revelation and directed all CIA employees to report to him any CIA "potential flap activities," past or present. This led to the compilation of a 693-page report (one page for each abuse) called "The Family Jewels." Seymour Hersh of the *New York Times* learned about one part of "The Family Jewels," Operation Chaos, and this is what was published on December 22, 1974 (Powers, 1979).

13. Ehrlichman (1982: 158–159) notes that during the first year of the Nixon presidency, the president repeatedly called for intelligence about domestic violence and bombings. Because of the poor quality of the FBI's investigative work, Ehrlichman soon discovered he could get better intelligence from the New York City Police Department intelligence unit. Jack Caulfield, a member of Ehrlichman's staff, was a former N.Y.C. policeman.

14. The Huston Plan was also revealed during the Senate Watergate Committee hearings in 1973. See note 10 in chapter 3 for a brief account of this plan.

15. The Church committee pointed out that there was a certain amount of duplicity in all of this. The various intelligence agencies had successfully concealed some of their secret programs from each other as well as from the White House. Some provisions of the Huston Plan were already in operation before 1970, and after President Nixon revoked his approval of the plan, the intelligence agencies still went ahead and expanded their collection programs (U.S. Senate, 1976b: 962–967).

16. A major part of the decline in the ratio of the size of the FBI and DOJ budgets in the early 1970s is accounted for by the funding of the Law Enforcement Assistance Administration (LEAA) in the DOJ budget. Under the Omnibus Crime Control and Safe Streets Act of 1968, LEAA was charged with the responsibility for assisting state and local governments in reducing crime and improving the quality of local criminal justice systems. This, however, does not undermine our measure of FBI organizational power, since it is significant that such responsibilities were placed with the Justice Department and not with the FBI. LEAA funding was eventually phased out in fiscal years 1979 through 1981, although a scaled-down Office of Justice Assistance, Research, and Statistics continued to be maintained.

Chapter 6

THE SCANDAL AND ITS AFTERMATH

Informed Justice Department sources disclosed today that what one of them called "illegal and unlawful" burglaries by agents of the Federal Bureau of Investigation had taken place in this country over a thirty-year period that began under the Administration of President Franklin D. Roosevelt and ended in 1966 (Crewdson, 1973a: 1).

While it is difficult to pinpoint a turning point in the FBI's road to scandal in the 1970s, the above revelation, perhaps more than any other, began the shift in attention away from the Watergate abuses of the Nixon administration to the abuses of the Federal Bureau of Investigation. Although the full meaning of this disclosure would have to wait until the Watergate scandal had run its course, one of the secrets of the Hoover FBI had been irreversibly leaked: the secret of black bag jobs, or surreptitious entries. Clearly, this disclosure was not a voluntary gesture on the part of the Justice Department but was a response to a statement made by President Nixon at a San Clemente news conference on the previous day that such burglaries took place "on a very large scale" during the Kennedy and Johnson administrations.[1] The Justice Department had been left in the rather uncomfortable position of either calling the president a liar or confirming his statement.

Up to this point in the scandal process, the public disclosures involved allegations of individual misconduct centering on the confirmation hearings of acting FBI Director Patrick Gray. Now, however, the organizational nature of FBI lawlessness had been disclosed. Surreptitious entries were not simply the result of overzealous agents but rather an "old, established investigative technique." President Nixon's San Clemente remark had unwittingly transformed the scandal process from a little scandal into a big scandal, to use Sherman's (1978) terms.[2]

It is again important at this point to place the politics of disclosure and the dynamics of scandal in some theoretical perspective. A crucial observation is that the fate of public disclosures about an organization—whether they remain little scandals or evolve into big scandals—depends on the relative power of the organizational actors involved. Organizations, unlike powerless individuals, have the resources to respond to imputations of deviance. Organizations become deviant in so far as they are not able to defend themselves and consequently are publicly labeled as deviant (Ermann and Lundman, 1987). Scandal itself becomes conditional on the power of competing organizational actors in the aftermath of public disclosures. The mobilization of scandal and promotion of disclosures as news is symptomatic of an underlying policy dispute between major social and political actors—that is, the elites.[3] The decision to disclose FBI lawlessness must be understood as part of a broader policy debate. As Molotch and Lester (1973: 9) express it, "The amazing thing about the Pentagon Papers, then, is not that Presidents tell lies, but that the *New York Times* was willing to expose that fact." While scandals may take on a life of their own as aggressive journalists pursue various angles of a story, there still must be parties willing to make disclosures in furtherance of their own agenda.

This willingness to promote discrediting information provided by an insider indicates the disclosure's usefulness to one of the parties engaged in a policy debate. The selective disclosure of official lawlessness in this way may help reinforce one segment of the elite's public definition of events. The absence of a public issue dividing elites would mean that revelation, even when provided by insiders, would not be publicly disclosed.[4]

Our task becomes one of seeing in the news—the disclosures, little and big scandals, competing definitions of events—the social organization that produces it (Molotch and Lester, 1973, 1974, 1975). To understand the FBI's scandal and reform in the 1970s, we must discover the underlying conflicts and policy disputes that gave rise to the disclosures, inquiries, and reactions to the disclosures. In sum, we must read into the record the organizational dynamics that produced it.

The Congressional Inquiries

In the wake of massive disclosures of abuse and improper activities by the U.S. intelligence agencies during the Watergate investigations and in the immediate post-Watergate period, the Senate and House established their own select committees, the Church and Pike committees,[5] respectively, to investigate these allegations and make recommendations for reforming the intelligence agencies. Both committees held extensive hearings in 1975, secured additional documents from the intelligence agencies, and issued final reports in 1976. The Pike committee was more assertive in its investigation, as it subpoenaed documents, resisted compromise, and refused to have its final report censored by the executive branch. The Church committee was more cooperative in its inquiry, negotiating with the agencies for material, rarely issuing a subpoena, and ultimately submitting its final report to intelligence agencies for review and declassification (Halperin et al., 1976: 2).[6] In the end, the Pike committee's final report was suppressed by the House itself and only its eleven recommendations were published.[7] The three volumes of the Church committee report were published in April 1976 along with its 183 recommendations for reforming the intelligence agencies.

By the Church committee's own admission, its inquiry was incomplete.

> Despite its legal Senate mandate, and the issuance of subpoenas, in no instance has the Committee been able to examine the agencies' files on its own. In all the agencies, whether CIA, FBI, NSA, INR, DIA, or the NSC, documents and evidence have been presented through the filter of the agency itself.
>
> Although the Senate inquiry was congressionally ordered and although properly constituted committees under the Constitution have the right of full inquiry, the Central Intelligence Agency and other agencies of the executive branch have limited the Committee's access to the full record (U.S. Senate, 1976a: 7).

Nevertheless, the Church committee conducted the most thorough investigation of the U.S. intelligence community to date.[8] It should be noted, however, that even at the height of the scandal there were limits to what the major actors in this drama were willing to disclose.

The policy debate in these congressional inquiries that related to the FBI centered on the FBI's role as an intelligence agency (Elliff, 1979).[9] At one extreme was the position that the bureau's intelligence function should be terminated and that there was no justification for intelligence operations beyond simple criminal investigations. At the other pole were those who advocated maintaining intelligence operations as preventive investigations to anticipate domestic violence; this was an indispensable function quite distinct from the reactive role played by criminal investigations. In the middle were those who sought a modified intelligence role for the FBI. The Church committee took the middle ground in its recommendations on this issue: "Preventive intelligence investigations" were appropriate for terrorist groups and hostile foreign intelligence activities (Elliff, 1979: 24).

When all was said and done, most of the recommendations focused on implementing this modified intelligence function of the FBI, which still provided for some preventive intelligence investigations quite apart from the bureau's law enforcement functions. The Church committee was especially concerned that the Congress frame statutes that would provide guidelines for the conduct of intelligence activities. In particular, legislative charters should be passed for defining the mission, authority, and limitations of intelligence operations (U.S. Senate, 1976a: 4). This was important because in the past, intelligence activities had relied overwhelmingly on executive authority. In addition, the Church committee emphasized the importance of strong and effective congressional oversight over the FBI and the intelligence agencies.

In its recommendations on domestic intelligence, the Pike committee urged that the FBI's Internal Security Branch be abolished and that the intelligence division be restricted to matters of foreign intelligence and counterintelligence. It recommended that all investigations involving the criminal activity of domestic groups be handled by the General Investigative Division, not the Intelligence Division. Furthermore, the Pike committee recommended that the investigation of terrorist groups be closely tied to violations of the criminal law and noted that the Justice Department has responsibility for determining when the political activities of domestic groups may be targeted for investigation as terrorist activities (U.S. House, 1975b: 2295).

The Reform of FBI Domestic Intelligence

By mid-1976 the congressional select committees had completed their difficult task of investigating the allegations of FBI and intelligence agency misconduct. It had been clear from the beginning of the disclosures, with the exception of the financial corruption scandal, that FBI abuses were concentrated in its domestic intelligence operations. In the aftermath of the scandal, would the appropriate congressional and executive authorities take action to implement the recommendations of the Church and Pike committees? What would be the impact of any reforms on FBI domestic intelligence—those activities that were at the heart of the Hoover FBI? Would the reforms be transitory or enduring?

Let us consider some of the reform measures that were taken. Even before the post-Watergate scandal involving the FBI and the intelligence agencies, the FBI's first permanent director after Hoover, Clarence Kelley, who was appointed in July 1973, had taken modest steps to reform the bureau. During his first year, he made efforts to improve relations with the Justice Department and introduced managerial reforms, what he called "participatory management." He also began to redirect bureau investigative resources into white-collar and organized crime, which would eventually become top FBI investigative priorities (Kelley and Davis, 1987).

The serious task of reorganizing domestic intelligence, however, was left until after the congressional inquiries. In August 1976 Kelley announced that investigations of domestic radical and terrorist organizations would be transferred from the Intelligence Division to the General Investigative Division, where they would be treated like all other criminal cases. Foreign counterintelligence investigations would remain in the Intelligence Division and would continue to be given high priority. Clearly, this reorganization of FBI domestic intelligence closely followed the recommendations of the Pike committee. On the day he announced these changes, Kelley also revealingly remarked that there were "some who harbor a feeling that the good old days during the time that Hoover headed the organization will someday come back. They won't" (Crewdson, 1976a: 1). Later, in his memoirs, Kelley confirms that these reforms were part of an ongoing bureaucratic power struggle. His attempts at moderating the intelligence programs were "viewed by some within the bureau as a compromise with 'anarchists,'" which "caused some hard feelings during my entire term as director of the FBI" (Kelley and Davis, 1987: 161).

While this might appear to be a cosmetic change, the rationale for the transfer of domestic intelligence investigations to the General Investigative Division was that the same norms employed in criminal investigations, relative to the rule of law, now be reinforced in domestic security cases (Elliff, 1979: 90). Such norms had been nonexistent in the Intelligence Division. For example, in his testimony before the Church hearings, Sullivan noted that regarding intelligence work, "this is a rough, tough, dirty business, and dangerous" and that legal norms were seldom considered (U.S. Senate, 1976b: 7; Halperin, et al., 1976: 226).

Along with these organizational changes, the bureau also began to discontinue many of its domestic security investigations, which declined dramatically from 21,000 in mid-1973 to fewer than 300 by the end of 1976 (Elliff, 1979: 92). The new strategy was to focus on organizations and key individuals in policymaking positions, not on the rank-and-file members; this was the "quality over quantity" approach. Neil Welch (1984: 219–222), the SAC of a number of major FBI field offices,[10] recalls how Kelley called him to Washington in the aftermath of the Church hearings to carry out the closing of the domestic security cases. Although there was resistance from the heads of the internal security sections and Hoover veterans, Welch concluded that 626 of the 4,868 original investigations he examined were justified and were authorized to remain open.

In the meantime, the Justice Department had been busy drafting guidelines on domestic security investigations. These went into effect on April 5, 1976, and came to be known as the Levi Guidelines, after Attorney General Edward Levi. They provided some clarification and standards for FBI domestic intelligence operations (Elliff, 1979). Under the guidelines, the bases for initiating investigations were articulated, the three levels of investigation specified (preliminary, limited, and full), as well as the investigative techniques appropriate to each level; the guidelines also delineated when investigations must or may be terminated (U.S. Senate, 1978: 98–99).

To fulfill the recommendations of the Church and Pike committees for better legislative oversight of the FBI and the intelligence agencies, the Senate established a permanent intelligence committee in May 1976; the House followed suit in July 1977 (*First Principles,* Mar./Apr. 1980: 5). In addition, both the Senate and House already had existing subcommittees of their Judiciary Committees having FBI oversight responsibilities. Although initially the Senate Intelligence Committee established itself as the major FBI oversight committee, with a carryover of some of the personnel and expertise from the Church committee, the Judiciary Committees eventually assumed the major responsibility for FBI oversight (Morgan, 1980). In particular, Don Edwards's House Subcommittee on Civil and Constitutional Rights emerged as the most critical of the congressional subcommittees in the area of oversight.

Presidents Ford (1976) and Carter (1978) meanwhile issued executive orders reasserting presidential power in the intelligence arena. With the exception of assassination, past abuses of the intelligence agencies were not specifically prohibited in these orders. They did reaffirm that the exclusive mission of the CIA was foreign intelligence and that the FBI had exclusive responsibility for domestic intelligence matters. This dichotomy between domestic and foreign intelligence, however, is difficult to maintain. Take, for instance, the section of the Carter order on "Restrictions on Certain Collection Techniques":

> Activities . . . for which a warrant would be required if undertaken for law
> enforcement rather than intelligence purposes, shall not be undertaken with-
> out a judicial warrant, unless the president has authorized the type of activity
> involved and the Attorney General has both approved the particular activity
> and determined that there is probable cause to believe that the United States
> person is the agent of a foreign power (Shattuck, 1983: 67).

Essentially, what this appears to mean is that when the attorney general has
"probable cause to believe" that a person in the United States is an "agent of a
foreign power," that person may be targeted by a variety of intrusive techniques,
including warrantless wiretapping, physical searches, and mail opening (Shattuck,
1983). Unfortunately, what constitutes an agent of a foreign power was never
defined in the Carter executive order. This domestic-foreign distinction is crucial
because U.S. citizens so designated as foreign agents are then beyond the reach of
the Fourth Amendment protections and the rule of law.

   Both the Ford and Carter executive orders also provided for the intrusive
surveillance of U.S. citizens both at home and abroad in many circumstances, even
if they are neither suspected of breaking the law nor of acting as an agent of a
foreign power. These orders also permitted the infiltration of domestic political
organizations under some circumstances. These executive orders, as they pertain
to the FBI, were to be implemented by attorney general guidelines, which may be
kept secret (Shattuck et al., 1982). With a few exceptions, the thrust of the executive
orders on intelligence was not to restrict the FBI and the intelligence agencies but
rather to reestablish executive authority over the conduct of such activities.

   The final element in the reform agenda that was called for by the
congressional inquiries was a statutory charter for the FBI and the intelligence
agencies. The task of drafting domestic and foreign intelligence charters rested with
the Intelligence and Judiciary Committees of both houses and the Justice Department. Four major bills involving intelligence charters were introduced in the 95th
Congress, but none were reported out of committee (Cardman, 1978: 8). When the
hearings on the FBI charter legislation began in 1978, there was widespread support
in the Congress, in the Carter administration, and in the FBI for such legislation.
As the policy debate unfolded, some of the key issues centered on whether
COINTELPRO-type activities should be prohibited. Should there be a criminal
predicate for domestic intelligence investigations? Should a judicial warrant be
required for the FBI use of intrusive investigative techniques, and should civil
remedies be provided for charter violations (*Civil Liberties*, Sept. 1979: 1, 3)? The
outcome of two years of hearings in various committees was the National Intelligence Act of 1980, which was essentially the Carter administration's version of an
intelligence charter. The act basically codified the system already in effect under
the executive orders and attorney general guidelines (*First Principles*, Mar./Apr.
1980: 1–11).[11] Civil libertarians criticized the bill for simply authorizing past
abuses (Halperin, 1980; Edwards, 1980). In fact, FBI Director Webster conceded
before the House Intelligence Committee that the proposed charter would permit
the use of disruptive techniques against domestic groups suspected of ties to foreign
powers (Lardner, 1980: 1).

   The advocates of this comprehensive intelligence charter abandoned their
efforts by mid-1980, as political support for such a measure collapsed.[12] A

legislative charter remains part of the unfinished business of the FBI scandal of the 1970s; a critical recommendation of the Church committee was not acted on.

The Decline in FBI Lawlessness?

Although failure to enact an FBI charter was a significant omission in the congressional reform agenda, it appears that most of the other major recommendations of the Church and Pike committees were implemented. The dominant view, at least in the immediate aftermath of the scandal, is that the reform measures had successfully rooted out the FBI abuses of the past. In perhaps the most thorough study of this postscandal period, Elliff (1979: 190) concludes, "These were not cosmetic reforms, but significant changes in the FBI's priorities and in its relationships with the Justice Department." Morgan (1980) also observes that much has been accomplished in FBI reform and, in fact, fears that reform might have gone too far in restricting domestic intelligence. About the same time, Wilson (1980) also notes the substantive changes that took place in the post-Hoover bureau, many of them in accordance with Congress.

Nevertheless, the suspicion lingers, particularly on the political left, that the FBI reforms were cosmetic and transitory and that a Hoover-style FBI will surface once the scandal is over. Nowhere perhaps is there more distrust than with the reformers' claim that domestic intelligence operations have declined. This area of bureau activity had, after all, been at the center of the Hoover FBI's lawlessness.

Figure 6-1 reveals a dramatic decline in FBI domestic intelligence between 1972 and 1978. While figure 6-1 traces changes in domestic intelligence according to the number of domestic intelligence matters received by the FBI, the decline in domestic intelligence is underscored by a number of other indicators: the number of domestic intelligence matters initiated decreased from a peak of

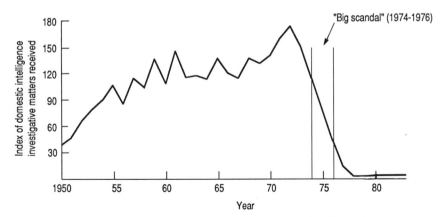

FIGURE 6-1. Changes in FBI Domestic Intelligence (1950-1983)
Source: U.S. Senate, 1975: 349-350; U.S. Attorney General, 1953-1954; U.S. House, Appropriations Hearings, 1977-1983; and U.S. Senate, Appropriations Hearings, 1981. See also source note for Figure 4-1.

3,464 in 1972 to 95 in 1977; the number of agents doing such investigations similarly decreased from 1,264 in 1972 to 143 in 1977; and the number of domestic intelligence informants declined from 1,885 in 1972 to 100 in 1977 (U.S. Comptroller General, 1976, 1977).[13]

It is also clear that FBI appropriations for domestic intelligence declined during this same period from approximately $40 million in fiscal year (FY) 1975 to $9.1 million in FY 1978.[14] The FBI continued to make budgetary reductions in domestic intelligence through FY 1982 although its percentage of allocations relative to other field programs bottomed out at about 2 percent in FY 1979 (U.S. House, Appropriations Hearings, 1976–1983).

While there can be little doubt that such a decline in FBI domestic intelligence occurred during the immediate post-Watergate era, there is some question as to why the decline occurred. The reasons for the decline from 1973 to 1975 offered by FBI officials are: (1) the reduced militancy of protest groups and (2) tightened criteria for initiating investigations. The continued decline after 1975 was attributed by FBI officials to the Levi Guidelines and the reorganization of FBI domestic intelligence (U.S. Comptroller General, 1977: 127–129). While the official reasons have surface plausibility, we have already noted that the major reforms in domestic intelligence did not occur until after the congressional inquiries had been completed in 1976. It is therefore difficult to attribute this rather significant decline in domestic intelligence to either the big scandal itself or to the reforms that accompanied it, since these events followed the onset of the decline in 1972 (see figure 6-1).

Another interpretation of figure 6-1 is that there was an anticipatory effect that preceded the actual scandal. During the Watergate era, and perhaps earlier, bureau activities having a significant flap potential were cut back. This appeared to be the case with COINTELPRO. While this might account for the decline in the FBI's most lawless activities, it would not explain the wholesale reduction in domestic intelligence that took place.

While the official version of the decline corresponds with the common-sense view of scandal—that organizational reforms follow disclosures and scandal—it is not consistent with the chronology of events. To further explore the meaning of the decline in FBI domestic intelligence, we must return at this point to our discussion of the politics of disclosure and the dynamics of scandal. We noted that the promotion of disclosures and the mobilization of scandal itself are conditional on the relative power of competing organizational actors engaged in major policy disputes. The nature of FBI reform in the 1970s is tied to an understanding of the underlying bureaucratic power struggles and policy debates that produced both the FBI scandal as well as the reform of its domestic intelligence functions. This includes bureaucratic conflicts within the executive as well as between the executive and legislative for asserting authority in the intelligence arena. To better grasp these underlying dynamics, there is yet another line of inquiry we must pursue. How the FBI and the Justice Department managed the disclosures of the Watergate era and the postscandal period will provide us with further clues in identifying the key actors and their policy disputes during this reform period.

The Management of Disclosures by the FBI and DOJ

Two periods of managing disclosures may be distinguished: (1) 1973 through 1976, the scandal period, which roughly corresponds to Kelley's tenure as FBI director; and (2) 1977 through 1980, the immediate postscandal period, which corresponds to Webster's early years as FBI director.

Each period had distinct news management and organizational problems. In the first period, the FBI and DOJ had to respond to the barrage of major disclosures, which was exacerbated by the 1974 amendments to the Freedom of Information Act (FOIA). At the same time, they had to deal with an entrenched FBI bureaucracy that still had many Hoover-era veterans who had been a part of the disclosed organizational practices.

In the second period, there were no new major disclosures although the FOIA constantly threatened to reveal new embarrassments. The problems of past disclosures remained, however, in the form of disciplining agents and officials who were still caught up in cases involving past abuse. In the view of older agents, these disciplined agents were victims of changing rules and were being prosecuted for performing their duties in good faith (Felt, 1979). However, more attention could now be focused on shaping a more favorable FBI public image—the "new" FBI.

The 1973–1976 Period

The FBI, during and after the Watergate investigation, under Director Kelley, developed an "open stance" policy toward the press (*New York Times,* Oct. 12, 1973: 51). At the same time, under pressure from the White House because of leaks about the Watergate investigation, the FBI attempted to minimize internal leaks to the press. In his memoirs, Nixon notes with alarm the leaks in 1973:

> It was as if a convulsion had seized Washington. Restraints that had governed professional and political conduct for decades were suddenly abandoned. The FBI and the Justice Department hemorrhaged with leaks of confidential testimony, grand jury materials, and prosecutorial speculation. And on Capitol Hill it seemed as if anything could be leaked and anything would be indulged, under the guise of righteous indignation over Watergate (Nixon, 1978: 851).

In August 1973, the FBI directed all of its employees to sign a written statement recognizing the confidentiality of the work of the bureau and acknowledging that the unauthorized disclosure of investigative information may result in criminal prosecution. The statement was a revised version of the FBI's traditional employment agreement, modified by the inclusion of language informing employees that violation could result in criminal or civil penalties (Crewdson, 1973b: 1).

In the meantime the Department of Justice was assuming a more assertive role in regard to the FBI. Beginning with Attorney General Richardson, and interim FBI Director Ruckelshaus (1972–1973), a series of negotiations were initiated designed to reform the FBI (*New York Times,* Mar. 31, 1974). A close working relationship, compared to the past, between the attorney general and FBI director continued under Saxbe, then Levi, and Clarence Kelley. Saxbe expressed this in his statements that the FBI wanted to be part of the DOJ again (*New York Times,* Jan. 16, and Nov. 30, 1974: 30). This new working relationship was delicate and by no means egalitarian. The DOJ was now clearly in a supervisory position to the FBI. This was later ensured by both the Ford (1976) and Carter (1978) executive orders on intelligence, which placed the attorney general in authority in relation to domestic intelligence matters as well as in issuing guidelines, procedures, and monitoring activity. The DOJ appears to have used this position to manage news and information about the FBI to ensure its dominance of the bureau.

By acknowledging the past abuses of the Hoover era,[15] and occasionally releasing documents or statements confirming those abuses, the DOJ was able to undermine the old guard Hoover-era veterans in the FBI bureaucracy who were an important counterforce in the struggle for control of the FBI. Under this strategy, Attorney General Saxbe disclosed a "four-year effort by the FBI to harass key blacks" (*New York Times,* Mar. 8, 1974: 16). He also made public a twenty-one-page DOJ report (Petersen Committee) on COINTELPRO (*New York Times,* Nov. 16, 1974: 23) that even Director Kelley took issue with in his defense of the FBI's past operations (*New York Times,* Nov. 30, 1974: 30; U.S. House, 1975c). Attorney General Levi disclosed the "wide scope of Hoover's secret files" (Horrock, 1975: 1), and ordered an FBI inquiry into the internal financial corruption of Hoover's Administrative Division[16] (Crewdson, 1976b: 1). While these press releases gave the appearance that the attorney general or a DOJ official were disclosing the new information to the public (a routine news event), we have already seen that in all of these instances, it was an outsider to the FBI and DOJ who initially disclosed the organizational practice. The DOJ press statement is usually in response to a FOIA request/lawsuit or a congressional inquiry, but in addition, the DOJ appears to be using the opportunity to mildly discredit the old FBI and, by implication, the Hoover old guard.

There is an important exception to this FBI/DOJ policy of managing the news. This exception was one of those accident news events that penetrated FBI and Justice Department public relations. The Socialist Workers Party lawsuit disclosed in July 1976 that the FBI had conducted illegal burglaries more recently than 1966, and that knowledge of this practice had been withheld from FBI Director Kelley by his subordinates. The implication of this is that the open press policy that had been developed in the fall of 1973, early in Kelley's administration, was called into question. Kelley's credibility depended on his having full knowledge and control of bureau activities. Kelley had to publicly admit that he could not flatly deny that FBI agents were engaging in illegal burglaries or other unlawful conduct (he had made such denials before), and he confessed, "I know that I was lied to" (*New York Times* editorial, Aug. 12, 1976: 30).

What is perhaps even more instructive is the manner in which the Department of Justice reacted to this apparent threat to Kelley's command of the bureau. Several days later, FBI agents (derisively known as the "dirty dozen" by their FBI colleagues) assigned to investigate the burglaries removed "file cabinet after file cabinet" from the bureau's Washington headquarters and the New York City field office. No advance warning was given to the bureau even though Kelley had committed the full cooperation of the FBI to the inquiry. The seized files were turned over to Department of Justice prosecutors who were investigating the illegal burglaries in the New York City area (*New York Times,* Aug. 20, 1976: 1). Kelley's credibility with the Department of Justice as well as the press was seriously damaged by this episode. Dissatisfaction with his control over the bureau also became a presidential campaign issue in the fall of 1976. Executive control of the FBI ultimately depended on a strong director; these incidents reflected the shakiness of Kelley's command.

The indictments of former Acting Director Gray and two other former FBI officials, Felt and Miller, which resulted from this Department of Justice inquiry into illegal burglaries, marked the first time that either a director of the FBI or a former bureau executive had been charged with a criminal act (Horrock, 1978: 1). No other disclosures of FBI organizational abuses produced criminal prosecutions. The Petersen Committee report of the DOJ concluded that no criminal investigation was warranted in connection with COINTELPRO (U.S. House, 1975c: 26–27). The DOJ report, which revealed financial corruption in the FBI, also indicated that no prosecutions were possible because of the statute of limitations; virtually all of the offenses had occurred more than five years before (Marro, 1978: 8). Similarly, there were no criminal prosecutions for the surreptitious entries before 1970. The DOJ inquiry had only investigated the illegal burglaries of the early 1970s.

The 1977–1980 Period

The FBI and the Department of Justice policy of managing public information after 1977 reflected some stability in the new FBI/DOJ relationship. While the FBI was no longer subject to a barrage of major disclosures, there appeared to be little interest or inclination by either the FBI or the DOJ to continue to acknowledge past abuses. Webster referred to the abuses of the past as "archeology" and "residuals" (Babcock, 1979: 2). Indeed, the new attitude seemed to be one of disclosing as little as possible.

In October 1977 the FBI adopted a policy of destroying certain investigative records more than five years old that, FBI agents privately indicated, would serve to prevent embarrassing revelations in the future (Kwitny, 1978: 1, 21).[17] Attorney General Bell risked contempt of court in 1978 by refusing to turn over eighteen FBI informant files to the court in the Socialist Workers Party suit. In 1979 Webster refused to allow the General Accounting Office to audit the FBI informant program despite congressional requests for the audit (Pear, 1980a: 21). Instead, the bureau conducted its own self-evaluation.

Halperin (1979: 16), observed that "both the FBI and CIA have launched public relations campaigns designed to, in effect, repeal the FOIA as it applies to them." FBI Director Webster argued, for example, that damage had been done to the FBI informant program and that there should be a ten-year moratorium on the release of investigative files (Halperin, 1979). In addition, Webster sought to have whole categories of records exempt from the FOIA: foreign counterintelligence, counterintelligence, organized crime, and terrorism (Pear, 1980b: 5; U.S. Senate, 1980b: 80). Furthermore, during this period, the Department of Justice refused to make public its report on former FBI informant Gary Thomas Rowe.

These events appeared to signal a new attitude toward public disclosures and openness toward FBI operations in contrast to the scandal era of 1973–1976. At the same time, Webster was being more successful than his predecessor in developing a favorable public image from the FBI's new priorities. The ABSCAM investigation brought public attention to the FBI's new emphasis on white-collar crime and public corruption (*Newsweek,* Feb. 26, 1980; *Time,* Feb. 18, 1980). The public announcement that the FBI had made a double agent out of a career KGB spy similarly brought attention to another of its top priority investigative areas, foreign counterintelligence (*New York Times,* Mar. 4, 1980)

By the late 1970s, the FBI/DOJ policy of managing disclosures and public information revealed stability in the bureaucratic power struggle to control the post-Hoover FBI. The bureaucratic power of the Hooverite old guard was effectively undermined by the earlier policy of mildly discrediting them through the acknowledgment of past abuses in congressional and DOJ inquiries or by forcing them into early retirement.

Most high-ranking FBI officials under Hoover had retired by 1973 (Felt, 1979). Others, including middle-level Hoover-era veterans, had been forced into retirement by the fifty-five-year age limit imposed by Congress in 1976 and made effective on January 1, 1978. It is estimated that approximately 650 FBI agents were forced into retirement in this manner (*New York Times,* Dec. 9, 1976).

In August 1979 Director Webster revised the top structure of the bureau, appointing three new executive assistant directors, none of whom were closely tied to Hoover. At the same time he announced the resignation of John McDermott, the only remaining high official linked with Hoover (*New York Times,* Aug. 13, 1979). This symbolically closed the Hoover era.

The Assessment of Reform

What emerges from the foregoing analysis is that the FBI of the 1970s was in the midst of a major bureaucratic power struggle involving social and political actors, both internal and external to the FBI, who sought control of the FBI. Also involved was a policy debate about authority to conduct intelligence operations and where discretion for such operations resided.

This debate was first manifested in the declining organizational power of the FBI in the early Nixon administration. This decline in power was closely followed by a dramatic rise in public disclosures revealing FBI misconduct. These disclosures evolved into a big scandal in which the FBI itself was labeled organizationally deviant. It is of interest that the disclosures of FBI misconduct, even past abuses, ceased once some stability was achieved in the postscandal FBI.[18] This stability was largely accomplished in the first years of Webster's tenure as FBI director.

The decade-long struggle to achieve executive control of the FBI and its operations could not have been accomplished without undermining the position of the Hoover old guard, which, in large part, was the purpose of the revelations of past abuse and the scandal itself. The task of reform, in this view, was to integrate the FBI into the executive, and particularly into the Justice Department. The Ford (1976) and Carter (1978) executive orders on intelligence clearly subordinated the FBI to the authority of the attorney general and, in effect, were measures to make the bureau an integral part of the executive. The Carter administration's FBI charter legislation (the FBI Charter Act of 1979), which was never passed, would have codified this new FBI organizational structure. In addition, Carter's comprehensive intelligence charter legislation (National Intelligence Act of 1980), again not passed, would have extended this process by defining the intelligence components of the FBI as part of the total intelligence community and placing them under the direction of the National Security Council and a Director of National Intelligence (*Congressional Record*, Feb. 8, 1980: S1319).

This view of FBI reform is reinforced by the observation that the FBI disclosures that were translated into public issues were not so much the organizational abuses of the past, which affected the rights of Americans (COINTELPRO, surreptitious entries, mail openings, and so forth), but rather the disclosures that related to issues of executive control of the FBI. During Watergate, for example, the central issue involving the FBI was the White House misuse of the FBI, which was part of the Judiciary Committee's second article of impeachment. As Chomsky points out, the Watergate break-in itself was a "tea party" compared to FBI abuses against radical dissenters (Perkus, 1975: 10). Again, when it was later disclosed that the FBI had engaged in illegal burglaries in the early 1970s, the public issue was not outrage for the victims, the SWP, or the friends and relatives of the Weather Underground but rather that the FBI was "out of control"—that is, executive control.[19]

Most of the FBI reforms were in one way or another linked to the question of executive control of the FBI. The ten-year term for the FBI director was enacted with the dual aim of insulating the director from political pressures as well as preventing the director from becoming too independent (U.S. Senate, 1974: 2). Both the Ford and Carter executive orders reaffirmed presidential power in the intelligence field and, like the proposed but abandoned charter legislation, ensured that the major discretion for FBI operations would remain within the executive. Most attempts to limit executive discretion in the postscandal period were rebuffed, even when they simply prohibited past organizational abuses. For example, an earlier intelligence reform bill that banned most of the past FBI abuses was never reported out of committee.[20] Similarly, Congressman Aspin's alternative proposal (H.R. 6820) to the Carter administration's comprehensive intelligence charter received the same fate. It, too, would have restricted certain intelligence activities. FBI Director Webster had argued that a statutory charter should be an affirmative statement of the FBI's mission and not a series of "Thou shalt not do this" and "Thou shalt not create this or that type of abuse" (*U.S. News and World Report*, Jan. 29, 1979: 54).

Even the reorganization of FBI domestic intelligence and the curtailment of such investigations were aimed at diminishing the authority of the FBI Intelligence Division and in assuming Justice Department control of FBI intelligence through the Levi Guidelines. There is nothing inherent in this reorganization that limits FBI domestic intelligence operations except government defensiveness in the post-Watergate climate. In its assessment of the impact of the Levi Guidelines, the General Accounting Office (U.S. Comptroller General, 1977) confirmed the dramatic decline in FBI domestic security investigations but pointed out that there was little change in the sources and techniques used in these operations. Consistent with its "quality over quantity" approach, the FBI was simply more carefully targeting its domestic intelligence investigations.

The FBI that emerged in the postscandal period was an agency much more firmly integrated into the executive branch of government, especially the Justice Department and the intelligence community. Although the reforms had been implemented ostensibly to curb FBI lawlessness, the thrust of the reform measures was simply to make the bureau more accountable to the executive. The days of the Hoover FBI, where the bureau had operated autonomously as a kind of private bureaucratic fiefdom, were officially over.

NOTES

1.   Nixon's statement was made in the context of a question about the constitutionality of the "plumbers'" 1971 burglary of Daniel Ellsberg's psychiatrist's office. The remark was part of the Watergate defense of showing that the abuses of the Nixon administration were not unique when compared to past presidential administrations.

2.   A "little scandal" is when the misconduct of individuals is not linked to institutionalized organizational practices. In a "big scandal," the organization itself is publicly labeled as deviant (Sherman (1978: 66).

3.   Herbert Gans's (1979) study of the national domestic news in the period 1967–1975 shows that between 70 and 85 percent of all domestic news involved "knowns"—basically, those people who occupy official positions and are well known to the public. In his analysis of news magazine columns in 1975, Gans reports that the president alone accounted for 23 percent of the domestic news; members of the House and Senate, 4 percent; other federal officials, 20 percent. State and local officials, business and labor leaders, and civil rights leaders were other prominent knowns in the news. These knowns, to use Gans's term, are what we are referring to as the dominant social and political actors in the news—or elites, for short.

Gans also analyzes the kinds of activities that make the news. In 1975 government conflicts and disagreements occupied 13 percent of news magazine columns; government decisions, proposals, and ceremonies, another 13 percent; crimes, scandals, investigations, 34 percent; and government personnel changes (including campaigning), 22 percent (Gans, 1979: 9–16).

4.   In so far as the press, especially the most politically influential press, is institutionally linked to dominant elites (Dreier, 1982), disclosures are not likely to be published in the absence of such conflict.

5.   Officially, the Church committee was the Select Committee to Study Governmental Operations with Respect to Intelligence Activities; the Pike committee was the Select Committee on Intelligence.

6. At the request of the intelligence agencies, three chapters were deleted ("Cover," "Espionage," and "Budgetary Oversight") as well as sections of other chapters (U.S. Senate, 1976a: iv).

7. The U.S. House voted 246 to 124 to suppress its own 338-page report on the intelligence agencies siding with the desires of President Ford and the agencies that the report should be censored by the executive (*New York Times*, Jan. 30, 1976: 1). Parts of the report were later leaked to the *Village Voice*.

8. There were eleven senators on the committee, chaired by Frank Church, who were assisted by a staff of one-hundred. The inquiry involved more than 800 interviews, over 250 executive hearings, and over 110,000 pages of documents (U.S. Senate, 1976a: 7).

9. John Elliff, formerly an associate professor of politics at Brandeis, was head of the Church committee's staff task force on domestic intelligence.

10. SAC is the FBI acronym for special agent in charge. At various times, Welch was the SAC in Buffalo, Detroit, and Philadelphia and was director in charge of the New York City field offices. He was a finalist for FBI director in 1978, but William Webster emerged as President Carter's choice. Welch retired in 1980 (Welch and Marston, 1984).

11. It is of some interest that the term *reform* does not appear in the title of the bill as it did in an earlier draft, the National Intelligence Reorganization and Reform Act.

12. The Carter administration's support for charter legislation weakened as the administration responded to the crises in Iran and Afghanistan. President Carter even called for the removal of "unwarranted" restraints on the CIA (*Civil Liberties*, June 1980: 1).

13. The indicator of domestic intelligence matters received was employed in figure 6-1, because data on this measure are available for the longest period of time. The other indicators, however, are highly correlated with our primary measure ($r = 0.9$ at a significance level of 0.001) and were used to estimate data for missing years.

14. The appropriations allocated to the FBI Intelligence Division were never revealed prior to fiscal year 1975 when the U.S. House and Senate Select Committees on Intelligence, in their 1975 hearings, obtained from FBI officials the estimate of $82 million (19 percent of total FBI budget). No further breakdown of the FBI intelligence budget was permitted, however, for "national security" reasons. Therefore, it was not possible at that time to ascertain the domestic and foreign intelligence portions of the budget. In subsequent years, the amount of domestic security funding has been separately reported, and it is now possible to estimate domestic security funding in FY 1975 from knowledge of the reduction of appropriations in subsequent years. It is also possible to estimate the foreign and domestic intelligence share of the budget by the relative proportion of investigative matters received in that year (8.3 percent for domestic, 11.7 percent for foreign).

15. The emphasis was always on past abuses and practices that had ostensibly been discontinued, whether it was COINTELPRO, Hoover's secret files, surreptitious entries, or the internal financial corruption of Hoover's Administrative Division. This emphasis was part of the DOJ strategy of mildly discrediting the old

guard Hooverites in the bureau executive—"keeping them in their place," so to speak.

16. The initial FBI investigation was characterized as a "whitewash" by DOJ sources. Attorney General Levi returned the report to Kelley with instructions to undertake a more extensive inquiry.

17. A 1979 lawsuit against the FBI and National Archives challenged this policy. Federal Judge Harold Greene directed seventeen experts from the National Archives, who received top security clearances, to examine a sample of bureau records going back to 1924 so they could recommend to him how much of them could be destroyed. In their eight-inch thick report, the archivists recommended that the bureau be required to keep, and ultimately turn over to the National Archives, 20 to 25 percent of its records, which consisted of approximately a billion pieces of paper on 25 million investigations. They also recommended that such records not be open to the public until fifty years after a case is closed (*New York Times,* Nov. 15, 1981: 73). In the fall of 1983, Judge Greene of the U.S. Court of Appeals ruled that FBI and National Archives officials had improperly destroyed FBI records and ordered that the FBI not destroy files of historical value without proper review by government archivists (*New York Times,* Oct. 2, 1983: 31; *Washington Post National Weekly,* Nov. 7, 1983: 37).

18. Even as early as 1976, toward the end of the big scandal, there was a growing backlash against the exposure of government secrets. This was evidenced in three U.S. House votes in the first half of 1976. We have already noted the House's 246 to 124 vote to suppress publication of the final report of the Pike committee. It also voted 269 to 115 to establish a special committee to investigate how portions of the report were leaked. In addition, the house voted 267 to 147 not to make public the size of the budget of the CIA (*Civil Liberties,* Apr. 1976: 4).

19. There is a parallel to this in the earlier reorganization of the old Bureau of Investigation in 1924. It was the corruption of the Harding administration and the questionable practices of Burns as bureau director that led to reorganization, not the Palmer raids in 1919–1920, which targeted aliens, communists, and the IWW (Ungar, 1975). It was, curiously, J. Edgar Hoover who coordinated the raids under Palmer and who was appointed director of the reorganized bureau.

20. This was the Federal Intelligence Agencies Control Act of 1977, H.R. 6051, introduced by Representatives Badillo, Drinan, Dellums, and Chisholm, among others, on April 5, 1977. This act prohibited political surveillance and preventive action against U.S. citizens, protected whistleblowers, banned intrusive investigative methods, and repealed the Smith Act and the authority of the attorney general to authorize domestic intelligence investigations. Paid informants in political groups were also banned (Shattuck and Berman, 1977: 1, 3).

Part Three
THE "NEW" FBI

Chapter 7

WHITE-COLLAR CRIME
AND THE "NEW" FBI

In the wake of massive disclosures and a major scandal in the mid-1970s, the Hoover FBI, as we have seen, came under public scrutiny and was subject to a major reassessment of its investigative priorities, particularly the traditional emphasis it had given to seeking out communists and subversives as well as chasing bank robbers and auto thieves. The rethinking of the Hoover FBI was aided by the Watergate scandal, which led to the unlocking of many FBI secrets, and was also assisted by post-Watergate revelations, which redirected public attention to the intelligence agencies themselves and not simply to the Nixon administration.

One of the outcomes of this scandal process was a reordering of the bureau's top investigative priorities. In the post-Watergate FBI, white-collar crime, organized crime, and foreign counterintelligence were officially pronounced the top priorities of both the Kelley and Webster FBI. There persisted, however, a suspicion that these were cosmetic changes and that a Hoover-style agency would soon resurface. This suspicion about the FBI may even apply to Hoover himself. Welch speculates that following Hoover's death in 1972, there were probably many who came to see him lying in state at the Capitol Rotunda who wished to confirm his death. "Thousands came to pay their respects, and an indeterminate number came to make sure he was really dead, an assurance denied by the closed casket" (Welch and Marston, 1984: 2).

In this and the next three chapters, we shall examine the nature and character of the changes in these investigative priorities, especially white-collar and organized crime, that are closely associated with the FBI reform of this period and with the emergence of a "new" FBI. We shall also be concerned with delineating the particular ways in which this "new" FBI is different from the Hoover FBI, which is critical for assessing FBI reform and for addressing the policy question at the heart of the scandal: the control of the bureau and its operations.

Although as early as the fall of 1974 Director Clarence Kelley identified white-collar crime as a "serious problem" in his "Message from the Director" column in the *FBI Law Enforcement Bulletin* (Sept. 1974), the public was largely oblivious to this new FBI investigative emphasis until Operation ABSCAM received national attention in February 1980. ABSCAM was an elaborate FBI undercover operation that involved FBI agents posing as an Arab sheik and his aides; these undercover agents attempted to buy political influence in Congress. While there was public outrage about the politicians who were caught by this "sting" operation, there was also a sudden public awareness of the new priorities of the bureau, particularly white-collar crime and public corruption, and the new techniques it employed in these investigations, namely, undercover operations. Media accounts of ABSCAM were consistently favorable and reinforced the image of a "new" FBI. *U.S. News and World Report* (Jan. 29, 1979), *Time* (Feb. 18, 1980), *Newsweek* (Feb. 25, 1980), and the *New York Times* (Mar. 16, 1980) all published major stories during this period showing that "the new FBI is watching" and that "the 'new' FBI is exorcising the ghost of J. Edgar Hoover." Operation ABSCAM came to epitomize the emerging public image of the "new" FBI.

During this period, Wilson (1980) notes that critics of the bureau may wonder whether the targeting of congressmen is a form of organizational retaliation for congressional inquiries into FBI misconduct. He argues that this is what one might expect from a Hoover-style agency, but that this is not what happened. In Wilson's view, ABSCAM was a genuine reflection of a changing FBI.

White-Collar Crime and the Hoover FBI

Operation ABSCAM is a logical starting point for this chapter because it contrasts how white-collar crime and public corruption were handled in the "old" and "new" FBI. The political influence buying that was targeted for criminal investigation in ABSCAM under Webster's FBI would likely have been handled differently by the Hoover FBI. Rather than disclosing political misconduct and making it the subject of investigation, such incriminating information was more useful to the "old" bureau when left unreported.

In the 1920s, Hoover informally began the practice of compiling dossiers on members of Congress. This practice was eventually systematized in the devel-opment of the personal and confidential files and the official and confidential files, which were highly sensitive files maintained in Hoover's office and kept separate from the bureau's central records (Elliff, 1979; Theoharis and Cox, 1988). As we have previously noted, Hoover's secret files on public officials were an important source of FBI organizational power and were also a source of abuse by both Hoover as well as presidents from Roosevelt to Nixon, who often sought information damaging to their political adversaries.[1]

After departing from the FBI, William Sullivan, who headed the Intelligence Division, subsequently disclosed some of the intimate tidbits presumably contained in the destroyed files, especially the ones on presidents. For example, writing in the *Washington Post Magazine,* Sullivan (1979b: 21) reveals that the FBI's legal attaché in Hong Kong discovered that in two trips Nixon took to Hong Kong in the 1960s he had established a friendship with a Chinese girl. Nixon subsequently assisted in the immigration of this same woman and her husband to Nixon's hometown. Even though Hoover had a longstanding friendship with Nixon, he subtly conveyed to Nixon that he possessed such information and that he would "never speak of it to anyone."

If this was the Hoover FBI's response to public corruption and improprieties, how were other areas of white-collar crime handled? If we examine the FBI annual reports in the late Hoover years, it is of interest that white-collar crime is not mentioned per se in the 1970–1972 annual reports. Accounting and fraud matters are mentioned, but they are listed under "other criminal investigations" in 1970–1971. In 1972 accounting and fraud matters first warrant a major subheading in the annual report. A content analysis of FBI annual reports reveals the marginal position white-collar crime occupied in the "old" FBI. The one area of white-collar crime that did traditionally attract attention was bank-related crimes, particularly bank fraud and embezzlement (Simon and Swart, 1984). Even this focus stems indirectly fromt the bureau concern with bank robbery, which came under its jurisdiction during the 1930s. What is clear is that white-collar offenses of any investigative complexity were avoided by the Hoover FBI. Hoover had built his empire focusing on crimes that were relatively simple to investigate and that produced impressive statistics: high percentage of crimes solved, large amounts of stolen property recovered, and so on (Cook, 1973). Crimes that did not lend themselves to producing impressive numbers were not included in the "old" FBI priorities.

The "old" FBI's avoidance of white-collar crime was, however, more basic. Traditionally, American society has not considered white-collar crime as crime. This point was, in fact, part of a major historical debate in criminology on the legal definition of crime (Sutherland, 1945; Tappan, 1947). The issue as to whether white-collar crime is crime reflects a double standard in criminal justice, where justice is administered differentially to street criminals and white-collar criminals. There is a legal and cultural blindness that makes it difficult for us to perceive the avoidable injuries and deaths produced by corporate and elite behavior as crime (Reiman, 1979; Box, 1983). The "real" crime problem has historically been the street crimes of the powerless and dangerous classes. This conception of the crime problem has traditionally been incorporated in the priorities and allocation of resources of law enforcement. This has been no less true of the Hoover FBI and the priorities Hoover used to build the FBI. The question remaining is whether the "new" FBI, which emerged in the aftermath of Watergate, actually did reverse this traditional neglect of white-collar crime along with the historical double standard of justice.

The "Discovery" of White-Collar Crime

The "discovery" of white-collar crime occurred during the mid-1970s at a time when the "old" bureau priorities had come under congressional scrutiny and when confidence in government generally was waning. Since the late 1960s, there has been a dramatic decline in public confidence in major American institutions, including the press, organized religion, the military, the executive branch of the federal government, Congress, labor unions, and big business (Lipset and Schneider, 1978). The national crises over the Vietnam War, civil rights, and Watergate all contributed to declining confidence levels and deep public distrust of government and big business (Simon and Eitzen, 1986). It was in this context and in the immediate aftermath of the Watergate scandal that the targeting of "establishment" crime seemed particularly favorable.

White-collar crime was first designated a top bureau investigative priority in fiscal year 1974. In its annual report that year, the FBI first denoted white-collar crime with a separate subheading in its program descriptions and summary of accomplishments.[2] Close examination of the 1974–1976 annual reports (U.S. Attorney General, 1974–1976) reveals that much of the emphasis continued to be on bank fraud and embezzlement, which were now included under white-collar crime. In 1974, 35.0 percent of the white-collar crime cases investigated were in the area of bank fraud and embezzlement. As evidence that white-collar crime was increasing, the FBI cited increasing convictions for bank fraud and embezzlement: in 1970, 712 convictions; in 1974, 1,200 convictions; in 1977, 1,700 convictions (U.S. Attorney General, 1971, 1975, 1978). Other kinds of investigations included under white-collar crime at this time were bribery, antitrust, perjury, conflict of interest, and fraud against some government programs. All of these investigative categories represented areas of investigation that the "old" FBI pursued. In one sense what was new about white-collar crime was the reclassification of these old crimes into a new category.

This reclassification of traditional FBI crimes into a white-collar crime category does not necessarily discredit Kelley's claim that such crime had become a top priority. If we examine resource allocation to these investigative areas, we find that an increasing proportion of FBI investigative resources were, in fact, allocated to white-collar crime in the immediate post-Watergate period. In 1975, 11.7 percent of total investigative matters received were in the white-collar crime area. This amount increased to 22.3 percent by 1979 (U.S. House, Appropriations Hearings, 1980).[3]

Is the whole, in this case white-collar crime, greater than the sum of its parts? Does the above reclassification of crimes represent a version of "old wine in new bottles?" The FBI reallocated some of its resources to white-collar crime but had not yet developed new investigative areas as part of this "new" top priority program. There was an additional problem, a conceptual and definitional one: What did the FBI mean by "white-collar crime"? Ultimately, the FBI and the Justice Department would have to come to terms with the meaning of white-collar crime. In early 1977, the Attorney General's White-Collar Crime Committee provided the following working definition: "White-collar offenses shall constitute those classes of non-violent illegal activities which principally involve traditional notions of deceit, deception, concealment, manipulation, breach of trust, subterfuge or illegal circumvention" (U.S. Department of Justice, 1980: 5).

As Simon and Swart (1984: 109) point out, this is a very expansive definition, including everything from welfare cheating by the poor to antitrust violations by upper-class businessmen. It does not specifically identify the types of cases being investigated. Part of the conceptual confusion is that white-collar crime is a sociological rather than legal category. What legal categories are to be included in the concept of white-collar crime? In 1980 the FBI included some seventy different legally defined crimes in its white-collar crime program (U.S. Department of Justice, 1980: 1a).

Another source of conceptual confusion is that the Justice Department's definition departs, and even obscures, the more traditional definition of white-collar crime, which defined such crime exclusively in terms of law violations of the upper class (Simon and Swart, 1984). White-collar crime in the "new" FBI is much more broadly conceived than when Sutherland first introduced the concept in 1939.[4]

In addition to white-collar crime, "public corruption" is first highlighted in 1978 as a separate category in the FBI's annual report. While the corruption of public officials was viewed as part of white-collar crime early in the Kelley FBI, the importance of public corruption as an investigative area increased in the post-Watergate period. A survey of FBI field offices in 1980 found corruption as the top-ranked white-collar crime priority; 54 percent of the field offices ranked it as their number 1 concern, and 16 percent, as their number 2 priority (U.S. Department of Justice, 1980: 12a). During the Kelley administration, public corruption emerged as the distinguishing feature of the "new" FBI in terms of the white-collar crime program.[5]

In spite of the FBI and the Justice Department's apparent pursuit of white-collar crime, there were congressional critics regarding the adequacy of the federal response to white-collar crime. In 1978 the Conyers subcommittee began a series of hearings on "White-Collar Crime: The Problem and the Federal Response." These hearings presented evidence that the federal response was underfunded, undirected, uncoordinated, and in need of the development of a national strategy and national priorities (U.S. House, 1979). It remained the task of the Webster FBI and the Carter Justice Department to more carefully marshal its white-collar crime resources.

Nevertheless, the "discovery" of white-collar crime was a significant, if not a surprising, development in the post-Watergate FBI, given the traditional omission of these crimes in our justice system. The "discovery" was, however, not just due to the efforts of Justice Department officials, but rather must be set against the background of a broader social movement against white-collar crime, which includes the media, consumer crusaders like Ralph Nader, some attorneys in official agencies, as well as an aroused public (Cullen et al., 1987: 3ff.). The FBI and the Justice Department simply provided an institutional setting for the movement.

Furthermore, it is revealing that the underlying concern of the Justice Department in this new emphasis on both public corruption and white-collar crime was that these offenses "undermine the strength and integrity of the country and its economy" (U.S. Attorney General, 1976). Webster reiterated this point in a 1980 law journal article, arguing that white-collar crime and public corruption strike "at the very fiber of our society by undermining trust and confidence in our political, governmental, and financial systems" (Webster, 1980: 279). FBI and Justice Department officials clearly acknowledge that their interest in white-collar crime is as a response to the political crisis engendered by the Watergate scandal and perhaps even to a more deep-seated crisis of legitimacy. The prosecution and conviction of white-collar offenders "reassert the ideology of equal justice and . . . they demonstrate the efficacy, autonomy, and neutrality of law and thereby contribute to the legitimacy of the state's authority" (Cullen et al., 1987: 13). White-collar crime enforcement in the immediate post-Watergate period had become a kind of antidote to the crisis of confidence and trust in the U.S. political economy.

White-Collar Crime in the Webster Era

The uncoordinated approach to and ill-defined concept of white-collar crime of the Kelley FBI made it necessary for the Carter Justice Department and the Webster FBI to establish national priorities in investigating white-collar crime. The development of a national strategy involved clarification of the conceptual and definitional problems and specification of law enforcement objectives. Seven national white-collar crime priorities were issued in a 1980 report by U.S. Attorney General Civiletti (U.S. Department of Justice, 1980: 48), as follows:

1. Crimes against federal, state, or local governments by public officials
2. Crimes against the government by private citizens
3. Crimes against business
4. Crimes against consumers
5. Crimes against investors
6. Crimes against employees
7. Crimes affecting the health and safety of the general public

The basic law enforcement objectives underlying these priorities, also stated in the 1980 report, were (1) to protect and enhance the integrity of the government and the economy, (2) to protect and enhance the well-being of the individual citizen, and (3) to enhance public respect for the nation's laws.

Writing about the same time in the *American Criminal Law Review,* FBI Director Webster similarly identifies the FBI investigative priorities in the white-collar crime field, which are consistent with the above DOJ priorities, and then proceeds to describe a five-pronged, coordinated approach to combating white-collar crime, which includes prevention, detection, investigation, prosecution, and sentencing. Webster identifies public corruption investigations as an area of special emphasis in the white-collar crime program and notes that FBI resources allocated to white-collar crime have been increasing (Webster, 1980). This is borne out by the appropriations data for the early Webster years. In FY 1978 the white-collar crime program appropriations constituted 17.3 percent of total FBI investigative appropriations, which amount increased to 25.3 percent in FY 1981 (U.S. House, Appropriations Hearings, 1979–1982).

After 1981, however, there is a major shift in the national strategy to combat white-collar crime. The top priority status given to white-collar crime by Kelley, and the subsequent clarification of white-collar crime priorities and objectives by the Carter Department of Justice, was fundamentally redefined by the Reagan Justice Department. Although the white-collar crime program continues to be identified as a top priority investigative category, appropriations and resources for the program have been sharply curtailed. Between 1981 and 1986, the appropriations allocated to white-collar crime, relative to total investigations, declined from 25.3 percent to 19.1 percent. The distribution of agent work-years in field programs similarly declined for white-collar crime during this same period: from 25.7 percent to 20.3 percent (U.S. House, Appropriations Hearings, 1982–1987). As the Reagan administration began to initiate its "war on drugs" and added drug enforcement to the FBI's responsibilities in January 1982, some resources for this program were diverted away from the white-collar crime program. Specifically, during 1982 agents transferred to narcotics investigations, now a joint responsibility with the Drug Enforcement Administration (DEA), came mostly from the white-collar crime program (U.S. House, Appropriations Hearings, 1984: 609; Taylor, 1984: 27).

The Reagan administration changed the course of the Webster FBI with regard to white-collar crime investigation. The early Webster FBI (before 1981) continued Kelley's priorities and attempted to bring greater coherence to the policies developed in the aftermath of Watergate. The Webster FBI after 1981, however, departed from those policies as the Reagan administration influenced the Justice Department in reordering its white-collar crime priorities and in redefining the meaning of white-collar crime.

The Transformation of White-Collar Crime in the Reagan Administration

In addition to reducing resources and appropriations for the white-collar crime program after 1981, the FBI reordered its white-collar crime priorities in July 1981 so that they were more in line with the Reagan administration's view of white-collar crime. Three major priorities were established to replace the seven priorities set forth in the 1980 Justice Department report. Fraud against the federal government was elevated to the highest priority, which was consistent with Reagan's frequently stated concern with eliminating fraud and waste in federal government programs. Public corruption in state and local government, however, was lowered to the second-ranking priority, and financial crimes were the third priority (U.S. House, Appropriations Hearings, 1985: 888).

The ascendance of fraud against government and the descendance of public corruption as priorities constitute a major shift of emphasis in the white-collar crime program, representing a change in emphasis from the corruption of the political elite to fraud by private citizens, particularly against federal government programs. This is certainly a far cry from the traditional sociological definition of white-collar crime, which focused on the crimes of the upper class and on corporate crime.

In 1983 Attorney General Smith created an Economic Crime Council as an advisory body within the Justice Department. This council further refined the white-collar crime priorities into six areas of national significance that the federal government should concentrate on:

1. Defense procurement fraud
2. Fraud against banks and other financial institutions
3. Money laundering
4. Investment frauds
5. Securities frauds
6. Health care frauds involving Medicare and Medicaid (U.S. Senate, 1987a, part 1: 59).

In these revised priorities, public corruption was eliminated as a top priority altogether, and the major thrust of the white-collar crime priorities is to protect the interests of major financial institutions or federal government programs.

This reordering of priorities, however, represents a much more fundamental change than simply reshuffling the order of crime categories; it is, in fact, a transformation of the underlying objectives of white-collar crime enforcement. White-collar crime ceases to be a moral problem, part of the crisis of confidence in institutions. Instead, white-collar crime enforcement is increasingly viewed in terms of its economic impact, as being an unnecessary expenditure or cost in the federal budget. In the aftermath of Watergate, federal response to white-collar crime and to public corruption, in particular, was to view these as threats to the integrity of the U.S. political economy. We already noted how the official "discovery" of white-collar crime was viewed as an antidote to this crisis of confidence.

After 1981 the Reagan administration began to reverse this perception of white-collar crime. The dominant public policy approach emphasized less government intervention in the economy, including the regulation of economic crime. In the Chicago School of economic philosophy, which was being espoused, such government interference is inherently anticompetitive and harmful to consumers (Isikoff, 1984). Even traditional antitrust laws are understood as a threat to U.S. competitiveness (Henderson, 1985). Economic concentration is no longer the fundamental antitrust problem but rather government intervention and regulation. In this context, public policy after 1981 began the process of deregulating white-collar crime. The deregulation trend expressed itself in a number of ways (Isaacson, 1981: 22–23):

1.   Consumer information—cancellation of regulations that would have required industries to post a list of chemicals to which their workers are exposed and cancellation of the *Car Book,* which provided comparative consumer information on automobiles.
2.   Safety standards—reduction of collision speed at which a bumper must protect a car, from 5 to 2.5 mph.
3.   Product evaluation—Reagan administration proposed elimination of the Consumer Product Safety Commission, which oversees some 15,000 products.
4.   Trade practices—relaxation of guidelines on corporate mergers, advertising, and so on.

The philosophical basis for deregulation had its pragmatic side, as the Reagan administration became concerned with the cost of regulations and the economic loss to the federal budget as a result of waste and fraud in social programs. For example, Murray Weidenbaum, Reagan's first head of the Council of Economic Advisors, conducted a study in 1979 that estimated the annual cost of regulation by fifty-five federal agencies at $102.7 billion (Green and Waitzman, 1979). This was a widely quoted figure at the time and was used to provide scientific support for the deregulation movement. Many of the benefits of regulation were ignored in the study, particularly those benefits difficult to quantify, such as lives saved and injuries avoided in health and safety regulations. Cost-benefit analysis became the scientific facade for deregulation. In addition to the costs of enforcing the rules and regulations of regulatory agencies, there were the unnecessary expenditures in federal social programs produced by waste and fraud. In a February 1981 address, President Reagan estimated such costs to be in the neighborhood of $25 billion (U.S. House, Appropriations Hearings, 1985: 888). This threat to the federal budget became one of the top priorities in the white-collar crime field during the Reagan administration.

Congressional hearings on white-collar crime in the oil industry revealed how the reordered white-collar crime priorities of the Reagan administration had affected the enforcement of law violations in the oil industry. The Dingell subcommittee (U.S. House, 1980b) began to disclose the scope of "daisy chain" operations in the oil industry during the 1970s. These were violations of federal price regulations created after the Arab oil embargo of 1973 to partially protect the American consumer from the astronomical increases in the price of international oil. A two-tiered pricing system was developed that distinguished between "old" oil and "new" oil. Old oil was from domestic wells previously discovered and in operation before the Arab embargo; its price was set at $5.25 a barrel. New oil, the product of new and more costly drilling, was allowed to reach the OPEC market level, then at $12 a barrel. The daisy chains were a variety of mechanisms the oil industry devised during this period to fraudulently "change" old oil into new oil and generally took the form of a series of paper transactions in "buying" and "selling" oil, which never moves, and marking up the price of the old oil in the process until it approaches the new oil price. Congressman Albert Gore expressed his view of the scope of the criminal fraud:

> One senior DOE attorney has added up all of the money that has been taken through these schemes and said that this is perhaps the largest criminal conspiracy in the history of the United States in terms of the amount of money that has been stolen from the American people (U.S. House, 1980b: 17).

The subcommittee hearings also looked into the possibility that there was a cover-up on the part of the government agencies responsible for enforcing these laws, namely, the Department of Energy (DOE) and the Department of Justice (DOJ), whose passivity in enforcing these price controls had aroused some suspicion. Although the press had publicized accounts of daisy chain operations as early as 1974, the DOE did not make a criminal referral to the DOJ until 1978.[6] As of April 1981, eleven firms and thirty-nine individuals had been convicted or entered pleas to felony or misdemeanor counts.

Total DOE alleged violations based on audits of the period 1973–1979 came to $13 billion. As of January 1981, $4 billion in settlements had been obtained, and the balance was still pending, involving over 200 compliance actions affecting mostly the top fifteen oil refiners. According to the Dingell subcommittee staff, about $7 billion of the remaining violations would not be pursued because of budget cuts in FY 1982 (U.S. House, 1981). At the hearings, Congressman Gore had difficulty understanding the wisdom of this policy. Under budget cuts proposed by the Reagan administration, about $40 million would be saved in the FY 1982 budget, but the public was going to lose approximately $7 billion in recovered charges and criminal penalties (U.S. House, 1981; Cook, 1981).

The federal response to daisy chains in the oil industry epitomizes the transformation of white-collar crime in the Reagan administration. This is not to say that the Carter administration had been particularly aggressive in its pursuit of violations of oil price regulations either. The Reagan administration, however, was bent on dismantling the DOE itself and the administrative mechanism for enforcing such price controls. This was not atypical of what has happened to much of the federal regulatory apparatus. Between 1980 and 1983, the total staff of the federal agencies with responsibility for consumer protection, workplace safety, environmental protection, and antitrust enforcement were cut by 19 percent (Coleman, 1985: 183). These agencies lost an additional 7 percent of their personnel between 1983 and 1986 (Coleman, 1987: 3). The vast majority of white-collar crimes falls under the jurisdiction of these agencies and the administrative law they enforce.

In addition to the weakening of the regulatory apparatus that handles violations of the administrative law, there was also a suspicion that the Justice Department in the 1980s was less than aggressive in its pursuit of criminal violations by white-collar offenders. In response to the Justice Department's apparent "soft" handling of several well-publicized cases involving General Dynamics, General Electric, and E. F. Hutton, the Senate Judiciary Committee began a series of hearings in February 1986 on the adequacy of its enforcement efforts.

At the hearings, DOJ officials rejected any criticisms that they were "soft" on white-collar crime or that they were influenced by politics or a "pro-business" orientation in their prosecutorial decisions. In fact, Deputy Attorney General D. Lowell Jensen included the controversial E. F. Hutton settlement as one of the Justice Department's recent significant prosecutions in his testimony (U.S. Senate, 1987a, part 1: 69–70).

One of the major concerns at the hearings, particularly in the E. F. Hutton case, was why only the corporation was charged with a crime and not high-level officials. Justice Department officials and prosecutors in the case argued that they did not have evidence to prosecute high-level executives, only two mid-level officials, and that to pursue the case against these two individuals would have meant foregoing immediate settlement with Hutton and engaging in a protracted court fight (U.S. Senate, 1987a, part 3: 17). Senator Metzenbaum, and to a lesser extent Senator Biden, were not convinced that the Justice Department had pursued the E. F. Hutton case to its fullest. Furthermore, Senator Metzenbaum argued that in the compendium of 400 recently prosecuted cases, which the DOJ had provided as evidence for its white-collar crime enforcement efforts, "there were not any real white collar criminals of any consequence, corporate criminals, that were prosecuted," only "some low-level people" (U.S. Senate, 1987a, part 3: 120).

As the hearings unfolded, it appeared that there was an expectation that the Justice Department's softness on white-collar crime would be revealed in its deliberate failure to prosecute top executives of E. F. Hutton. This was not the case, as various Justice Department officials, as well as the determined prosecutor in the case, provided rather convincing justifications for their decisions not to prosecute any E. F. Hutton officials. The senators appeared to come up empty handed in their search for softness and the traditional double standard in dealing with white-collar crime. What was missed in the inquiry, however, was that the double standard was manifest, not in a conscious, deliberate, prosecutorial decision but in a more subtle, institutional bias in the system. What prevented high-level officials at E. F. Hutton from being prosecuted had more to do with limitations and loopholes in the criminal law when applied to organizational behavior, the need for strategies to investigate the internal affairs of corporations, the ability of top officials to insulate themselves from widespread corporate practice, and federal court decisions that narrowed the options for prosecutors. A double standard exists, but it takes a more subtle, systemic form, not the blatant favoring of elite defendants the senators sought to find.

Whatever the fruits of the Judiciary Committee's inquiry, the expectations, even from members of the committee, seemed to be that not much of substance would be disclosed at these hearings. Senator Biden's opening statement at the March 11 hearings appears to reflect the view that these were "what has been characterized as a dull set of hearings thus far. But they are dull by design. . . . . We have been interested in getting the facts before we make judgments" (U.S. Senate, 1987a, part 1: 99). In fact, the six hearings that were held went largely unnoticed by the media, and the unfinished hearings were put on hold (Kurtz, 1986a, b).[7]

White-Collar Crime Enforcement Appraised

In this chapter we have traced the evolution of white-collar crime enforcement from the Hoover FBI, to the Kelley and Webster FBI in the aftermath of Watergate, and to the FBI, still under Webster, during the Reagan administration. This course was one of avoidance under Hoover, to top priority in the Watergate era, to benign neglect during the Reagan period.

We still need to address the question of whether the "new" FBI reversed the traditional neglect of white-collar crime as well as the historical double standard of justice. In answering this question, we must distinguish between the "new" FBI, which emerged in the aftermath of Watergate, and the "new" FBI of the Reagan administration.

The period of the "discovery" of white-collar crime during the mid- and late 1970s did represent a departure from the "old" priorities under Hoover. To a degree, what was involved was a reclassification of traditional FBI crimes into a white-collar crime category. The appropriations data are clear, however, that in this post-Watergate period of dwindling bureau resources, the FBI was disproportionately increasing its investigative resources to this new top priority. While conceptually white-collar crime remained rather nebulous during this period and enforcement efforts lacked a national strategy, a new area of investigative emphasis was eventually carved out: public corruption. The attack on public corruption became the distinguishing feature of the FBI's white-collar crime program and a kind of federal response to the crisis of confidence in post-Watergate America.

The publicity following Operation ABSCAM in 1980 signalled to the public that there was a "new" FBI. Even during this period of heightened investigative emphasis on white-collar crime and public corruption, the concern for white-collar offenders was not confined to the law violations of the upper class. The operating definition of white-collar crime employed by the Justice Department was broad and expansive, including all social strata and not simply the economic and political elite. Furthermore, there was a conspicuous absence of concern for organizational crime in the FBI's newfound top priority of white-collar crime. The Justice Department conceived of white-collar crime as a problem of individuals rather than of organizational structure and as a problem of fraud and deception rather than of violent crime, which it is in some of its manifestations.[8] It is of interest that during the period of "discovery," one of the major areas of organizational crime, antitrust enforcement, remained relatively constant.[9] Moreover, during the Reagan years, there was a "virtual surrender to the corporate offenders" in the area of antitrust (Coleman, 1987: 4).

The "new" FBI's threat to the traditional double standard of differentially administering justice to street criminals and white-collar criminals was slight and transitory. The concept of white-collar crime, only discovered by the Justice Department in the mid-1970s, was eclipsed and quickly transformed by the Reagan administration in the early 1980s, even though such crime remained a top priority.

But there is more to white-collar crime investigation than simply the new priorities that differentiate the Kelley and Webster FBI from the bureau of J. Edgar Hoover. The evolution of white-collar crime and public corruption as top investigative priorities reflects an organizational responsiveness to executive policy direction that did not exist under Hoover. This is not to say that the bureau has become politicized in the narrow sense but rather that the FBI's overall policies and priorities take direction from bureaucratic superiors in the executive, namely the attorney general and president, in a way that was not true in the Hoover FBI. In the autonomy of the Hoover FBI, investigative priorities were much more a function of Hoover's predilections than what was desired by the attorney general or the prevailing administration. In this sense, the contemporary FBI has become more responsive to its "political masters," to use Weber's term (Gerth and Mills, 1958: 232).

The continual reordering of priorities within the white-collar crime program reflects that new responsiveness. In the Ford and Carter administrations, white-collar crime enforcement served an important symbolic function by providing a rather unique way of dealing with the national crisis of confidence in the aftermath of Watergate.[10] By giving the appearance, if not the reality, of taking action against white-collar offenders, the federal government not only responded to widespread public concern, and even outrage, over white-collar crime but also contributed to the legitimacy of the state by symbolically reaffirming traditional ideas of equal justice and neutrality of laws (Cullen et al., 1987: 20ff.). While the Reagan administration recognized the symbolic value of white-collar crime enforcement and continued it as a top priority program, Reagan simultaneously redefined what was meant by the term. White-collar crime enforcement became less a response to the crisis of confidence and more a way to protect federal government programs from fraud, waste, and abuse as well as a way to protect financial institutions from fraud. On the whole, however, white-collar crime in the Reagan years was viewed as a regulatory problem that could be translated into a cost-benefit equation—the costs versus the benefits of regulation—and did not pose the same moral problem as street crime. If the costs of regulation exceed the benefits, the result is the deregulation of white-collar crime. The trend during this period was one of deregulation: to reduce the resources of regulatory agencies entrusted with enforcing the violations of the administrative law.

Clearly, the FBI is only one component of the federal government's total white-collar crime program. There are numerous regulatory agencies that have relatively independent jurisdiction over a wide range of business and professional matters: the environment, the workplace, consumer products, drugs, food, transportation, and so forth. In addition, the U.S. attorney offices throughout the country have responsibility for developing and prosecuting federal cases, including cases of white-collar crime; U.S. attorneys are the field arm of the Justice Department. Since the early 1980s, U.S. attorneys as well as the FBI have taken direction on policies and priorities in white-collar crime from the Economic Crime Council, an advisory body within the DOJ (U.S. Senate, 1987a, part 1: 59).

While we have emphasized the responsiveness of the Kelley and Webster FBI in comparison to the Hoover bureau, we should be careful not to overstate our case. This does not mean that the contemporary FBI is totally at the whim of its political superiors in the executive; the bureau still operates with some measure of autonomy. For example, on August 21, 1986, the FBI's Miami office sent an eight-page internal memorandum to Director Webster. The memo criticized the U.S. Attorney and Justice Department's decision not to prosecute Pratt and Whitney for $22 million in overcharges on defense contracts from 1979 through 1984 and also criticized Air Force officials of gross negligence for permitting such overcharges (spent on fishing and golf trips, lavish banquets, football tickets, and so on). The DOJ's four-year investigation of Pratt and Whitney was, however, closed in 1986 with no charges brought (Kurtz, 1987). Since prosecutors have enormous discretion in deciding what cases to prosecute, we cannot be sure what the real reasons were in this case. It does appear, however, that the cases the bureau pursues may not always be consistent with the agenda of its "political masters" in the Justice Department and the executive.

The tension between bureau autonomy and executive control is an ongoing dilemma in the "new" FBI, but what is clear, nevertheless, is that the contemporary bureau operates in a very different political and administrative context than the Hoover FBI. This theme will be further pursued in the next chapter, as we explore Hoover's "strange reluctance" (Cook, 1973) to investigate organized crime and the sudden reversal of this position in the post-Hoover years.

NOTES

1. Chapter 3 provides further discussion of the political uses and misuses of these files. Chapter 5 elaborates on how Hoover's files, long rumored to exist, were made public.

2. It is of some interest to note that references to white-collar crime in the 1974 annual report are all qualified with quotation marks: "white collar." The implication seems to be that such crimes are not exclusively committed by those from white-collar backgrounds.

3. The number of white-collar crime investigative matters received actually declined between 1975 and 1979, from 78,918 to 58,823 (U.S. House, Appropriations Hearings, 1976–1980), but this was a slower rate of decline than that of total FBI investigative matters. It should be pointed out that overall FBI investigative resources were decreasing during this period (U.S. House, Appropriations Hearings, 1976–1980).

4. In two recent studies of white-collar crime by the Bureau of Justice Statistics (1986, 1987), the Justice Department has continued its departure from the traditional sociological meaning of white-collar crime by employing forgery, counterfeiting, fraud, and embezzlement as the white-collar offenses in its official research. While these offenses are white-collar crimes, they are not a fair representation of Sutherland's domain of white-collar crime, and they do not begin to tap the full scope of the sociological meaning of white-collar crime (Coleman, 1985: 2–5). They are certainly not the crimes of political and economic elites.

5. Financial crimes, which include bank fraud and embezzlement, were still, however, the second-ranked white-collar crime priority in 1980; 33 percent of the FBI field offices ranked such crime as their number 1 concern, and 39 percent, as their number 2 priority (U.S. Department of Justice, 1980). This attitude reflects the persistence of some of the "old" bureau priorities. In 1986 financial crimes still

occupied 56 percent of agent time within the white-collar crime program, with bank fraud the top priority within that category (U.S. House, Appropriations Hearings, 1987).

6. There is a five-year statute of limitations on these offenses. The conviction of Conoco in 1978, the first company to be convicted, was on the final day of the statute of limitations. Conoco had, in fact, turned itself in to the DOE after an internal audit, and had it not been for an inquiring U.S. attorney in Houston, Tony Canales, the case might have been lost. The case had been initially assigned to a DOJ attorney who did not have enough time to pursue the Conoco case, according to Deputy Assistant Attorney General John Keeney (U.S. House, 1980b).

7. At the first hearing, Strom Thurmond, the chair of the Judiciary Committee, and Joseph Biden, the ranking Democrat on the committee, left before the lead-off witness finished his opening statement. By the time Deputy Attorney General D. Lowell Jensen finished his testimony, only three of the committee's eighteen senators remained. By the time Sen. John East took the microphone, senatorial attendance had dwindled further and provoked the following comment: "I would propose—I guess to myself, since I'm the only one here—that we might take a recess of ten minutes" (Kurtz, 1986a: 14).

8. The view of white-collar crime as nonviolent crime continues to be advanced by DOJ officials. In his testimony before the Judiciary Committee, Deputy Attorney General D. Lowell Jensen conveyed the meaning of white-collar crime as denoting "a broad range of nonviolent criminal activity that either threatens or injures important governmental, economic, or social interests" (U.S. Senate, 1987a, part 1: 26).

9. Antitrust convictions fluctuated slightly between 1974 and 1980, but on the whole remained at a relatively low-priority level, not unlike the Hoover FBI. In 1974 there were 128 convictions; in 1975, 72; in 1976, 165; in 1977, 143; in 1978, 107; in 1979, 173; and in 1980, 94 (U.S. Attorney General, 1975–1981).

10. Recent opinion polls show that public trust and confidence in government today are about as low as in the Vietnam-Watergate years. In 1974, 37 percent of a national sample said they trusted the government most of the time or always; this bottomed out at 30 percent in 1978, and in 1986 the level of trust was still at only 40 percent. This is in contrast to the relatively high levels of trust in the mid-1960s—65 percent in 1966 (Sussman, 1986: 37).

Chapter 8

ORGANIZED CRIME ENFORCEMENT IN THE "OLD" AND "NEW" FBI

The transformation of bureau investigative priorities, which was part of the FBI reforms of the 1970s, is usually cited as evidence that the post-Watergate FBI is, indeed, new and different from the old Hoover bureau. Perhaps the change that would have been least anticipated by those familiar with the "old" FBI was the elevation of organized crime to a top investigative priority in the mid-1970s. This new, top status for organized crime is all the more remarkable given Hoover's traditional neglect of it. Until 1957 J. Edgar Hoover denied the existence of organized crime and even after that refused to acknowledge the Mafia as an organization. Beginning in 1963, with the Valachi Hearings, La Cosa Nostra, or LCN, became the FBI's term of choice in referring to traditional organized crime, and this practice has continued to the present. Why and how organized crime underwent this sudden turnabout and became institutionalized as a top priority in the "new" FBI is the focus of this chapter.

Before we come to terms with this recent transformation of priorities, it is necessary to first ask the question: Why did the Hoover FBI neglect organized crime enforcement? As we shall see, the answer to this question will provide further insight into the political and administrative milieu of the post-Watergate FBI.

Organized Crime and the "Old" FBI

The Hoover FBI's failure to combat organized crime, what Cook (1973) called a "strange reluctance," has been a matter of speculation for some time. Some might argue that we may never know the reasons for this reluctance, since Hoover is deceased and therefore cannot tell us what his motives were. While it may not be possible to definitively answer this question, it is possible to approach the problem by reconstructing the historical context in which the "old" FBI established its priorities. Without prying into Hoover's motives or discovering a previously undisclosed document, it is possible to develop a good sense of how the FBI's "strange reluctance" came about. First, however, let us review some of the hypotheses that have been offered thus far.

Cressey (1969: 21ff.) identifies "five interlocking hypotheses" related to Hoover's failure to recognize organized crime as a national problem and his denial of the existence of the Mafia until around 1963.

1. Hoover was jealous of Harry Anslinger, director of the Federal Bureau of Narcotics, who had shown concern over the Mafia since the 1930s but particularly during and after the Kefauver hearings of 1950–1951.
2. The Apalachin Mafia gathering in New York state in 1957 forced Hoover to recognize that a Mafia existed, but he waited until a new name, La Cosa Nostra, was given to the organization before officially acknowledging it. This new name surfaced in the Valachi hearings in 1963 and allowed Hoover some measure of face saving.
3. Attorney General Kennedy ordered Hoover to begin a move against organized crime, and Hoover simply followed the orders of his Justice Department superior in initiating investigations of organized crime during the early 1960s.
4. Hoover had no statutory jurisdiction in investigating organized crime activities until the Kennedy years.
5. The information from wiretaps and bugs in 1960 to 1961 convinced Hoover of the danger of organized crime.

Cressey (1969: 23) dismisses all but one of these hypotheses and argues that hypothesis number 4 has the "greatest likelihood of validity." He further points out that Hoover himself indicated this as the reason for his reluctance in 1966, which gives some plausibility to this hypothesis.

This hypothesis, however, has been challenged by Turner (1970), who argues that legislation passed during the 1930s firmly placed much interstate crime under FBI jurisdiction and could have provided a legal basis for combating organized crime on several fronts had Hoover been so predisposed. William Hundley, former chief of the Organized Crime Section of the Department of Justice, also adheres to the view that if Hoover had wished to move against organized crime, he would have had the necessary support for doing so (Cook, 1973: 162).

We have come full circle back to Cook's (1973) question: Why this "strange reluctance"? Cook himself suggests a number of plausible explanations. The myth of FBI invincibility was built on a foundation of statistics showing a high percentage of convictions and, each year, an ever larger number of fugitives located and stolen property recovered. The targeting of a formidable adversary such as organized crime would dilute these statistics and undermine the FBI image of infallibility. In addition, Cook speculates on the political risk that investigating organized crime might pose for the FBI. The possibility that members of Congress and other leading politicians have connections to organized crime could affect the bureau's own legislative power base should it seriously investigate organized crime and the accompanying political corruption.

Messick's (1972: 49) observations on Hoover also lend credibility to Cook's thesis:

> John Edgar Hoover in the course of his career has shown great wisdom in his choice of targets. The international Communist conspiracy has, of course, been his favorite, but he has gone after bankrobbers and kidnappers with equal zeal. In doing so he stepped on no important toes, made enemies of no important segment of the financial or political establishment.

In addition to the political risk to the bureau, Rhodes (1984) also notes that Hoover feared the potential of organized crime investigation to corrupt his agents.

Ungar (1975) points out that in addition to organized crime, the FBI was also reluctant to get involved in narcotics and civil rights enforcement. The Hoover reluctance to pursue civil rights issues extended into the Kennedy years (O'Reilly, 1988). The common element in how the bureau allocated its resources, according to Ungar, was avoidance of the toughest problems.

More recently, Powers (1987: 332ff.) argues that Hoover's reluctance to take on organized crime was due to his fear that FBI autonomy and independence would be compromised. Insofar as an effective strategy against organized crime would require considerable coordination among numerous agencies, the result would be a diminution in Hoover's authority.

Demystifying the Organized Crime Problem

While these observations on the FBI's reluctance to investigate organized crime may not provide a definitive answer to our question, they do provide an important insight into the process by which law enforcement allocates its resources and why it targets some crimes and not others. The conventional wisdom regarding the central purpose of our criminal justice system (including the FBI) is that it exists to protect us against the most serious threats to our person and property (Reiman, 1979). This wisdom makes an "objectivity" assumption about the nature of danger in our society; that is, there are certain crimes (murder, rape, robbery, and so on) in our society that indisputably constitute the real crime problem and are intrinsically the most harmful. As Box (1983: 3) clearly argues, there is no doubt that these common-law crimes are *a* crime problem, but considering them to be *the* crime problem is a social construction of reality that may serve broader social functions, for example, to deflect attention from other serious avoidable deaths and injuries, such as those connected with corporate crime, that may in fact be more "objectively" harmful. This "mystification," as Box (1983: 12) calls it, is crucial in the allocation of law enforcement resources and in the targeting of particular crime problems, providing the ideological basis for what constitutes the real threats to person and property. Top political officials, the media, and law enforcement itself all contribute to the mystification of crime in our society.

In his essay "God and the Mafia," Hawkins (1969) astutely shows how much of our past thinking about the Mafia and organized crime was based more on metaphysics and theology than on science. Hawkins argues that the evidence for the existence of a single nationwide structure of organized crime—such as a Mafia that dominates organized crime—is highly tenuous and ultimately rests on an article of faith that such a nationwide structure exists. The analogy to the arguments supporting or denying the existence of God is striking. In this sense, the FBI's reluctance is simply a failure to share in this particular belief system and metaphysics about organized crime.[1]

This understanding of the process of mystification has largely been absent in previous speculations as to the FBI's reluctance to combat organized crime. Earlier hypotheses centered on Hoover's personal motives or on the organizational constraints of the FBI. These are not unimportant considerations, but there is a level of analysis that has been neglected. This level relates to the social and political forces that shape our consciousness of the crime problem and which crime problems are defined as the most threatening in any particular historical era.

Smith's (1975) tracing of the "Mafia mystique" provides a useful starting point in this analysis. He observes that the Mafia label disappeared in the period between World Wars I and II. The terms *gangster, racketeer,* and *organized crime* were alternately used during that period. This is not simply a matter of substituting synonymous terms for the same phenomenon; the different labels also convey different meanings.

> To the extent that the gangster was identified narrowly with robbery, the label understated the scope of activities generally attributed to criminal associations at this time. Most obviously, it failed to account for bootlegging and other illegal businesses; it also bypassed a range of extortionate enterprises. To accommodate a wider view, "racketeering" became a more common label (Smith, 1975: 66).

The terms *gangster* and *racketeer* both emphasize the imagery of the individual criminal (robber, kidnapper, and so on) and not the organization of their enterprise. Nash (1972: 82–83) contends that Hoover refused to distinguish between gangsters who operated as part of lone gangs and those who were part of syndicated crime, lumping them all together as "hoodlums."

In referring to Don Whitehead's *The FBI Story,* Cook (1973: 141) notes the absence of any mention of the top organized crime figures of the 1930s: "Where are names like Charles (Lucky) Luciano, Frank Costello, Joe Adonis, Albert Anastasia, Bugsy Siegel, Tony Accardo, Meyer Lansky, Vito Genovese? Where— oh, where—is the Mafia?" As noted, the Mafia label, with its connotations of ethnicity, conspiracy, and organization, was not the prevailing label or image of the 1930s, so in this sense the question is an unfair one. Cook's observation, however, that the FBI neglected pursuing these major organized crime figures has some validity.

This neglect again must be understood in terms of the consciousness of the crime problem of the 1930s. The terms *gangster* and *racketeer* were more all encompassing in their portrayal of the "crime wave" of the late 1920s and early 1930s than were those organized crime figures we would identify today with the Mafia. Walker (1980: 182) argues that Hollywood transformed the gangster into a national folk hero in a succession of gangster movies such as "Little Caesar" (1930), "The Public Enemy" (1931), and "Scarface" (1932). At the same time a series of sensational crimes in the early 1930s stirred public concern about crime. The 1932 Lindbergh kidnapping became a major media event and contributed to the kidnapping scare that swept the country. Similarly, the bank robberies of John Dillinger, Pretty Boy Floyd, Bonnie Parker and Clyde Barrow, Machine Gun Kelley, Ma Barker, Alvin Karpis, and Baby Face Nelson generated much publicity. The other component of the gangster/racketeer image was the organized criminals, especially in Chicago and New York City, who transformed the vices, particularly bootlegging, into big business in the 1920s. This transformation was accompanied by much violence—the "beer wars" of the 1920s and the Castellammarese War (1930–1931)—which received much media attention and helped establish the basic infrastructure of organized crime in the United States (Inciardi, 1975).

The FBI Priorities of the Depression Era

It was in this context that J. Edgar Hoover, the master bureaucrat, saw an opportunity to exploit the "gangster as hero" to the political advantage of the bureau. The antidote to the glamorization of gangsters was the "cop as hero."

> He skillfully manipulated the media and transformed a group of otherwise ordinary criminals into national "public enemies." . . . Heroes, of course, need to do battle against great enemies. So Hoover inflated the reputation of the Dillingers to make bureau exploits all the more impressive (Walker, 1980: 184).

The exploitation of the crime problem for bureaucratic self-serving ends is certainly not unique to the FBI or to law enforcement. For Hoover, this exploitation was part of a grander strategy of transforming the FBI into the law enforcement agency par excellence. The establishment of the National Police Academy (1935), the inauguration of the *FBI Law Enforcement Bulletin* (1932), the opening of the bureau's scientific crime laboratory (1932), and the rapid expansion of fingerprint files during the 1930s all established the FBI as the premier law enforcement agency for its professionalism and crime-fighting efficiency.

The question still remains why Hoover selected Dillinger-type gangsters as public enemies instead of the organized crime figures mentioned by Cook. John Dillinger, Bonnie and Clyde, and the other gangsters of the Depression era who chose bank robbery as their primary criminal pursuit were of a different stripe than the gangsters involved in bootlegging and vice. The Dillinger-type gangsters operated in close-knit gangs and were the ideological descendants of the bandits of the American West. These gangsters were fourth- and fifth-generation Americans whose origins and criminal exploits were concentrated in rural America. As it turned out, their Depression-era banditry was short lived (less than a decade) as a result of the decline of the frontier and federal efforts to combat bank robbery (Inciardi, 1975: 94–97). In contrast, the gangsters of organized crime had their origins in the street gangs of urban ethnic neighborhoods. Prohibition provided the impetus to the development of a more sophisticated organized crime structure in major cities, with the illegal distribution of alcohol at the structure's center. Although Prohibition ended in 1933, the crime syndicates that had been formed persisted in their provision of other illegal goods and services. The question of Hoover's neglect of these crime syndicates has two parts: (1) Why the original neglect in the 1920s and 1930s? and (2) Why the continued neglect, especially in the post–World War II years?

In regard to the original neglect, the jurisdictional argument must be taken into account. The FBI did not have enforcement responsibility for the National Prohibition Act; in 1920 this job fell under the jurisdiction of the U.S. Treasury Department (Lowenthal, 1950). However, even when Hoover was given the belated opportunity to enter the arena of Prohibition enforcement by President Roosevelt in 1933, he vigorously opposed consolidation of his bureau with that of the Prohibition Bureau (Whitehead, 1956: 91).

Bootlegging was at the core of the crime syndicates of the 1920s and early 1930s and provided the economic basis for cooperation among organized criminals in various cities (Inciardi, 1975). While, as Turner (1970) asserts, the FBI during this era could have been more aggressive in pursuing Prohibition enforcement, this argument does not take into account the relative organizational power of the bureau of that period vis-a-vis the executive branch or the bureau's rivalry with other law enforcement agencies. It must be remembered that the FBI of the 1920s experienced a scandal and reorganization (1924), which placed it on the defensive, and it was not until the mid-1930s that it began to achieve the distinguished reputation that came to be associated with the post-World War II bureau. This, indeed, was Hoover's great accomplishment of the 1930s. The FBI therefore was not in a strong position to compete with its bureaucratic rivals over law enforcement turf. The path of least resistance for the bureau was to carve out its own jurisdictional turf in interstate crime, namely kidnapping and bank robbery. In the wake of the Lindbergh kidnapping, Congress passed the "Lindbergh Law," which made kidnapping a federal offense. Congress subsequently passed legislation in 1934 that made bank robbery a federal offense.

As we have noted, the selection of crime targets is also critical to enhancing the status of law enforcement agencies. Public enemies must be conquerable. Clearly, kidnappers and bank robbers were politically weaker than the gangsters of the crime syndicates, who were enmeshed in the corruption of the local urban political machines. Cook (1973: 145) notes:

> The famous kidnappers were not the big names of the underworld. Bruno Richard Hauptmann, the kidnapper of the Lindbergh baby, was an impoverished carpenter; Angelo John LaMarca, executed for kidnap-murder of the Weinberger baby on Long Island in the late 1950s, was an impecunious laborer driven to the border of insanity by debts.

Messick's (1972) and Cook's (1973) arguments about the wisdom of selecting targets with minimal political risk appear to apply for the bureau of the Depression era, which was only beginning to establish itself as the paragon of law enforcement professionalism.

According to Sherrill (1973), there was an additional reason for Hoover's selection of the Dillinger-type gangsters as public enemies of the 1930s. The sympathy these gangsters found among segments of the public, given the animosity toward banks during the Depression, was particularly infuriating to Hoover, and this romanticization of bank robbers added to Hoover's determination to enhance the FBI's image. Clearly, all of these factors combined to account for the bureau's original neglect of organized crime during the Depression.

The Postwar Priorities of the FBI

How, then, can we account for the continued reluctance of the FBI to combat organized crime in the post–World War II era, when the bureau's position of preeminence in law enforcement was unquestioned? The issue is further complicated by the fact that the Depression-era gangsters on whom Hoover had built the bureau's reputation had been mostly apprehended; the phenomenon of this rural outlaw banditry was waning (Inciardi, 1975). It would appear that the conditions for channeling resources toward organized crime were ripe. As we know, this did not happen even though the bureau had apparently fallen on hard times, by 1938, when five field offices were closed and one-half of its investigative staff were laid off (U.S. Attorney General, 1938: 159).

The national security concerns that emerged during World War II and the McCarthyism of the postwar years allowed the FBI to elaborate a new national menace of espionage, sabotage, and domestic subversion by communists. Internal security and communists became the new FBI public enemies of the postwar years, and bureau resources were allocated accordingly. Halperin and colleagues (1976) estimate that one-third of the bureau's total investigative force was doing internal security work during the McCarthy era.

But what about organized crime? Why did Hoover select the communist menace over the Mafia menace? On one level, the answer is simple: there was no Mafia menace in the postwar years while the communist threat mushroomed into a full-blown public hysteria in the early 1950s. But even before this, in 1939, Roosevelt's executive order on internal security restored intelligence functions to the FBI, and a new General Intelligence Division was established. The internal security work the FBI pursued after World War II became a logical extension of the national defense activities it had conducted during the war. Internal security and domestic intelligence became the major source of organizational power for the postwar FBI (Bernstein, 1976; Theoharis and Cox, 1988).

Theoharis (1971) argues that much of the anticommunist hysteria was generated by the Truman administration as a way of gaining public support for the Marshall Plan and its containment foreign policy. Congressional conservatives later exploited this public alarm as a political tactic to discredit the New Deal and to generate the internal security scare that became known as McCarthyism. The communist menace provided the FBI with an attractive target for its own resources. There was high-level government support for combating the communist threat, and Hoover, from his earlier years as chief of the General Intelligence Division, already had experience doing battle with the radicals and anarchists of the Red Scare era in 1919 to 1920 (Lowenthal, 1950; Murray, 1955; Preston, 1963).

By comparison, the Kefauver hearings of 1950 through 1951 were struggling to establish organized crime as a national, and even international, menace. The Kefauver committee concluded:

> Behind the local mobs which make up the national crime syndicate is a shadowy, international criminal organization known as the Mafia, so fantastic that most Americans find it hard to believe it really exists. . . .
>
> The Mafia, however, is no fairy tale. It is ominously real, and it has scarred the face of America with almost every conceivable type of criminal violence (Kefauver, 1951: 14, 19).

As Smith (1975) observes, the Kefauver hearings rediscovered the Mafia on the national scene and initiated the transformation of the gangster and racketeer of the Depression era to the Mafia of the postwar years. The Mafia label, however, did not stick at the time of the Kefauver hearings, but it did inspire the beginning of a series of reports and investigations, culminating in the 1967 Presidential Task Force Report on Organized Crime (Smith, 1975).[2] Although the Mafia menace, as portrayed in the Kefauver hearings, was consistent with the paranoid style of politics of the McCarthy era, there was not a broad base of support in the political arena or in the media for the idea. The major advocate for the Mafia as the force behind a single national crime syndicate was the Federal Bureau of Narcotics (FBN).[3] The FBN provided evidence and testimony for the Mafia link to organized crime at both the Kefauver hearings and the later McClellan Committee hearings in 1957 to 1958 (Smith, 1975).

Cressey (1969) argues that the FBN and the FBI were in bureaucratic competition for federal budget support. Harry Anslinger, director of the Federal Bureau of Narcotics, had long been an archrival of Hoover's but unlike Hoover seemed to be constantly in a losing battle against narcotics trafficking. In this respect, the FBN might have needed to portray a supercriminal opponent, the Mafia, as a justification for its failure to control narcotics traffic (Smith, 1975: 289–290). The role of Anslinger and the FBN in manufacturing the marijuana scare of the 1930s has been well documented (Lindesmith, 1965; Becker, 1963). The outcome of that earlier publicity campaign was passage of the Marijuana Tax Act of 1937, which brought the control of marijuana under federal jurisdiction—specifically under the Federal Bureau of Narcotics. It is therefore not unreasonable to see the "failure" of the Mafia menace in the 1950s against this background of bureaucratic competition and the "success" of the communist menace more consistent with the ideological needs of both foreign and domestic policy in the postwar years. The Mafia menace would have to wait until the mid-1960s before it would capture the national imagination.

The FBI Priorities of the 1960s

By all accounts, in the years following the McCarthy era and into the 1960s, Hoover continued to be reluctant to commit FBI resources to the investigation of organized crime. William P. Rogers, U.S. Attorney General in the late 1950s, indicated in an interview with Demaris (1975: 149) that the FBI had to be brought into organized crime "kicking and screaming." Since the FBI launched its Top Ten Fugitives Program in 1950, for example, hundreds of criminals have made the list, but only one was linked to organized crime and he was never caught (Turner, 1970: 166). The official FBI (that is, Hoover) line during this period was that the Mafia as an organization did not exist and that the individual Mafiosi were "just a bunch of hoodlums" (Sullivan with Brown, 1979a: 117). It is not that Hoover did not recognize organized crime but that he saw it as a local police problem, outside his jurisdiction and consisting of individual hoodlums. He did not share the conspiratorial view of the Mafia and organized crime advanced by the FBN at the Kefauver and McClellan hearings. It should be pointed out that the FBI was not alone among law enforcement agencies in having this blindspot. The Johnson Crime Commission's survey of seventy-one cities to determine the extent of state and local enforcement activity against organized crime found that only nineteen cities acknowledged having organized crime. Of those nineteen, only twelve had specialized units for organized crime investigation (President's Commission on Law Enforcement, 1967b: 12).

This blindspot in bureau priorities may have reflected a reluctance to investigate a politically risky and powerful criminal adversary, as some have alleged (Cook, 1973; Messick, 1972), but it primarily reveals a complacency in the priorities that had served the FBI well during the postwar years. These priorities had established the bureau as an extraordinarily independent and powerful agency in the federal government. Neil Welch, a veteran FBI agent, makes the observation that Hoover was not interested in discovering organized crime as an FBI target (Welch and Marston, 1984: 82). He was not interested because he did not need organized crime; his old priorities had already demonstrated their success. In 1959 Hoover opposed a coordinated federal effort against organized crime, indicating that he had neither the manpower nor the time for such an effort (Smith, 1975: 202).

According to Sullivan (1979a: 118), who rose to the number 3 position in the bureau during the 1960s, the 1957 Apalachin gathering of Mafia "hit the FBI like a bomb." The FBI policy of nonrecognition of the Mafia could no longer be maintained, and the bureau was now open to much criticism and embarrassment. Sullivan (1979a: 120) further notes his surprise at one aspect of Hoover's response to this crisis:

> I had nothing to do with criminal investigation at that time—I was chief of the Research and Analysis Section investigating communism, espionage, and the Klan—so I was surprised when Hoover called me into his office to talk about the Mafia and even more surprised when he accepted my offer to do some research on organized crime for him.

The outcome of Sullivan's research was a two-volume study of organized crime that showed the existence of the Mafia and that it had been in operation for many decades. After reading the internal FBI study, Hoover privately conceded that the Mafia existed, but he did not allow copies of the study to be circulated outside of the bureau (Sullivan with Brown, 1979a: 121). This is a revealing footnote because it suggests that Hoover may not have been well informed about the Mafia and organized crime at this time and that he genuinely did not see it as a national menace.

The FBI response to the Apalachin meeting became more a problem of managing public relations than one of reordering priorities. The FBI initiated a Top Hoodlum Program[4] in which each field office was to designate the top ten hoodlums in its area. In 1959 the New York City field office still only had four agents assigned full time to organized crime, in contrast to the 400 assigned to internal security (Turner, 1970: 173–176).

It required internal pressure within the Justice Department in the early 1960s to gradually get Hoover to commit FBI resources to organized crime investigation. This pressure initially came from Attorney General Robert Kennedy, who had acquired a special interest in organized crime from his days as committee counsel for the McClellan Committee.[5] Based on his experiences on the committee, Kennedy wrote *The Enemy Within* in 1960, which examined racketeer influence in unions. It is of some interest to note that Kennedy referred to gangsters and mobsters in his writing on organized crime, not the Mafia (Smith, 1975).

It also required a new series of organized crime hearings from 1963 to 1964, which were conducted by Senator McClellan's Permanent Subcommittee on Investigations, to motivate the FBI and to generate support for organized crime legislation. The principal witness in these hearings was an organized crime informer, Joseph Valachi, who introduced La Cosa Nostra to the American public and provided a "breakthrough" in the secrecy surrounding organized crime. These hearings helped get some of the Justice Department's anticrime proposals through Congress, in particular Kennedy's wiretap and witness immunity legislation (Smith, 1975). This legislation served to undermine some of the traditional basis for the FBI reluctance in this area by providing legislation that gave the bureau expanded powers, especially over interstate gambling and bookmaking (Cook, 1973).

The hearings also symbolized the ascendance of the conspiratorial view of organized crime that placed the Mafia, or La Cosa Nostra, in control of a nationwide structure of organized crime.[6] By 1966 even J. Edgar Hoover began to acknowledge this national menace. In his testimony before the U.S. House Appropriations Subcommittee in that year, Hoover discussed La Cosa Nostra as a nationwide criminal cartel that controls organized crime in many of our largest cities (President's Commission on Law Enforcement, 1967b: 6–7).

The *Task Force Report on Organized Crime* (1967b) of President Johnson's Crime Commission gave official sanction to the above view, which was further reinforced by Donald Cressey's *Theft of the Nation* (1969). In the arena of popular culture, Mario Puzo's book *The Godfather* (1969), and later the movie, demonstrated the "reality" of "organized crime as an evil, alien, conspiratorial entity comprised of Italians bearing the 'Mafia' label" (Smith, 1975: 277). A 1971

Harris poll showed that 78 percent of the U.S. public accepted this theory (Woodiwiss, 1988: 145).

Despite all these efforts at the federal level to mobilize public opinion on organized crime, the FBI's efforts still appeared rather meager throughout the 1960s. According to Ramsey Clark, attorney general in the late 1960s:

> The conflict between Attorney General Kennedy and the FBI arose from the unwillingness of the Bureau to participate on an equal basis with other crime control agencies. The FBI has so coveted personal credit that it will sacrifice even effective crime control before it will share the glory of its exploits. This has been a petty and costly characteristic caused by the excessive domination of a single person, J. Edgar Hoover, and his self-centered concern for his reputation and that of the FBI (Clark, 1970: 64–65).

In a 1985 interview with Michael Woodiwiss (1988: 168), Clark further revealed that President Johnson asked him to persuade Hoover to take over jurisdiction of drug enforcement; this was at a time in 1968 when federal resources in drug control were being reorganized. Clark said that he did not even attempt the impossible knowing quite well that Hoover would not expose his agents to the corrupting influence of drug enforcement. Although during the 1960s gambling was viewed as the most profitable of organized crime activities, drug trafficking was emerging as an important source of organized crime revenues.

The concept of the federal strike force was developed in 1967 to combat organized crime in major cities on a highly coordinated basis. Investigators from numerous federal agencies were required to work as a team or task force (Clark, 1970). Even though indictments of organized crime figures increased during the 1960s, it was not because the FBI had contributed its fair share of investigative resources.[7] In 1971 columnist Jack Anderson reported that the FBI had assigned only four agents to the Justice Department's seventeen-city drive against organized crime; other federal agencies had provided 224 investigators (Cook, 1973).

However, this reluctance to cooperate with other federal agencies was not unique to organized crime enforcement. The ill-fated Huston Plan in 1970 was in large part due to the FBI's unwillingness to cooperate with other intelligence agencies. In fact, in March 1970 Hoover severed formal liaison ties with the CIA and, shortly after, with the other intelligence agencies as well (U.S. Senate, 1976b).

It seems clear that the bureau priorities of the postwar years were deeply entrenched; the disproportionate allocation of resources to internal security was solidly institutionalized. Attorneys general, congressional hearings, and even the creation of a Mafia menace in the mid-1960s could not substantially alter the FBI, or J. Edgar Hoover, from its course. In this respect, the Hoover FBI had become quite insulated and unresponsive to its "political masters" in the executive.

Internal security and FBI domestic intelligence had become too integral a part of the source of bureau organizational power to reorder FBI priorities in any significant way. Ungar's (1975: 403) observations on the bureau seem to support this point: "In Hoover's last years, he began to carry on about organized crime as if he had personally discovered it. But it is probably true that until the Director died, the Bureau could not make a full commitment to fighting it." This is also confirmed in Ehrlichman's (1982: 163) memoirs on the Nixon years (1969–1974). The former presidential adviser reports that "whatever the reason, both Mitchell and Nixon were unsuccessful in asking Hoover to turn his agents loose on the Mafia."

Organized Crime as a Top FBI Priority

If the thesis being advanced here is correct, it would mean that in order for organized crime to become a genuine bureau priority, the "old" bureau priorities, and basis for FBI organizational power, would have to be challenged. Hoover's death, as Ungar (1975) asserts, may have been a precondition for such a change, but much more was required to unravel the "old" priorities. As we have already seen, it was ultimately a series of major public disclosures during the early 1970s, the Watergate scandal itself, and finally post-Watergate revelations that led to FBI reform. Since most of the disclosed FBI abuses were associated with its internal security responsibilities, this area of FBI operations was most seriously questioned. One of the outcomes of the scandal was the dramatic erosion of the FBI's internal security apparatus, and this served to undermine the postwar basis of the bureau's organizational power (Elliff, 1979; Poveda, 1985; U.S. Controller General, 1976, 1977). It was in this context that a shift in priorities was possible.

While there can be little doubt that such a decline in FBI domestic intelligence occurred during the immediate post-Watergate era,[8] the question is whether the reduction of resources for domestic intelligence was, in fact, shifted to the new bureau priorities, particularly to organized crime. Did the bureau match its rhetoric with its resources? In order to assess this question, we need to determine when these new priorities were implemented within the FBI. While difficult to pinpoint exactly, the turning point appeared to occur in August 1975, when the quality-over-quantity approach to investigations was extended to all FBI field offices. This approach consisted of a decreased involvement in less complicated investigative matters along with an increased emphasis on selected high-priority criminal and security matters, including organized crime, white-collar crime, and foreign counterintelligence (U.S. House, Appropriations Hearings, 1976: 476, 497).

If we examine a number of different measures of FBI investigative activity relative to organized crime during this period, there are some indications that the bureau's top priority status for organized crime was not matched by the resources allocated to this program. Investigative matters received by the FBI in its organized crime program totaled 29,504 in 1975 and declined to 18,141 in 1979 (U.S. House, Appropriations Hearings, 1976–1980). The number of convictions of organized crime figures similarly declined during the late 1970s. After peaking at 1,417 in 1975, the number of convictions decreased to 628 in 1979. This is perhaps surprising, since such convictions had been steadily rising since 1967 (U.S. Attorney General, 1968–1980).

A somewhat more unobtrusive measure of FBI activity in regard to organized crime is the percentage of the FBI's annual report that describes its organized crime investigations. Insofar as this reflects FBI emphasis in this area of investigation, there was a gradual increase in the percentage of the annual report that focuses on accomplishments in its organized crime investigations. In 1974, 5.5 percent of the annual report concentrated on organized crime; by 1979 this figure had increased to 8.3 percent of the annual report.

Finally, a content analysis of the articles in the *FBI Law Enforcement Bulletin* during Kelley's tenure as director (August 1974 to March 1978) reveals that only one of the 251 articles was related to organized crime investigation. This is certainly not impressive for an organization that emphasizes organized crime as a top priority and that presumably wishes to stress this point in the law enforcement community.

How can we make sense of this ostensibly contradictory data? Was Kelley really shifting FBI priorities or simply formulating "new" priorities as a public relations ploy? Furthermore, was Kelley continuing Hoover's neglect of organized crime in spite of public pronouncements to the contrary?

The answer to these questions lies in an understanding of the post-Watergate FBI and its organizational environment. It is important to realize that the FBI of Clarence Kelley, unlike that of Hoover, was in a no-growth situation in the late 1970s. Although actual FBI appropriations were increasing in absolute terms, these dollars were constant relative to inflation. The number of FBI special agents was actually decreasing during this period, from 8,490 in 1975 to 7,904 in 1979. Similarly, the number of investigative matters received by the FBI declined by 61 percent in the late 1970s (U.S. House, Appropriations Hearings, 1976–1980). In short, the bureau was confronted with a major loss in its investigative capacity. This situation was further compounded by a diminishing of the FBI's organizational power in this post-Watergate era.[9]

During this era of dwindling resources, bureau strategy under Kelley was, as we have seen, to drastically reduce its domestic intelligence operations, the source of most of the abuses under Hoover, and to more carefully target its resources in other investigative areas. This became known as the quality-over-quantity approach, where the quality of caseload was stressed over quantity. Diminishing resources also provided the economic basis for a more proactive approach to investigations in which the undercover technique was increasingly employed as a way to more carefully target resources. The "old" FBI had relied on reactive case-by-case investigations of separate offenses. The proactive undercover technique eventually became the hallmark of the "new" FBI. Undercover operations were initially used in organized crime investigations but by the early 1980s had been extended to most of the investigative areas under the FBI's jurisdiction (U.S. House, 1984: 1).

In this context, we need to examine whether organized crime, which had been designated as a top FBI priority in 1975, received its fair share of FBI resources commensurate with its top priority status. This is somewhat difficult to determine, since appropriations for the organized crime program were not separately identified in congressional appropriation hearings until FY 1978. However, organized crime investigative matters received were reported commencing in 1975. We have already noted that there was an overall decline of 61 percent in bureau investigative matters received between 1975 and 1979. While there was also a decline in such investigative matters for organized crime, it was not as great (38.5 percent). From 1975 to 1979, organized crime investigative matters constituted a growing proportion of total FBI investigative matters—4.4 percent in 1975, 6.9 percent in 1979 (U.S. House, Appropriations Hearings, 1976–1980). It does appear that in spite of declining resources, the bureau was beginning to reorder its investigative capacity in line with its newly stated priorities.

In the post-Watergate period, organized crime provided an attractive target and priority because it combined the concern over political corruption with another clear-cut menace—the Mafia—which the Johnson Crime Commission had already transformed into a national crime syndicate with conspiratorial overtones. In addition, the seeds for this new priority had been planted several years earlier. In 1967 Neil Welch, special agent in charge (SAC) of the Buffalo office, launched a covert operation targeting Buffalo organized crime figures. His undercover operation was concealed from other agents in his field office as well as bureau headquarters. The outcome of this first full-time undercover surveillance by FBI agents was the arrest of ten organized crime figures. Welch was subsequently transferred to the Detroit, Philadelphia, and New York City field offices during the 1970s. With each new assignment, he reorganized each field office into target squads and case squads, employed undercover operations, and emphasized organized crime, corruption, and white-collar crime over internal security investigations (Welch and Marston, 1984). Ironically, what began as a "subversive" operation under the Hoover FBI became established practice and a top priority in the Kelley era.

Organized Crime in the Webster Era

While the birth of organized crime as a top FBI priority, after decades of neglect, was in the context of FBI scandal and dwindling investigative resources, the FBI of the 1980s found itself on different ground. William Webster, who became FBI director in 1978, not only continued Kelley's priorities but also was able to pursue them under more favorable conditions. It was during Webster's administration of the FBI that the public increasingly became conscious of a "new" FBI. After 1980, FBI resources again started to increase both in absolute and relative terms. The number of FBI special agents were again on the rise between 1980 and 1985, increasing from 7,804 to 8,739. The bureau investigative work load, as measured by agent work-years, similarly increased by 22.8 percent during that same period of time (U.S. House, Appropriations Hearings, 1981–1986). Finally, the FBI appeared to be regaining some of its organizational power, lost in the previous decade, as its percentage of DOJ appropriations rose from 25 to 30.4 percent (U.S. Bureau of the Budget, 1981–1986).

In this context of expanding resources, the FBI continued to disproportionately allocate resources to organized crime as one of its top priority investigative programs. This is especially evident when we consider that the FBI's role in the Reagan drug war was coordinated through its organized crime program and some thirteen (Organized Crime Drug Enforcement) task forces that included other federal agencies. By 1986 the bureau's organized crime program, including its drug investigations, occupied 24.2 percent of agent time in its field programs, a substantial increase since 1980 (U.S. House, Appropriations Hearings, 1987).

Quite aside from the question of resources is the investigative strategy toward organized crime that was developed in the Webster era. The Webster-era strategy for combating organized crime was first formulated in the 1960s in the aftermath of the Valachi hearings and Johnson's Crime Commission. The Valachi hearings provided the impetus for passage of Kennedy's anticrime proposals regarding wiretapping and witness immunity. The 1967 Crime Commission similarly provided the basis for the Omnibus Crime Control and Safe Streets Act of 1968 and the Organized Crime Control Act of 1970. Both of these acts gave expanded powers to the Justice Department in its pursuit of organized crime figures.

Albanese (1985) argues that much of this organized crime legislation was passed on the assumption that there is a nationwide Mafia conspiracy, and the legislation accordingly provides the tools to deal with this threat. Presumably, if such a centralized bureaucratic structure exists, it would, indeed, be a formidable law enforcement adversary.[10] It would also seem to follow that if law enforcement is provided with sufficient resources and investigative tools for the task, such a national crime syndicate could be dismantled by removing its top leaders. The primary strategy of the Justice Department and the FBI has been precisely this: to target the top leadership of La Cosa Nostra. At the House Appropriation Hearings in 1979, bureau officials stated the purpose of the Organized Crime Program as follows: "The thrust of investigations within the Organized Crime Program are targeted against the Syndicate, the largest organized criminal group known to be operating illegally within the United States" (U.S. House, Appropriations Hearings, 1979: 859). The FBI annual review of accomplishments on organized crime during this period largely consists of a listing of convictions of organized crime figures. In 1982, for example, this listing includes an impressive number of convictions of high-level syndicate members in Kansas City, New Orleans, Los Angeles, Cleveland, Chicago, Tampa, Philadelphia, Detroit, Boston, Milwaukee, and New York City (U.S. House, Appropriations Hearings, 1983). In the early 1980s, the leadership in seventeen of twenty-four La Cosa Nostra families had been indicted or convicted (President's Commission on Organized Crime, 1986b: 47).

In 1979 the FBI began to develop a data base for organized crime (Organized Crime Information System—OCIS) to enhance its investigative and intelligence capacity on syndicate leaders. It also began to make use of the RICO statute (Racketeer Influenced and Corrupt Organizations), which was part of the Organized Crime Control Act of 1970. Before 1978 only thirty-seven individuals had been convicted under RICO (Rhodes, 1984: 75). The increasing use of RICO in the early 1980s allowed the Justice Department to pursue the crime syndicates themselves as well as the top leaders.[11]

By 1981, the FBI acknowledged, in effect, that organized crime was not a monolithic national structure when it expanded its Organized Crime Program beyond La Cosa Nostra to include "nontraditional" groups, including motorcycle gangs and other ethnic organizations involved in organized crime. Nevertheless, the bureau continues to focus on La Cosa Nostra as the organized crime group with the most power and influence. More than 70 percent of agent time within the Organized Crime Program is still devoted to the LCN (U.S. House, Appropriations Hearings, 1987).

The basic strategy in the mid-1980s remained the same: to remove the top organized crime figures "from the street" (U.S. House, Appropriations Hearings, 1985: 1088). Webster argues that this has the effect of reducing the invincibility of the top leadership, undermining the code of silence, and ultimately weakening the structure of organized crime itself (U.S. House, Appropriations Hearings, 1984: 617).

While the post-Watergate FBI was serious in its efforts to combat organized crime, it was not without its critics. In 1977 a General Accounting Office (GAO) evaluation of the federal strike forces combating organized crime revealed confusion in the federal strategy. According to the GAO report, the federal government still had not developed a strategy and there was no agreement on what organized crime is and, therefore, on whom or what the government is fighting. A 1981 GAO follow-up evaluation found that progress had been made in coordinating federal efforts and in setting priorities for strike forces; the report recommended concentrating resources on high-level organized crime figures (Albanese, 1985: 107–110).

The President's Commission on Organized Crime also criticized federal efforts against organized crime, in spite of the impressive accomplishments noted by Attorney General Smith and FBI Director Webster at the 1983 hearings.[12] Federal efforts were characterized as fragmented and lacking adequate coordination. The commission argued that it was not enough to go after individual figures; a new strategy was needed because of the "insidious and systemic nature" of organized crime. The commission attributed the ineffectiveness of the existing strategy to lack of political will, fixed responsibility, and a national plan of attack. The commission's principal recommendation was to develop "a national strategy to remove organized crime from the marketplace" (President's Commission on Organized Crime, 1986a: 5–6, 307ff.). In response to the criticisms by the commission, the FBI indicated that since December 1987 it has employed a "national strategy" against the LCN; this is an extension to the national level of the bureau's attack against organized crime as a criminal enterprise.[13]

While the FBI and Justice Department's strategy against organized crime is evolving, there continue to be signs that the strategy of "taking out the top leadership," even at the national level, has not brought the expected results. At the Senate subcommittee hearings on the status of organized crime (U.S. Senate, 1988), Senator Nunn read from the summary statements of FBI field reports from several cities (Chicago, Miami, Newark, Kansas City, New York City, Detroit). These reports indicated that the impact of enforcement efforts and prosecutions on LCN criminal activities was minimal, although there was an impact on the hierarchy of the LCN. The replacement effect of younger, less disciplined members quickly rising in the LCN hierarchy appears to have led to a "new breed" of leadership that is more prone to violence, especially in some cities. The FBI field reports further noted that the LCN was left with assets and structure intact.

There can be little doubt that the Webster FBI continued organized crime as a top investigative priority, both in its allocation of resources and in its formulation of a strategy, to reduce the incidence of organized crime, although this strategy may be flawed. Webster himself has commented on the bureau's record in this area: "I think when I look back, when my time to leave comes, I will look back on this effort as being one of the proudest achievements of the FBI in its history" (U.S. House, Appropriations Hearings, 1984: 617).

The "New" FBI and Organized Crime

It seems clear that the bureau that emerged in the post-Watergate era was real in its commitment to combating organized crime. Establishing organized crime in the mid-1970s as a top priority was not simply a public relations ploy. There is, however, still a lingering question: How can we account for the sudden shift in bureau priorities, from neglect under Hoover to organized crime as a top priority in the "new" FBI. We have already noted the changing organizational needs of the bureau in the aftermath of Watergate as its "old" priorities had been discredited, especially in the internal security area, which resulted in a reassessment of FBI operations and the identification of new priorities. This, however, does not explain why organized crime was identified as a priority. There is also the question of why the Mafia menace itself arose as a national threat in the mid-1960s, even though various groups had been warning of its dangers since the Kefauver hearings of the early 1950s.

An important clue to both of these questions is provided in the Johnson Crime Commission's view of the threat of organized crime. The fundamental danger is in organized crime's accumulation of capital and profits outside of governmental control. This, in combination with the use of this illegally gained wealth to enter the legitimate economy and to corrupt public officials, is at the core of the organized crime threat (President's Commission on Law Enforcement, 1967b: 1–2). The bottom line is that traditional American values and institutions are subverted by this activity: crime is a source of upward mobility and a basis for economic and political power (Smith, 1975: 333). The forging of the Mafia menace during the 1960s becomes a way of personifying this threat and, of course, of oversimplifying it at the same time.

While organized crime groups existed in previous decades, they had been viewed in a very compartmentalized way, as exclusively involved in illegal goods and services—bootlegging, gambling, prostitution, narcotics, loan sharking, labor racketeering, and so on. While there was moral ambivalence about these illegal activities, since these goods and services were meeting a public demand, organized crime nevertheless was operating in its own illegal economic domain. The legal and illegal marketplaces in this view were sharply delineated. By the 1960s, this compartmentalized view began to break down. The links between organized crime, public corruption, and the legal economy became manifest. In his classic essay "Crime as an American Way of Life" (1964), Daniel Bell alluded to this overlap between the "captains of crime" and the "captains of industry" and to the functions of organized crime in American society—"the queer ladder of social mobility."

This discovery of the expansion of organized crime outside the traditional arena of illegal goods and services gave rise to the Mafia threat of the 1960s. As Donald Cressey writes:

> While organized criminals do not yet have control of all the legitimate economic and political activities in any metropolitan or other geographic area of America, they do have control of *some* of those activities in many areas. . . .
> We recognize a danger. We cannot be sure of the degree of the danger any more than the observer of the beginnings of any other kind of monopoly can be sure of the degree of danger (Cressey, 1967: 25).

American capitalism had an unwelcome competitor in the legal marketplace. The alarm over this discovery resulted in federal efforts to begin to contain this competitor who had access to billions of dollars of illegally accumulated wealth. The federal strike forces developed in 1967, and the organized crime legislation passed in 1970, must be understood in this context.

This concern over the penetration of organized crime into the legal marketplace has continued into the present. In 1983 President Reagan formed a President's Commission on Organized Crime "to study the nature and scope of organized crime in the United States" and to report on any new developments. In one of the commission's reports, *The Edge: Organized Crime, Business, and Labor Unions* (1986a: 1), the concern over organized crime's influence in the marketplace is clearly stated:

> Organized crime in America is entrenched in the marketplace. It owns and operates legitimate businesses, and in some areas of the country, it controls segments of entire industries. Throughout the economy, organized crime distorts the cost of doing business through theft, extortion, bribery, price fixing, and restraint of trade.

Released as part of the final report was a study by Wharton Econometric Forecasting of Philadelphia on "The Income of Organized Crime." This study shows in an empirical way how organized crime affects the legal marketplace and estimates that the existence of organized crime reduces the GNP by $18.2 billion per year, reduces employment by 414,000 jobs, and raises consumer prices by 0.3 percent (President's Commission on Organized Crime, 1986b: 487). The Wharton study does appear, however, to take a middle road on the threat organized crime poses, taking issue with those who argue that organized crime is a large and growing part of the national economy. The study also disagrees with the other extreme position that organized crime is not a large problem—that it is a fabrication by law enforcement for its own self-serving ends (President's Commission on Organized Crime, 1986b: 419).

The threat, however, is no longer one of a monolithic Mafia danger but instead encompasses a diversity of organized crime groups in addition to La Cosa Nostra. In its final report, *The Impact: Organized Crime Today* (1986b), the commission warns that "we must broaden our perspective" beyond the traditional preoccupation with the Mafia and realize that the problem of organized crime has become much more pervasive. It then proceeds to identify a plethora of "nontraditional" organized crime groups, including four outlaw motorcycle gangs, five prison gangs, Japanese "Yakuza" groups, Colombian cocaine rings, and Cuban crime cartels. Nevertheless, the LCN remains the dominant group in organized crime, with its superior network of contacts and political influence. The underlying goal, with regard to all organized crime groups, remains the same, however: to reduce or eliminate organizes crime's influence and impact on the national economy and other major institutions.

In hindsight, Hoover's neglect of organized crime, especially prior to the 1960s, is much more understandable. His "old" priorities created one of the most powerful agencies in the federal government. Organized crime, however, turned out to be more than "just a bunch of hoodlums"; it became an unwelcome competitor in the legitimate economy. Equally understandable is the "new" FBI's sudden concern over La Cosa Nostra and, more recently, other organized crime groups. The "new" FBI's designation of organized crime as a top priority is part of the broader federal effort to contain the influence and penetration of organized crime groups in the political economy of the United States.

The evolution of organized crime as a top investigative priority, like white-collar crime, reflects a "new" FBI that is more responsive to the policy concerns of the prevailing administration. It no longer has the organizational autonomy of the Hoover FBI to exhibit a "strange reluctance" to areas of enforcement that a presidential administration might deem top priority, whether that be organized crime, white-collar crime, or drug law enforcement. In the following chapter, we shall see some indications that bureau autonomy is reemerging, as evidenced by the FBI's resistance to overtures by the Reagan administration to "unleash" the FBI on terrorists, domestic and foreign. The Webster FBI's dissent on the war on terrorism reveals still another distinguishing aspect of the contemporary bureau.

NOTES

1. Since Hawkins's 1969 essay, the evidence that nearly all LCN families are under the authority of a "national commission" has been firmly established (President's Commission on Organized Crime, 1986b: 37). It has also become more apparent in the last decade that organized crime takes many forms besides the traditional Mafia structure. This, nevertheless, does not discredit the central point here, which is that much of our thinking about crime, including organized crime, is based more on faith than on fact. Walker's (1989: 10ff.) discussion of crime control theology also makes this same point.

2. This evolution of the Mafia label can be traced by counting the number of articles under the entry "Mafia" in the *New York Times Index*, 1950–1973. In 1950 and 1951, at the time of the Kefauver hearings, the number of entries were five and eleven, respectively. They remained low (about four entries per year) until 1963, the year of the Valachi hearings, when the number of entries jumped to sixty-seven. The list of Mafia entries continuously increased during the 1960s, peaking at 359 in 1969, and declined during the early 1970s (Smith, 1975: 292).

3. The Federal Bureau of Narcotics (FBN) was established in 1930 and was the forerunner agency of the current Drug Enforcement Administration (DEA). Harry J. Anslinger became the first head of the FBN and, like Hoover, enjoyed a long reign as its director until 1962. He had previously served with the National Prohibition Unit, which was responsible for enforcing the Volstead Act (Lindesmith, 1965).

4. It should be noted that the FBI still did not officially recognize the term *Mafia* but instead continued to adhere to the term *hoodlum*. The sudden official use of *Mafia* would have been tantamount to admitting the blindspot in FBI priorities.

5. President John F. Kennedy had also been a member of the committee.

6. This is further reflected in the increasing use of *Mafia* in the national media in the post-Valachi era, as measured by entries in the *New York Times Index*. In 1963 there were 67 "Mafia" entries; in 1964, 57; in 1965, 81; in 1966, 98; in 1967, 148; in 1968, 182; in 1969, 359 (Smith, 1975: 292).

7. In 1960 there were 19 indictments of organized crime figures; 687 in 1964; 1,107 in 1967; and 1,166 in 1968 (Clark, 1970: 65).

8. Refer to chapter 6 for a more complete discussion of the reform of FBI domestic intelligence and of the decline in such activities.

9. A measure of the FBI's organizational power is the ratio of the FBI budget to the DOJ budget. Throughout the 1970s, FBI appropriations fluctuated between 20 and 23 percent of the DOJ budget. This, again, was unlike the Hoover FBI of the 1950s and 1960s, which had consistently maintained an FBI budget of over 40 percent of the DOJ budget (see table 3-1).

10. The controversy surrounding the existence of a monolithic Mafia organization is analogous to the elite-pluralist debate in sociology and political science. The underlying question is the same: How concentrated is political power? Is it centralized in a ruling elite (the "national commission"), or is it dispersed among numerous interest groups (the twenty-four LCN families)? Some research on organized crime suggests that organized crime is much more entrepreneurial than the Mafia myth would have us believe (Smith, 1975; Rubinstein and Reuter, 1978; Block, 1979; Reuter, 1983). My reading of the evidence is that organized crime in the United States is a more dispersed, that is, a more pluralist phenomenon than the elite-conspiratorial view allows. This is further reinforced if one takes into account the emerging nontraditional organized crime groups.

11. RICO provides federal investigators and prosecutors with the legal tools to pursue patterns of criminal activity, criminal organizations, and their profits, not just organized crime figures. More specifically, it prohibits the profits derived from illegal activity to be used in any enterprise. It also prohibits the use of any enterprise to commit a pattern of criminal activity. The concept of enterprise is employed broadly in the statute to include legal and illegal enterprises; as defined in the statute, an enterprise can be "an individual, a partnership, a corporation, an association, a union, or any legal entity capable of holding a property interest." The RICO statute provides for criminal sanctions as well as civil remedies (Abadinsky, 1981: 181–187).

12. Attorney General Smith testified that 2,609 members and associates of organized crime had been convicted since 1981 (President's Commission on Organized Crime, 1983: 17).

13. This extension of the bureau's organized crime strategy was announced by Director William Sessions at the Senate hearings on the status of organized crime (U.S. Senate, 1988). Sessions replaced Webster as head of the FBI in November 1987.

Chapter 9

THE "NEW" FBI, TERRORISM, AND THE REAGAN ADMINISTRATION

The area of FBI operations that continues to evoke the greatest public suspicion is its domestic security and intelligence function. As we have seen, these operations were at the center of the Hoover FBI's lawlessness and were prominent in the revelations of the Watergate years. In the "new" FBI of the 1970s, domestic intelligence took a back seat to the three top investigative priorities of organized crime, white-collar crime, and foreign counterintelligence.

In this chapter we shall examine the role of the Reagan administration in at least partially undoing these reforms by attempting to "unleash the FBI," and the FBI's resistance and accommodation to these efforts. The question of the permanence of the mid-1970s reforms takes on renewed significance with the disclosure in early 1988 of an extensive FBI surveillance from 1981 through 1985 of U.S. citizens and groups opposed to the Reagan administration's policies in Central America (Shenon, 1988b).[1] Whether this disclosure signifies the revival of Hoover's policies of surveilling political dissidents engaged in First Amendment activities must be understood in relation to the debate in the early 1980s over the nature and scope of domestic terrorism. It is important to realize that the FBI, at least initially, resisted the Reagan administration's definition of the threat posed by domestic terrorism. The outcome of this debate gives us insight into the place of domestic security and terrorism investigations in the FBI of the Reagan administration. It also is revealing of the political and administrative context in which the contemporary bureau operates.

The FBI Dissent Over Domestic Terrorism

The erosion of the FBI's internal security apparatus, which had been the postwar basis of bureau organizational power, was a crucial element of FBI reform in the aftermath of Watergate. The decline in FBI domestic intelligence operations during this period is well documented.[2] By the late 1970s, domestic security had been incorporated into the FBI Terrorism Program and represented the preventive intelligence function of the program.[3] Director Webster indicated that in 1978 he changed the designation from "domestic security" to "terrorism" because in his mind there was no difference in the two terms (U.S. House, 1987a: 38). In the Webster FBI, "domestic terrorism" became the primary designation for FBI activities formerly labeled "domestic security," "domestic intelligence," "internal security," or "domestic subversion" operations.

At the appropriations hearings for FY 1982, the FBI indicated the following changes and prospects for the Terrorism Program: "The Terrorism Program will be decreased by 21 positions and $286,000 in 1982. If terrorism activity continues at its present level, it is believed that this reduction will necessitate a reorganization and redirection of the remaining resources" (U.S. House, Appropriations Hearings, 1981: 808). This downward trend in domestic security and terrorism appropriations represented a continuation of reforms initiated during the Watergate era.

This trend, however, was suddenly reversed in FY 1983. Not only were such program reductions ended but domestic terrorism began to account for an increasing share of agent time in the FBI field programs. In 1982 only 2 percent of agent work-years in field programs were accounted for by domestic terrorism; this amount increased to 3 percent in FY 1983 and 5 percent in FY 1984 (U.S. House, Appropriations Hearings, 1983–1985).[4] Furthermore, on October 1, 1982, terrorism was elevated to a national priority program along with organized crime, white-collar crime, and foreign counterintelligence (U.S. House, Appropriations Hearings, 1983: 940).

It is this sudden turnabout in FBI priorities and apparent resurgence in FBI domestic intelligence that will concern us. Why was the FBI Terrorism Program transformed from a priority 3 program, which is a low priority in the bureau hierarchy of field programs, to a priority 1 program, the highest investigative priority, in a very brief period of time during the early 1980s? In the 1978 appropriations hearings, FBI Director William Webster indicated that the bureau was at "rock bottom" in the domestic security and terrorism area (U.S. House, Appropriations Hearings, 1978: 673). In fact, in FY 1979 the FBI had a $2 million surplus in its Terrorism Program (U.S. House, 1980a: 5). As previously noted, these program reductions continued through FY 1982, because the FBI itself maintained as late as April 1981 that "this program continues to utilize resources at a rate less than the funded level" (U.S. House, Appropriations Hearings, 1981: 991). Yet in the following fiscal year, the Terrorism Program was transformed into a top investigative priority.

This reordering of priorities within the FBI carried with it much broader social and political implications as to how the domestic battle against terrorism would be waged by the Reagan administration and how the terrorist threat would be defined and presented to the American public. This struggle for ideological hegemony of the terrorist threat was played out in various congressional subcommittee hearings as the Reagan administration attempted to impose its ideological view of terrorism on FBI operations. The competing views of the terrorist threat focused on three issues: (1) the adequacy of resources and appropriations for terrorism, (2) the attorney general guidelines on domestic security operations, and (3) the nature of domestic terrorism. As we shall see, FBI Director Webster and other bureau officials dissented from the Reagan administration on each of these issues. A closer examination of each issue will reveal the nature of that dissent and the outcome for the Reagan administration's war on terrorism.

On the Adequacy of Terrorism Resources

The FBI of the immediate post-Watergate period, unlike the Hoover FBI, was in a no-growth situation. Although actual FBI appropriations were increasing in absolute terms, these funds were roughly constant relative to inflation. The number of FBI special agents was decreasing during this period, as was the number of investigative matters received by the FBI in the late 1970s (U.S. House, Appropriations Hearings, 1975–1980). The bureau's budgetary situation was certainly not enhanced by its loss of organizational power in the post-Watergate era.[5]

In this context of dwindling resources and investigative capacity, domestic intelligence operations were drastically reduced. The 91.5 percent decline in domestic intelligence investigative matters received from 1975 through 1979 overshadowed the 61 percent decline in overall FBI investigative capacity. As noted earlier, FBI Director Webster indicated the bureau was at "rock bottom" in the domestic security and terrorism area by the late 1970s. However, after 1980 FBI resources again started to increase both in absolute and relative terms. The number of FBI special agents was on the increase between 1980 and 1985; the bureau investigative work load, as measured by agent work-years, was similarly increasing; finally, the FBI appeared to be regaining some of its organizational power, which had been lost in the previous decade.[6] The question remained whether the more favorable budgetary and political conditions of the 1980s would also lead to a restoration of domestic intelligence operations on their former scale or whether the Webster FBI would persist with the priorities set following the mid-1970s scandal.

For the answer to this question, our inquiry turns to several congressional subcommittee hearings in the late 1970s and early 1980s. As early as 1978, less than two years after the Church and Pike committees final reports on FBI and intelligence agency abuses, some congressmen were raising questions as to the adequacy of FBI efforts in the domestic security and terrorism area. At the appropriations hearings for FY 1979, Congressman Joseph Early showed concern over the FBI's proposed reductions in domestic security and terrorism. The FBI was requesting a 27 percent reduction in appropriations and a 30 percent decrease in personnel. Early asked FBI Director Webster if he could adequately do the job with that reduction. Webster replied in the affirmative and explained that the FBI was concentrating on "the tough cases, the cases that involve terrorism, bombing and massive violence." Early was apparently not satisfied with Webster's justification for the reductions, since he indicated that he would not support them (U.S. House, Appropriations Hearings, 1978: 655–673).

The following year, in the appropriations hearings for FY 1980, Director Webster was again called on to defend his continued reductions in the Terrorism Program. Webster argued:

> The reduction in the Terrorism Program is partly due to the effectiveness, I think, of our work and that of cooperation with local law enforcement. The number of terrorist bombings last year was very substantially reduced from the previous year. We are not spending all the money that the Congress had allocated for us for fiscal 1979 (U.S. House, Appropriations Hearings, 1979: 925).

In his testimony, Webster, in fact, projected a budget surplus in the terrorism program for FY 1979.

At the Edwards subcommittee hearings on FBI oversight earlier in the same month,[7] Congressman Drinan similarly questioned FBI officials on the reason for this $2 million surplus and the adequacy of resources for the Terrorism Program. Sebastian Mignosa, who headed the domestic security and terrorism section, assured Drinan that his program had sufficient resources and that he did not need or want more appropriations (U.S. House 1980a: 11).

In May 1980 the Edwards subcommittee held hearings on the federal government's capability in dealing with terrorist incidents. In pursuing the question of the adequacy of resources, Congressman Edwards asked FBI Assistant Director Charles Monroe,[8] "Why are you going to spend less money on antiterrorism in the coming year than you did this year?" Monroe replied:

> That is based primarily on statistics, sir. For those who analyze budgets, the primary data is statistics. It's hard to justify something that might happen. There is a trend going down and the trend does not justify our saying based on speculation, based on accurate statistics, that we need more money—I think that the money we are asking for this year is realistic (U.S. House, 1980c: 45–46).

In the previous month Congressman Early again had criticized Director Webster during the appropriations hearings for the low priority the FBI gave to terrorism.

> I used to think of it as a great agency. I see that now you are trying to promote public relations. You publish more charts and more reports, but from where I view the FBI, I am not impressed.

> You said you set priorities, but you cut the funding level for terrorism investigations. You also cut money from the legal attachés. They would be my top priorities. Why do you see other crime as more important than domestic terrorism? (U.S. House, Appropriations Hearings, 1980: 152).

Webster's response was, in part, based on statistics, which no doubt further irritated Early. Webster observed that terrorism incidents in the United States had been on the decline and that the FBI would spend more if necessary: "My sense of it is that we have enough resources in our terrorism program or I would ask for more" (U.S. House, Appropriations Hearings, 1980: 153).

In the 1982 appropriations hearings, Director Webster produced the statistics he used to justify reductions in the Terrorism Program. These confirmed that terrorism in the United States had declined from 111 terrorist incidents in 1977, to 69 in 1978, 52 in 1979, 29 in 1980, and 42 in 1981 (U.S. House, Appropriations Hearings, 1982: 1205). At these hearings, Webster further distinguished between domestic terrorism investigations and international terrorism investigations. While the number of agents assigned to the former had decreased during the preceding two years, the number of agents assigned to the latter had increased. For the first time, Webster requested the same level of funding for the domestic Terrorism Program in FY 1983 as in the previous year, even though he continued to insist that "the number of domestic terrorist incidents has gone way down" (U.S. House, Appropriations Hearings, 1982: 1146). He emphasized that the problem was in the international terrorism area, where incidents were up: "Our problem today is with the foreign groups, with the Armenians, with the Croatians, the Jewish Defense League, the anti-Castro Cubans, the Omega 7 groups. Those are the active ones" (U.S. House, Appropriations Hearings, 1982: 1146).

In spite of Director Webster's, and other FBI officials', consistent defense of program reductions in the Terrorism Program, what began as inquiries and criticisms of the adequacy of FBI efforts in this area in the late 1970s turned into outright alarm with the advent of the Reagan administration in 1981. Reagan's transition team and the Heritage Foundation, which had prepared a report on intelligence for the new administration, advocated increased domestic spying, loyalty-security programs, and the revival of congressional internal security committees (Peterzell, 1981a, 1981b; Donner, 1982). The Heritage report voiced alarm about the current state of the union, claiming that "the threat to the internal security of the Republic is greater today than at any time since World War II" (Peterzell, 1981a: 1). The report further proposed that the FBI initiate domestic intelligence investigations of a wide range of political groups, including terrorist organizations, but also political groups involved solely in lawful activity. Groups listed as likely targets by the Heritage report included foreign immigrants, radical and New Left groups, and even the "anti-defense and anti-nuclear lobbies" (Peterzell, 1981a: 2).

As the crescendo of alarm and the rising specter of terrorism were raised by the Reagan administration, the FBI, in spite of its own evidence to the contrary,[9] elevated terrorism to the status of a national priority program on October 1, 1982. At the March 1983 appropriations hearings, the bureau for the first time requested an increase in funding for the Terrorism Program: an additional twenty-five positions and $830,000 to fully staff a Hostage Rescue Team in FY 1984 (U.S.

House, Appropriations Hearings, 1983: 851). FBI officials never accounted for the apparent contradiction between the sudden elevation of terrorism to a top priority program and their testimony of former years. Although not directly addressing this contradiction, an official explanation was offered in the 1983 appropriations hearings relating to the need for more resources: "In recent years, the threat of terrorism to the security of the United States and to the President of the United States has steadily increased. To successfully counter the increasing threat, a redirection of FBI resources was considered necessary by the FBI" (U.S. House, Appropriations Hearings, 1983: 940).

Furthermore, two years earlier (April 2, 1981), Congressman George O'Brien of Illinois had pointedly asked Director Webster whether the FBI was making a new policy on terrorism or whether the administration was doing so. Webster's reply made it clear that the impetus for change was coming from his bureaucratic superiors: "Under the instructions of the Attorney General, the FBI is currently reviewing both the foreign counterintelligence [FCI] and domestic intelligence guidelines" (U.S. House, Appropriations Hearings, 1981: 984).

Our inquiry into the turnabout of FBI priorities on terrorism will now look at the second area in which the FBI appeared to dissent from the Reagan administration's view of the terrorist threat: the attorney general guidelines on domestic security operations. The arena for this clash of opposing views on terrorism was the newly established Subcommittee on Security and Terrorism of the U.S. Senate Judiciary Committee.

The Attorney General Guidelines on Domestic Security Operations

One element in the reform of FBI domestic intelligence during the mid-1970s was the establishment by the attorney general of a set of guidelines that would govern domestic security investigations. These were implemented in 1976 and came to be known as the Levi Guidelines, after Attorney General Edward Levi. These domestic security guidelines were viewed by the Reagan administration as a major obstacle to the expansion of domestic intelligence.

In 1982 the Senate Subcommittee on Security and Terrorism, chaired by Sen. Jeremiah Denton, began a five-part series of hearings on the Levi Guidelines with the aim of assessing their impact on domestic intelligence and modifying them accordingly. In Senator Denton's opening statement, he revealed his concern that in the reordering of priorities in the mid-1970s, domestic security and terrorism "may have fallen through the cracks" and that various domestic groups might "hide themselves among other groups in areas well protected by the First Amendment and thereby escape the scrutiny of the Bureau" (U.S. Senate, 1982a: 2).

Senator East, also a member of the subcommittee, was similarly highly critical of the Levi Guidelines. In his prepared statement, he asserted that "they have virtually destroyed an adequate internal security function in the FBI" and that their adoption "has undermined our ability to track, prevent, and apprehend persons and groups that threaten the internal security of the country, including terrorist and terrorist support groups" (U.S. Senate, 1982a: 34).

FBI Director Webster's testimony was in marked contrast to that of the two senators. "It is difficult to measure the effect of these guidelines on our operations, but we believe they have served us reasonably well" (U.S. Senate, 1982a: 8). Webster also remarked that "my problem today is not unleashing the FBI, my problem is convincing those in the FBI that they can work up to the level of our authority" (U.S. Senate, 1982b: 19).

During the ensuing questioning, Senator Denton asked Webster if the bureau was out of the domestic intelligence business. Webster explained that the FBI takes a "quality-over-quantity" approach to its investigations and that its domestic security operations are carefully targeted on key organizations and individuals in leadership positions. Webster emphasized that "in addressing the domestic security area, we found that we had been engaging in manpower allocations that were not really producing anything of significance and that vast amounts of money were being paid out for information that was not productive" (U.S. Senate, 1982a: 13).

One year earlier, before a Senate appropriations hearing, Webster had also spoken approvingly of the Levi Guidelines:

> We have not found ourselves unduly restricted by the domestic security guidelines with respect to terrorist activities. In fact, the guidelines as a whole give strength and confidence to the activities because our agents are more convinced, as a result of those guidelines, that they will not be second-guessed and subjected to discipline or prosecution (U.S. Senate, 1981: 563).

Although Webster voiced some reservations about the Levi Guidelines and noted that the bureau was cooperating with the Department of Justice on their revision, the thrust of his testimony at the Denton subcommittee hearings was that the guidelines were working "reasonably well" and that he did not share the same alarming concerns of Denton and East. Nevertheless, the subcommittee hearings continued. At the June 25 hearings, two retired Hoover-era veterans, W. Mark Felt and Ed Miller, were brought in as expert witnesses on intelligence.[10] Their views on the Levi Guidelines coincided with those of Denton and East. Felt asserted that "we are confronted with an enormous security gap" in the internal security area and that the Levi Guidelines were just part of this gap. Miller also believed the Levi Guidelines to be too restrictive (U.S. Senate, 1982a: 75–76).

In spite of the apparent satisfaction of Webster with the Levi Guidelines, Attorney General William French Smith issued new domestic security guidelines in March 1983 that, on their face, gave the FBI additional authority to conduct domestic security and terrorism investigations. FBI and Justice Department officials were reluctant to characterize the Smith Guidelines as a loosening of the restrictions that had been imposed by the Levi Guidelines. In fact, Senator Denton specifically asked Webster whether the Smith Guidelines had this effect. Director Webster was evasive and refused to get drawn into the semantics of whether restrictions had been loosened, even after some persistence on the part of Denton. Webster did, however, finally offer that the guidelines did not "unleash" the FBI

(U.S. Senate, 1983b: 15). About a month later, before the Edwards subcommittee, Webster did concede that "the guidelines allow us greater flexibility during the early stages of an investigation. . . . They do permit us, consistent with that obligation, to seek an early interdiction of unlawful violent activity" (U.S. House, 1987a: 25).

The Denton subcommittee held hearings on the new Smith Guidelines a few days after they went into effect. Assistant Attorney General D. Lowell Jensen elaborated on the major provisions of the Smith Guidelines: the guidelines for terrorist enterprises were integrated with the guidelines for criminal investigations; the "criminal enterprise approach," similar to that used in organized crime investigations, was adopted; statements that advocate criminal activity or an apparent intent to commit a crime could be investigated; and the continued monitoring of groups that may be temporarily inactive was allowed (U.S. Senate, 1983b: 8–10). The Smith Guidelines also did away with the three levels of investigation permitted in the Levi Guidelines. The new guidelines only distinguish between preliminary inquiries and full investigations. Preliminary inquiries (with a ninety-day time limit) permit agents to "follow up on allegations or information indicating the possibility of criminal conduct in order to determine whether a full investigation is warranted" (U.S. House, 1987a: 12).

In light of Director Webster's earlier statements on the Levi Guidelines, it was of particular interest to see how Webster would view the revisions. At the Denton hearings, Webster attempted to put the revisions in context: "The new domestic security guidelines do not reflect any major changes in policy or shift in direction; they are merely part of the normal evolutionary process in the development of effective and workable rules" (U.S. Senate, 1983b: 11). He also pointed out that the FBI and the Department of Justice had spent eight months working on the revisions, suggesting that the guidelines were a joint venture and not simply imposed on the bureau from above.

In its final report on the impact of the Levi Guidelines, which was released seven months after the Smith Guidelines were implemented, the Denton subcommittee reaffirmed the need to revise the Levi Guidelines. In its conclusions and recommendations, the subcommittee asserted the importance of deleting the criminal standard as a basis for initiating a domestic security and terrorism investigation. The subcommittee argued that the criminal standard is an "inappropriate intrusion of a law enforcement concept in what is properly and primarily an intelligence activity" (U.S. Senate, 1984: 30). The report called for restoring domestic security investigations as an intelligence, as opposed to a law enforcement, activity. Interestingly, J. Edgar Hoover is cited as a source in support of maintaining this distinction.

While the subcommittee's report was aimed at the Levi Guidelines, it did not address itself to the revised guidelines. Although the Smith Guidelines do appear to expand FBI authority, they do, however, retain the criminal standard and incorporate terrorism investigations in the concept of a "criminal enterprise" and as part of the broader guidelines for criminal investigations. This crucial element of the revised guidelines was quite consistent with Webster's long-term view of domestic security investigations, which he had previously expressed before the Denton subcommittee: "What we are looking for is criminal conduct. The question is whether or not words, unaccompanied by conduct, can be the subject of investigation" (U.S. Senate, 1982b: 18).

He reiterated this idea before the Edwards subcommittee: "We are not interested in constitutionally protected advocacy of unpopular ideas or lawful political dissent." However, Webster cautioned, "But it must be made clear to our agents that statements which taken in context present a credible threat of crime should not be ignored" (U.S. House, 1987a: 25). Nearly three years later, in discussing terrorism investigations before the same subcommittee, Webster continued to stress that "the important aspect of terrorism in my mind is emphasizing the criminal aspect of it. . . . I have some resistance in my mind to reinjecting into the equation political motivation unnecessarily" (U.S. House, 1987b: 122).

The debate over the adequacy of the Levi Guidelines and their revision by Attorney General Smith in 1983 reflects the continuing efforts of the Reagan administration to impose its view of domestic terrorism on FBI operations and, indeed, on the American public. The unsettled question is still whether these efforts were successful. Will the FBI use its expanded authority? Will it resurrect the Hoover-style domestic security investigations as intelligence operations to combat terrorism? This question relates to our third area of conflict: the nature of domestic terrorism. The FBI and the Reagan administration again had differing views on the character of domestic terrorism in the 1980s.

The Nature of Domestic Terrorism

During the various subcommittee hearings, FBI officials presented a consistent picture of domestic terrorism in the early 1980s. Terrorist incidents in the United States were declining.[11] Most of these incidents were caused by groups that had "foreign quarrels, foreign problems, foreign origins" (U.S. Senate, 1982b: 9). The vast majority of terrorist activity in the United States between 1977 and 1981 was accounted for by Puerto Rican, Cuban, and Jewish groups (U.S. Senate, 1982b: 71). According to the FBI, many home-grown groups, which had previously been under domestic security investigation, were no longer viable organizations, and their investigations were closed in the late 1970s. These groups included the Weather Underground, the Republic of New Africa, the Black Liberation Army, and the Symbionese Liberation Army (U.S. Senate, 1982b: 39–43). Furthermore, the FBI did not see any organizational linkages among various terrorist groups. While conceding that there might be connections between individuals in some of these groups, Webster contended that "there is no known coalescing of an ideological synthesis among these groups, nor do we have any sense that they have become effective" (U.S. Senate, 1982b: 10).

Also, integral to the FBI view of domestic terrorist groups is that they are well-established organizations with goals and identities well known to the bureau. FBI special agent Carter Cornick, a specialist in terrorism investigation, expressed the following view of terrorist groups at the Edwards subcommittee hearings: "The groups themselves, particularly the ones which I think we are here to talk about this morning, are well established; their goals are well known; their modus operandi is reasonably known" (U.S. House, 1980c: 46). It follows from this view of domestic terrorism that terrorism stems from ongoing organizational enterprises, the activities of which are generally known to the bureau. As we saw, the concept of "criminal enterprise" was incorporated in the Smith Guidelines. The emphasis in combating terrorism is on targeting these terrorist enterprises in order to detect criminal conduct; domestic security and terrorism investigations are a special form of criminal investigation, with the emphasis on conduct rather than ideology. As Webster noted in 1982, "They should be pursued as organized criminal enterprises" (U.S. Senate, 1982a: 11). This continues to be the FBI strategy, as affirmed by Oliver Revell, executive assistant director, at the 1986 oversight hearings on terrorism: "We should put our resources into detection of those groups involved in violence and prevention of those specific acts rather than trying to fortify the entire structure of the United States" (U.S. House, 1987b: 179).

Moreover, the FBI, in its approach to domestic terrorism, is not particularly concerned with the isolated individuals or groups that might engage in terrorism unless they are part of a terrorist enterprise. As special agent Cornick indicated:

> I might say that our main thrust or our main efforts have been toward these people [that is, established groups]. So, therefore, we have not run into the problem of the suspicious individual—that is, the problem of the isolated, singular incident where we would be restricted under the present guidelines (U.S. House, 1980a: 46).

In marked contrast to the FBI's approach to domestic terrorism is the more expansive concept of terrorism espoused by the Reagan administration and some congressional conservatives. This view was well articulated by Senators Denton and East in the Subcommittee on Security and Terrorism hearings. In his opening statement at the hearings, Senator Denton described a complex structure and network of terrorist groups and organizations that operate on many fronts, overtly and covertly, and are linked in numerous kinds of interrelationships. Senator Denton's account of the terrorist threat is much more global than that of the FBI's.

> When I speak of a threat, I do not just mean that an organization is, or is about to be, engaged in violent criminal activity. I believe many share the view that the support groups that produce propaganda, disinformation, or "legal assistance" may be even more dangerous than those who actually throw the bombs (U.S. Senate, 1982a: 4).

In this view the criminal standard for terrorism investigations prevents the FBI from monitoring activities that may be legal and nonviolent yet constitute a threat of subversion through their support of terrorist activities. The final report of the Denton subcommittee hearings on the Levi Guidelines addressed this issue: "A key element of subversion therefore is the intention to make use of legitimate processes and institutions for illegitimate ends, to 'work within the system to destroy the system'—for example, to exploit the First Amendment. . . ." (U.S. Senate, 1984: 33).

Interestingly, Senator Denton asked Director Webster during the hearings about subversives who were not terrorists. Webster's answer again reveals the FBI view of the terrorism threat.

> Well, the word *subversive* is one that we don't see very often in the Bureau any more because of its difficulty in defining. One man's subversive is another man's freedom fighter. And we would prefer to make our judgments in allocating resources on the basis of conduct or activity (U.S. Senate, 1983b: 28).

Earlier in the same hearings, Denton asked Webster about the difference between domestic security and terrorism. Webster's reply was that "for our purposes they are interchangeable." He elaborated, however, on the distinction that *domestic security* is the older term and has connotations of the widespread surveillance activities of the past. Webster indicated that the bureau prefers the term *terrorism* because it avoids these connotations (U.S. Senate, 1983b: 24).

It is precisely on this point that the two views of the terrorist threat diverge. The FBI opts for the narrower view of terrorism, which focuses on criminal conduct. The Reagan administration, however, advocated a more expansive concept of terrorism, which encompassed criminal and noncriminal activities. It follows from this latter view of terrorism that the appropriate means of combating terrorism are through intelligence operations rather than criminal investigation.

Triumph of Ideology or Bureaucracy?

Throughout this chapter we have traced the efforts of the Reagan administration to inculcate its ideological view of the terrorist threat in FBI operations. We have followed this debate and conflict in relation to three issues: (1) the adequacy of resources for terrorism investigation, (2) the attorney general guidelines on domestic security operations, and (3) the nature of domestic terrorism. At the inception of our analysis, we noted the apparent reversal in FBI priorities regarding domestic terrorism during the early years of the Reagan administration. At this point, we need to evaluate the Reagan administration's success in undoing the modest reforms in FBI domestic intelligence that were instituted in the mid-1970s.

It is clear that the Reagan administration did succeed in reordering FBI priorities so that terrorism was elevated to a national priority program in October 1982. The administration also reversed the downward trend in appropriations for domestic security and terrorism that began in 1972. Reagan's executive order on intelligence (E.O. 12333), issued in December 1981, gave the FBI expanded authority to gather "positive intelligence" (Berman, 1985: 1), and the revision of the Levi Guidelines in March 1983 similarly gave the FBI broader authority to conduct domestic intelligence operations in the United States.

What is not so clear is the extent to which the FBI has acquiesced to the influence of the Reagan administration and its view of the terrorist threat. During the late 1970s and early 1980s, FBI officials appear to have played down the domestic terrorism issue, consistently pointing to the decline in terrorist incidents in the United States, and FBI Director Webster has had repeatedly to defend his reductions in the terrorism program through FY 1982. While the percent of agent time spent on domestic terrorism has increased from 2 percent in FY 1979 to 5 percent in FY 1984,[12] this is still significantly below the percentage of agent time spent on other top priority field programs—for example, 17.9 percent for organized crime, 20.3 percent for white-collar crime, and 11.5 percent for drug investigations (U.S. House, Appropriations Hearings, 1987: 1906–1918). Moreover, if we examine the allocation of resources within the FBI's Terrorism Program for domestic security,[13] since only this segment of the program is involved in intelligence activities, we observe a slight increase in this category, from 10.3 percent in FY 1980 to 16 percent in FY 1984 (U.S. House, Appropriations Hearings, 1981: 540; U.S. House, Appropriations Hearings, 1985), yet this preventive/intelligence phase of the program remains a relatively small part of the total Terrorism Program.

Furthermore, while the FBI participated in the revision of the Levi Guidelines, it was able to retain the criminal standard in the new guidelines even though the Smith Guidelines gave the FBI expanded authority in political surveillance activities. Although Webster stated before the Denton subcommittee, several days after the Smith Guidelines were implemented, that the guidelines did not represent a major policy change, it appears, nevertheless, that the new guidelines were useful to the FBI in reaffirming its authority in this area and in reassuring agents in the field as well.

In one important respect, however, the FBI seems to have expanded its domestic intelligence operations in departure from its organizational practices under the Levi Guidelines. The disclosure of FBI surveillance of political dissidents in the early 1980s, particularly those opposed to the Reagan administration's policies in Central America, indicates a much greater willingness on the part of the bureau in the Reagan years to intervene in the ambiguous area of First Amendment–protected activities. This, in fact, was hinted at by Webster in his testimony on the new guidelines when he conceded that they do permit "an early interdiction of unlawful violent activity" (U.S. House, 1987a: 25). This expansion of domestic security and terrorism operations appears to be primarily at the "preliminary inquiry" level of investigation, where the Smith Guidelines permit FBI "interdiction" based on "advocacy of criminal activity" or "allegations or information indicating the possibility of criminal conduct." This approach has opened the door not only to earlier FBI intervention in its surveillance activities but also to the increasing use of intrusive techniques (informants, undercover agents, and so on) at this stage. That such surveillance activities are departures from past practice seems supported by the FBI dismissal in 1987 of a twenty-two-year veteran agent, John C. Ryan, for his refusal to conduct a domestic security and terrorism preliminary inquiry of a pacifist group, Silo Plowshares, which opposed U.S. foreign policy in Central America.[14]

Although the data are still sketchy, it appears that most of the FBI's expansion in the domestic terrorism area during this period was at the preliminary inquiry level. The bureau's own statistics on the number of organizations targeted for full investigation under the domestic terrorism program reveal no discernible trend during the early 1980s.[15] No comparable data are available in regard to the number of individuals or organizations targeted in preliminary inquiries. Since FBI appropriations and agent time spent on domestic terrorism did increase during this period, it suggests that most of these resources were channeled into the first of the two levels of investigation.

The disclosures in the Committee in Solidarity with the People of El Salvador (CISPES) investigation in 1988 raise still another possibility of how the FBI may have increased its domestic intelligence activities under the pretext that the targeted group was a foreign agent. A group designated as an "agent of a foreign power" or as an "international terrorist" organization permits the FBI to use a different set of investigative guidelines in targeting such groups; the Smith Guidelines pertain only to domestic terrorist groups. International groups are investigated under a much less restrictive set of guidelines—the foreign counterintelligence (FCI) guidelines—which are classified. As Steven Pomerantz (1987: 16), chief of the FBI Terrorism Section, noted, "International terrorists who may be operating in the United States are considered hostile foreign elements." There is, therefore, a dual standard in the investigation of terrorist groups, depending on whether they are categorized as "domestic" or "international." The latter designation allows the FBI much greater latitude in the use of intrusive investigative techniques, including warrantless searches, and, furthermore, the investigation need not be linked to criminal activity (Center for Constitutional Rights, 1987: 8). The authority for such domestic intelligence operations derives from Reagan's 1981 executive order on intelligence (E.O. 12333).

Documents released under the Freedom of Information Act to the Center for Constitutional Rights indicate that CISPES was targeted as an international terrorist group. Initially, in 1981–1982, the FBI based its investigation on the predicate that CISPES was an agent of a foreign government. When this fact could not be substantiated, the bureau closed and then reopened the investigation from 1983 to 1985 under the foreign counterintelligence and international terrorism label, on the suspicion that CISPES was a terrorist group (Buitrago, 1988). Despite several years of intensive FBI surveillance, eventually involving fifty-two field offices, criminal charges were never brought against CISPES or any of its members. One possible implication is that the investigation was a political, rather than a criminal, investigation; CISPES was highly critical of the Reagan administration's policies in Central America.[16] Some of the released internal FBI files suggest such a political purpose. One memo from the New Orleans field office to FBI headquarters, dated November 12, 1983, states: "It is imperative at this time to formulate some plan of attack against CISPES and, specifically, against individuals, [deleted] who defiantly display their contempt for the U.S. government by making speeches and propagandizing their cause while asking for political asylum."[17]

Some of these allegations against the FBI were, in effect, confirmed by FBI Director Sessions in September 1988 when, as a result of an internal inquiry, he announced before the Senate Select Committee on Intelligence that six FBI special agents were being disciplined by the bureau for their mismanagement of the CISPES investigation.[18] Sessions indicated that the major problem occurred in October 1983, when the decision was made to expand what had been a fairly limited investigation to field offices throughout the country. While CISPES was suspected of having links to terrorist groups, this fact was never established, and the investigation was terminated in June 1985. In Sessions's view, the investigation became "unnecessarily broad," and the FBI supervisors of the case used poor judgment in expanding the investigation. The internal inquiry confirmed that the CISPES investigation produced 178 spin-off investigations, including nine other groups and 169 individuals (Shenon, 1988a: 20).

It is difficult to determine at this time whether the FBI's investigation of CISPES is an aberration or part of a broader pattern of organizational misconduct in its FCI and international terrorism investigations, which appear aimed at circumventing the domestic security guidelines. Director Webster's testimony at appropriations hearings during the 1980s indicates that resources allocated to international terrorism were increasing (U.S. House, Appropriations Hearings, 1982: 1205; 1985: 1076). This is not surprising, given the concern over international terrorism during this period. It is of interest, however, that the FBI Terrorism Program was reorganized in 1984 so that the domestic and international program elements were consolidated, although they remained under separate guidelines (U.S. House, Appropriations Hearings, 1984: 626). One consequence of this consolidation is that, budgetarily, it is no longer possible to distinguish between the allocation of resources to domestic and to international terrorism. Beginning in FY 1985, the Terrorism Program budget was subsumed under "other field programs" in the FBI's budget justifications to Congress. The thrust of this reorganization seems to be a blurring of domestic and international terrorism investigations as well as growing secrecy in relation to both programs. It is, nevertheless, clear that FBI operations in both domestic and international terrorism expanded during the early 1980s; what is unclear is the extent to which international terrorism investigations may have been used as a pretext for domestic intelligence gathering in circumvention of the Smith Guidelines. To further cloud the issue, in his request for additional positions for domestic terrorism in FY 1988, Webster volunteered that since 1983, the FBI has had to redirect resources from the international portion of the Terrorism Program to address domestic terrorism needs (U.S. House, Appropriations Hearings, 1987: 2007). This is surprising, given the bureau's role in playing down domestic terrorism during the 1980s and may reflect ambiguity in the FBI's definition of domestic and international terrorism.

On balance, it appears that although the FBI initially dissented from the Reagan administration on the terrorism issue, the bureau did eventually reach an accommodation with the administration on combating domestic terrorism. The Reagan administration, however, did not succeed in "unleashing" the FBI, as it had apparently set out to do. Domestic intelligence in the Reagan years was not restored to the place of prominence it once enjoyed during the Hoover FBI. Although terrorism was elevated to a top investigative priority, the allocation of resources to domestic terrorism remained well below that expended on other top priority programs.

At the House appropriations hearings for FY 1986, Congressman Early continued to be dismayed about the FBI's position on the domestic terrorism issue. The following exchange with Director Webster illustrates Early's bewilderment and frustration in determining precisely how the FBI had responded to the administration's concerns over terrorism:

Mr. Early: "Isn't domestic terrorism really one of your prime functions?"

Mr. Webster: "That is why it has been designated as one of the top priorities."

Mr. Early: "But we haven't given you the money. You designate it, but you didn't get the money in the last few years."

Mr. Webster: "We have been very careful about not seeking to expand our domestic security work beyond real terrorism. At one time the FBI's budget—years ago we were spread out in so many places, in so many school boards, and the Socialist Workers Party, and so on, that we were not getting a return for that effort, and we were resoundingly criticized for intruding into organizations.

Now, of course, the concern is back about terrorism. The reality of terrorism in this country is that we have dealt with it very well with the resources that we have. Your figures, of course, have to do with domestic terrorism. Our budget for international terrorism and our utilization of that budget has gone way up" (U.S. House, Appropriations Hearings, 1985: 1076).

The Failed Terrorism Scare

It seems appropriate at this point to add a historical footnote to the debate over the terrorism issue in the early 1980s. While we have focused on the FBI dissent and its eventual accommodation to the terrorism concerns of the Reagan administration, these events had broader social and political implications. During the early 1980s, as the Reagan administration was sounding the terrorism alarm, some on the political left anticipated a new Red Scare or McCarthy era (Peterzell, 1981b; Donner, 1982).

Given the benefit of hindsight, we can try to understand why this did not occur. If the above analysis is correct, the role of the FBI seems pivotal in this regard. While the Reagan administration, some conservatives, and the media can raise the specter of terrorism, they cannot achieve widespread acceptance of their ideological view of the terrorist threat without the corroboration of the FBI. As the bureau has noted repeatedly at its annual appropriations hearings, it is the principal agency that responds to terrorism within the United States; 99 percent of all terrorist activities fall within the investigative responsibility of the FBI. An agency with such a virtual monopoly of information about terrorism and internal security cannot be taken lightly. Without the support of the bureau, a terrorism scare in the 1980s could not achieve credibility.

The role of the FBI in the Reagan years is in sharp contrast to the role played by the Hoover FBI in the McCarthy era and the Palmer Justice Department in the Red Scare of 1919–1920. In those two earlier periods of internal security alarm, the FBI and Justice Department reinforced the alarm and, indeed, magnified and exaggerated the threat that radicals, aliens, and communists posed for internal security (Poveda, 1982). In the incipient alarm sounded by the Reagan administration in the 1980s, the Webster FBI instead exerted a calming influence by playing down the domestic terrorism issue. No less a critic of the FBI than Congressman

Edwards has praised the bureau in this respect: "The FBI and Judge Webster deserve a lot of credit for keeping a cool head about terrorism in the United States" (U.S. House, 1987b: 171). The absence of FBI Director Webster's support for an internal security panic in the 1980s represents a critical difference from this era and the previous internal security scares in this century.

How can we account for this rather unexpected role the Webster FBI has played in the Reagan era? Ostensibly, it would appear that a terrorism scare would serve the bureau's interest by providing a fertile ground for new appropriations and resources. This undoubtedly would have been an issue that the Hoover FBI would have exploited. Such was not the case, however.

It must be understood that the legacy of the modest Watergate reforms remained with the Webster FBI. In Webster's first two years as director, he had the unenviable task of disciplining agents and officials who were still caught up in cases involving past abuse. In the view of older agents and officials, these disciplined agents were victims of changing rules and circumstances, and they were being prosecuted for performing their duties in good faith. The Webster FBI was understandably reluctant to get drawn into the same kind of activities that had tarnished the image of the bureau only a few years before. It was in this context that the Webster FBI reasserted its autonomy by resisting being "unleashed" by the Reagan administration and offering a moderate dissent from the administration on the terrorism issue. The organizational interests of the FBI simply did not coincide with the broader policy objectives of the Reagan administration in the early 1980s. Additionally, the role of Director Webster was pivotal to exhibiting a sense of balance between due process and crime control values during an era when crime control values were ascendant, whether it be in regard to common-law criminals or terrorists. While the bureau eventually accommodated itself to some of the concerns of the Reagan administration—the elevation of terrorism to a top priority, revision of the Levi Guidelines, and the increased allocation of resources to terrorism—it did demonstrate that the "new" FBI was not totally responsive to its political masters. The FBI had carved out an area of organizational autonomy within the executive.

Furthermore, the FBI's post-Watergate priorities had already begun to reshape the public image of the bureau. The successes in public corruption cases such as ABSCAM, the arrests of major Mafia figures in organized crime, and the development of major espionage cases in foreign counterintelligence all contributed to the new foundation of the transformed Hoover FBI and to a highly favorable public image. Undoubtedly, the Webster FBI did not wish to jeopardize this new image.

The disclosures of the Watergate years appear to have succeeded, at least temporarily, in divorcing the FBI's internal security apparatus from its organizational power base. However, it should also be emphasized that the legal authority for conducting domestic intelligence operations was never rescinded, COINTELPRO-type activities were never specifically prohibited, and during the Reagan era, as we have seen, the authority for conducting domestic intelligence was again expanded.

NOTES

1. A New York lawyers' group, the Center for Constitutional Rights, obtained about 1,200 pages of documents through the Freedom of Information Act that disclosed extensive surveillance of groups opposed to the Reagan administration's Central American foreign policy. The Committee in Solidarity with the People of El Salvador (CISPES) was originally targeted, but the investigation expanded to include more than one-hundred organizations, according to the center. The documents reveal the use of undercover agents, informants, and the surveillance of peaceful demonstrations during the investigation (Shenon, 1988b: 1, 18).

2. All of the major indicators of such activities point to a dramatic decrease. The number of domestic intelligence investigative matters initiated decreased from a peak of 3,464 in 1972 to 95 in 1977; the number of agents doing such investigations similarly decreased from 1,264 in 1972 to 143 in 1977; and finally, the number of domestic intelligence informants declined from 1,885 in 1972 to 100 in 1977 (U.S. Comptroller General, 1976, 1977).

3. In FY 1980, 12 percent of the anticipated appropriations for the FBI Terrorism Program was allocated to domestic security, that is, the preventive intelligence function. The remaining allocations went to the reactive functions of the program, which were criminal investigations of bombings, sabotage, espionage, and so on. This is in contrast to 1974, when preventive intelligence comprised 87.8 percent of intelligence matters (U.S. House, Appropriations Hearings, 1979: 787).

4. According to Robert Ricks of the FBI Terrorism Program, approximately 6 percent of FBI field agents were allocated to terrorism investigations in FY 1986 (C-SPAN, Feb. 11, 1987).

5. A measure of the FBI's organizational power is the ratio of the FBI budget to the Department of Justice budget. Throughout the 1970s, FBI appropriations fluctuated between 20 and 23 percent of the DOJ budget. This, again, was unlike the Hoover FBI of the 1950s and 1960s, which had consistently maintained an FBI budget of over 40 percent of the DOJ budget. The Webster FBI of the early 1980s showed a steady growth in its share of the DOJ pie, reaching 30.4 percent in FY 1985 (U.S. Bureau of the Budget, 1950–1986).

6. The number of FBI special agents increased from 7,804 to 8,739 between 1980 and 1985; total agent work-years increased 22.8 percent during the same period of time (U.S. House, Appropriations Hearings, 1981–1986).

7. Congressman Don Edwards is chair of the Subcommittee on Civil and Constitutional Rights of the House Judiciary Committee. His subcommittee has FBI oversight responsibilities and has been one of the congressional subcommittees most critical of FBI operations in recent years.

8. As assistant director of the criminal investigative division, Monroe's responsibilities included the Terrorism Program.

9. The number of terrorist incidents in the United States had increased somewhat in 1982 to 52, but declined again to 31 in 1983. The level of terrorist incidents, by the FBI's own figures, was still well below the levels of the mid-1970s (U.S. House, Appropriations Hearings, 1982: 1205; 1984: 626).

10. Both retired from the FBI in 1973. Felt was the number 2 man in the bureau at that time, under Acting Director Gray, and Miller was head of the Intelligence Division. They were both indicted for authorizing illegal break-ins and were convicted in 1980. They were subsequently pardoned by President Reagan.

11. This continues to be the bureau position. In a C-SPAN interview Feb. 11, 1987, Oliver Revell, executive assistant director, reported that there were seventeen domestic terrorist incidents in 1986. This represents a downward trend from the level of such incidents in the 1970s and early 1980s, although there were only thirteen incidents in 1984 and seven in 1985 (U.S. House, 1987b: 280). In a recent article in the *FBI Law Enforcement Bulletin,* Revell (1987: 2) asserts that "the number of active groups and the relative terrorist threat in the United States has not increased. There has not been a terrorist act committed by an international terrorist group in the United States since 1983."

12. In FY 1985 the domestic and international terrorism programs were consolidated and both are subsumed under "other field programs" in the budget. It is, therefore, no longer possible to separately identify the resources allocated to domestic terrorism—or to the total Terrorism Program, for that matter—at least from this source.

13. "Domestic security" within the terrorism program refers to those activities the FBI calls "preventive." These operations correspond to the domestic intelligence portion of the program as opposed to the reactive portion, which involves criminal investigations of bombings, espionage, and so forth.

14. This group is a loose-knit group of peace activists whose members were suspected of vandalizing military recruiting offices in the Chicago area. Ryan was familiar with members of the group, whom he knew were committed to nonviolence. He also refused to conduct the inquiry because he did not view the case as one involving domestic terrorism (*Progressive,* Jan. 1988: 14; CBS "60 Minutes: Ryan of the FBI," May 15, 1988).

15. In February 1980, eighteen organizations were targeted; ten, in February 1981; eleven, in February 1983; nineteen, in March 1984; thirteen, in February 1985; and twenty-one, in February 1987 (U.S. House, Appropriations Hearings, 1980–1987).

16. Director Webster denies that such investigations have a political purpose. In discussing the approximately one-hundred FBI "visits" to U.S. citizens returning from Nicaragua, he argued that the FBI has a legitimate foreign counterintelligence (FCI) interest in agents of Nicaragua and that the FBI's task, as mandated by E.O. 12333, is to pursue that interest. He added that it is not a matter of the FBI favoring or opposing the Contras but a matter of its FCI responsibilities, which he could not discuss in open session (U.S. House, 1986b: 8)

17. Document HQ 128X1. This document, along with a number of other files obtained through the FOIA, was provided to me by the Center for Constitutional Rights.

18. All of the agents were mid- to low-level supervisors. Three of the supervisors were suspended for two weeks without pay and internal probation; the other three received written reprimands. The six supervisors who were disciplined had managed the CISPES investigation at FBI headquarters in Washington, D.C., and at the Dallas field office (Shenon, 1988a: 20).

Chapter 10

THE HIGH-TECH, PROACTIVE FBI

In our examination of the "new" FBI, we have focused on the changing investigative priorities of the post-Hoover FBI. Clearly, the top priorities that emerge after Watergate, especially organized crime, white-collar crime, and public corruption, differentiate the "new" from the "old" bureau. Critics of the "new" FBI sometimes fear the revival of some of the "old" priorities and the re-emergence of a Hoover-style agency, especially in the area of domestic security and terrorism. While there is some basis for this concern, as we saw in the last chapter, to some extent this concern misses the essence of the "new" FBI, which has developed its own organizational style, distinctive investigative methods (which pose dangers of their own), and a glorifying myth extolling its new technologies.

This chapter will examine some of these less-noticed changes in the post-Hoover FBI, particularly the development and use of new investigative techniques and their policy implications for control of the bureau. These more subtle elements of the "new" FBI include nothing less than the development of a new FBI mystique anchored in computer technology—national information systems on criminal records, artificial intelligence, and criminal profiling—and in the increasing use of undercover operations. The development of these investigative techniques conveys an image of an all-knowing, all-seeing agency that now possesses the technological solution to the crime problem, or at least will in the future. A 1980 *Newsweek* story on the FBI captured some of that mystique in its title: "The New FBI Is Watching"; as Burnham (1984) puts it, we have gone "from G-man to cursor-man."

The Roots of the High-Tech FBI

The G-man myth of the Hoover FBI was based on the bureau's prowess in scientific law enforcement and managerial efficiency, as well as its professionalism. Hoover established the FBI's crime laboratory in 1932 and, during the same period, secured bureau control of the federal fingerprint files, which at that time numbered fewer than one million fingerprints. As a result of his advocacy of the importance of fingerprints in criminal investigations, these files grew astronomically during Hoover's tenure. By 1974 there were more than 159 million fingerprint files in bureau records (Walker, 1980: 187–188). The idea that the FBI of the 1930s had modern science on its side was certainly an element in the myth of an invincible FBI. By the 1970s, however, with the collapse of the G-man myth and the growing realization of the disparity between myth and reality of FBI conduct, it also became apparent that these earlier efforts at introducing scientific law enforcement had not kept pace with technological and scientific advances.

William Sullivan, a former FBI assistant director, recounts in his memoirs the low opinion many field agents in the Hoover years had of the FBI crime lab. Although the FBI publicized the lab as "the greatest law enforcement laboratory in the world," this, according to Sullivan, was nothing but "a show-business spiel." While the lab's equipment and activities looked impressive, it was "all illusion." The crime lab was not staffed with top scientists who had kept up with the latest scientific developments, and the famous laboratory files were really "incomplete and outdated" (Sullivan with Brown, 1979a: 95–99).

Similarly, when Clarence Kelley became FBI director in 1973, he found the FBI's computers and data management systems to be "antiquated." Kelley asserts that they were not even comparable to the computers in Kansas City, where he had been police chief (Kelley and Davis, 1987: 305). A few years later, a panel of computer experts faulted the National Crime Information Center (NCIC)[1] of the bureau for having "obsolete equipment resulting in deteriorating service" and for lacking "competent and professional computer managers for the system" (U.S. Senate, 1980a: 100). This same panel also acknowledged that Director Webster was beginning to correct some of these problems.

In the mid-1970s, at the height of the intelligence agencies scandal, both the Rockefeller Commission (1975) and the General Accounting Office (U.S. Comptroller General, 1976) criticized the FBI for having no evaluation and analysis capability in connection with its domestic intelligence operations. While the targeting of individuals and groups in such operations was massive in terms of quantity, the selection of targets for intelligence gathering and disruption was largely ad hoc and unsystematic.[2] In addition, there was little follow-through in terms of either evaluation or analysis for those domestic intelligence operations that were carried out.[3] The GAO found Hoover's domestic intelligence operations "incomplete" in this respect and implied that the intelligence gathered in this manner was not particularly useful to the Justice Department or to the executive branch in making decisions on national security.

While these technological, scientific, and information system deficiencies in the Hoover FBI only came to the surface in the mid-1970s, the impetus for correcting them and for modernizing the bureau can be traced to the late 1960s. The law-and-order crisis of this period generated considerable political pressure for solutions to the problems of urban disorder and violence. The President's Commission on Law Enforcement and the Administration of Justice, established by Lyndon Johnson to study and make recommendations on improving the criminal justice system, found that fragmentation and lack of coordination among the criminal justice agencies was one of the key obstacles to effective law enforcement (President's Commission on Law Enforcement, 1967a). In its *Task Force Report: Science and Technology* (1967c), the President's Commission offered a solution to this fragmentation, recommending, among other things, the formation of a national criminal justice information system to aid decision making by criminal justice officials and to improve coordination among the components of the system. The social and political conditions were thus ripe for the development of a more sophisticated, technological approach to crime, with the federal government playing a lead role.

It was during this period that the FBI established its National Crime Information Center (NCIC), which in its trial phase in 1967 had terminal connections to only fifteen police agencies and possessed some 23,000 records of wanted persons and stolen property (Laudon, 1986: 43). The FBI's Identification Division also began the process of automating its 94-million criminal fingerprint files in 1972. This long-term project, called Automated Identification Division System (AIDS), did not reach completion until the end of 1987.[4] This system required the development of techniques for reading and searching fingerprint cards rather than the manual processing of them. The FBI's processing time on fingerprint inquiries has been reduced accordingly from twelve days to one day (U.S. House, Appropriations Hearings, 1987: 1817).

The FBI's development of a national computerized criminal history (CCH) databank encountered criticism and objections during the 1970s. Some officials in the Nixon, Ford, and Carter administrations as well as some members of Congress objected to such a national depository of criminal records (Burnham, 1983: 67).[5] The FBI scandal of the 1970s also delayed development of a national CCH under bureau control in that doubt had been cast on FBI trustworthiness. By 1980, however, the political climate was changing, as concern over street crime was being revived. Attorney General Smith's Task Force on Violent Crime (1981) recommended the construction of a file on all those arrested in the United States (Burnham, 1983: 63). The building blocks for a national CCH were now largely in place.

It is this high-tech aspect of the post-Hoover bureau, of which a national CCH is one element, which began slowly under Kelley (1973–1978) and accelerated rapidly in the Webster FBI (1978–1987), that has become one of the hallmarks of the "new" FBI. We shall consider the promise this computerization holds for the future of the FBI, examine in some detail some selected programs that are part of this process, and consider the efficacy of these developments.

The Computerization of the FBI

In 1981 the FBI formulated a long-range automated data processing (ADP) plan that reflected a ten-year outlook through 1991 on its strategy for computerizing the FBI. In the bureau's own words, it is a program "to apply state-of-the-art information technology in a cost-effective manner across virtually all functional areas, including investigation, law enforcement services, resource management, and executive decision making" (U.S. House, Appropriations Hearings, 1982: 1211). While the program aims to bring computer technology to all organizational areas,[6] the main focus is on applications to the bureau's top investigative priorities. Director Webster expressed this at the FBI's 1985 judiciary hearings: "Computerization of priority investigative program data and the resultant analytical capability that process provides are keys to our future success" (U.S. House, 1986b: 4).

In order to implement the ADP plan, it was anticipated that the bureau would spend $317 million by 1991 (U.S. House, Appropriations Hearings, 1982: 1212). Between fiscal year 1980 and 1985, the ADP portion of the FBI budget grew by 195.4 percent, in contrast to the 56.3 percent growth of the total FBI budget (U.S. House, Appropriations Hearings, 1981–1986). FBI spending for computerization has also increased at a faster rate than most other federal agencies, including the Defense Department and the Department of Health and Human Services (Burnham, 1984).

For FY 1988 the FBI requested $13 million for construction of an Engineering Research Facility, the purpose of which would be to design special types of equipment for modern forensic and investigative work. As Webster put it, this facility would adapt "cutting edge technology for law enforcement" (U.S. House, Appropriations Hearings, 1987: 1877). It is clear that the FBI does not view computers and technology as marginal to bureau operations but rather as a central ingredient in the "new" FBI.

A National Computerized Databank of Criminal Records

Historically, there has been resistance by both the states and the Congress to the development of a national centralized depository for criminal records (a national CCH). SEARCH, a consortium of U.S. criminal justice practitioners, is one such group that is opposed to the centralization of criminal history records at the federal level. Instead, SEARCH advocates an option where the states have their own organization for the interstate exchange of criminal history records, which are stored in the respective states. In SEARCH's view, federal agencies could participate in this organization on the same basis as other agencies. The FBI would continue to keep a national fingerprint file, but with no criminal history data, and it would also be a repository for federal criminal history data (U.S. Senate, 1980a: 96–101).

One of the FBI's lesser-known achievements during the 1980s was the establishment of a national databank under the guise of "modernization," with the accompanying rationale that administrative efficiency would be enhanced. In 1982, with the support of the Reagan administration, the bureau created a new file in the NCIC computer called Triple I (III). As a political compromise with the states, many of whom already had their own CCH systems, this new file was only a pointer system, not an actual depository of criminal records. Criminal justice agencies with access to the NCIC computer could make inquiries to the III file with respect to a particular suspect who has been arrested. Triple I will then specify whether the individual has been arrested in another state and "point" the user to the identity of that state. The actual criminal history records of the suspect may then be directly obtained from that state, not from the III file.[7]

At the same time, the FBI's automation of its criminal fingerprint files entered the second phase (AIDS II), and by 1983 the files were being made available to law enforcement agencies through the III file.[8] These AIDS files, which have historically accumulated in the Identification Division, also contain criminal history data. The integration of these two FBI information systems (III and AIDS) means that by the end of the 1980s, as the AIDS program is completed, the FBI will have established a de facto national CCH. It is estimated, assuming that states continue furnishing fingerprints and criminal records to the Identification Division, that some 40 million Americans who have been arrested for any crime could have their criminal histories entered in this national databank (Gordon and Churchill, 1984: 497). As of January 1987, the FBI was in possession of criminal fingerprint records on 23.6 million persons (U.S. House, Appropriations Hearings, 1987: 1961).

What is the justification for such a national databank of criminal histories containing the files of about one-third of the labor force? Again, if we go back to President Johnson's Crime Commission, the purpose is to aid the decision making of criminal justice officials and to reduce the fragmentation of the criminal justice system by better coordinating information among its components. A national CCH will enhance the effectiveness of the system by providing timely information to criminal justice officials who need to make decisions on detention of a suspect, bail, prosecution, sentencing, and so on. The FBI also claims that the greater mobility of American criminals and the interstate nature of many crimes make such a databank necessary if we are to apprehend such offenders (Laudon, 1986: 386). Whether the promise of a national CCH holds up under critical scrutiny will be addressed later.

Profiling and Artificial Intelligence

In June 1984 the FBI established the National Center for the Analysis of Violent Crime (NCAVC), partly in response to the Reagan administration's renewed concern over violent crime (U.S. House, 1986a: 6). One of the two units at the center provides investigative support to law enforcement agencies by developing new investigative techniques to aid in solving violent crimes, many of which involve the application of computer technology to various investigative problems (Depue, 1986).[9]

One of the investigative techniques being continuously refined at the NCAVC is psychological profiling. Profiling is defined by the FBI as:

> an investigative technique by which to identify the major personality and behavioral characteristics of the offender based upon an analysis of the crime(s) he or she has committed.... Profiling unfortunately does not provide the identity of the offender, but it does indicate the type of person most likely to have committed a crime having certain unique characteristics (Douglas and Burgess, 1986: 9).

As of 1987, psychological profiling has been generally applied to serial violent crimes, particularly those involving murder, rape, and child abduction or molestation. The purpose of profiling is not to determine why an offender is engaged in a pattern of serial violence but rather what the personal characteristics of such an offender are, as inferred from what the offender does during and after the criminal act. Based on research on prior cases and on convicted offenders, FBI profilers have developed statistical profiles of the probable characteristics of offenders in particular types of cases (Porter, 1983; Hazelwood, 1987; Enter, 1987).[10]

A more recent program is the Violent Criminal Apprehension Program (VICAP), which became operational in May 1985. It consists of a nationwide data information center on certain violent crimes, particularly those that involve serial violence and that are apparently random, motiveless, or sexually oriented. VICAP serves as a pointer system to agencies that report similar patterns of violence occurring in disparate jurisdictions. The system alerts agencies to the possibility that an unsolved crime in one locality may be related to a similar crime in another jurisdiction (Howlett, Hanfland, and Ressler, 1986).

Clearly, both profiling and VICAP are intended as investigative aids to unsolved violent crimes and lend themselves particularly to cases where violent offenders are highly mobile and the crimes transcend legal jurisdictions. VICAP attempts to identify offenders through the discovery of similar patterns of violence in different jurisdictions; profiling seeks to identify offenders by inferring personal characteristics from the criminal acts themselves.

Yet another development in the application of computer technology to crime investigation is the use of artificial intelligence (AI). In 1984 Director Webster approved an initiative to apply AI to the bureau's investigative needs (U.S. House, Appropriations Hearings, 1986). At the cutting edge of computer technology, AI, "the computer emulation of human intelligence," seeks to develop an expert system embodied in a computer program that will institutionalize investigative knowledge and experience that can then be applied to decision making in various investigative areas (U.S. Congress, 1988: 28–29). For example, one AI expert system being developed at the NCAVC will assist investigators in solving violent crimes and thus will allow the NCAVC to "eliminate useless investigative paths which historically have proved fruitless" and to "preserve and recall knowledge of similar cases, criminal personality profiles, and research studies" (Icove, 1986: 29).

In the summer of 1986, the FBI operationalized the first of these expert systems, Big Floyd, which will be used in labor racketeering cases (Schrage, 1986). Other AI expert systems are being developed in other investigative areas, including organized crime, narcotics intelligence, and counterterrorism. The FBI wants to develop the capability to track terrorist individuals and groups in order to anticipate and react in a more timely manner to terrorist incidents. The bureau requested $12 million for FY 1987 to fund its various AI initiatives (U.S. House, Appropriations Hearings, 1986: 184, 192, 261).[11]

Perhaps the most compelling reason for the development of AI expert systems in various investigative areas is that it preserves the acquired knowledge and expertise of top investigators in the FBI's institutional memory. In this manner, the loss of expertise due to turnover and retirement is minimized.

Undercover Operations

Although at first glance the shadowy world of undercover operations may not appear to have much in common with the high-tech world of artificial intelligence, profiling, and computer information systems, there is a theme that links these developing investigative techniques of the "new" FBI. Undercover operations, as well as the applications of computer technology discussed above, are part of a new management style in law enforcement. The Anglo-American tradition of policing in the U.S. has historically emphasized a reactive style of policing. Law enforcement should create a visible presence in their communities to serve as a deterrent to crime and to respond to citizen complaints about crime. The vast majority of police activity today continues to be in response to citizen reports of crime. In recent years, however, there has been a noticeable shift away from reactive policing, especially in regard to certain investigative areas. In the emerging proactive style of law enforcement, the police are more aggressive in discovering law violations, not content to simply respond after the fact. In proactive policing, the task of law enforcement is to anticipate crime and sometimes even to target potential, high-risk offenders.[12] In some very fundamental respects, proactive law enforcement represents a departure from the traditions of Anglo-American policing (Marx, 1985, 1988).

It is important to understand the development of these law enforcement technologies in the context of the new proactive ethos. In particular, we shall trace the emergence of this ethos in the "new" FBI in relation to the expansion of its undercover activities. Traditionally, undercover police work has been limited to the vices, particularly narcotics and prostitution, and to the political surveillance of subversive groups. Such undercover practices were virtually unknown in the "old" FBI in that Hoover had a long-standing policy that prohibited special agents from playing undercover roles (Sullivan with Brown, 1979a).[13] In the Hoover FBI, informants or wiretaps would typically be used to detect or anticipate criminal conduct; FBI agents were not used in an undercover role.

As we saw, the seeds for complex undercover activities within the FBI were planted by Neil Welch in the late 1960s when, in a covert operation, he targeted organized crime figures in Buffalo (Welch and Marston, 1984). This was probably the first use, unbeknown to FBI Director Hoover, of FBI agents in a full-time undercover surveillance since World War II. Ironically, what in the late 1960s was a "subversive" investigative practice within the bureau, ten years later became a standard investigative technique. Like computer technology, undercover work is at the cutting edge of the "new" FBI.

It was Director Kelley's introduction of the quality-over-quantity concept in the mid-1970s that began the process of changing the bureau's basic strategy of investigations. Faced with dwindling resources and investigative capacity, he had to channel FBI resources where they would be most effective, which meant identifying investigative priorities and selecting crime targets to which limited resources should be applied. The FBI could no longer rely on producing statistical accomplishments as it had under Hoover (quantity), but it now had to focus its activities on selected targets for maximum results (quality). In this quality-over-quantity approach, Kelley emphasized imaginative approaches in investigating crime targets, including the use of undercover agents (Kelley and Davis, 1987: 310–313).

After 1975 the larger FBI field offices were reorganized so that high priority was given to proactive investigations that employed agents in target squads. The first undercover operations were antifencing "sting" operations that were joint operations with local law enforcement and were funded by the LEAA (Law Enforcement Assistance Administration); ten such operations were conducted in 1975 and 1976. The bureau's first request for funds explicitly for undercover operations was in 1976, for $1 million for FY 1977 (U.S. Senate, 1983a: 1).

FBI Director Webster continued to be an advocate of the undercover technique and proactive law enforcement. During his tenure (1978–1987), undercover operations expanded rapidly and were viewed as indispensable to the "new" FBI's priorities. Between 1977 and 1981, the undercover technique was extended to white-collar crime, public corruption, and organized crime and by 1984 had become "nearly coextensive with the FBI's jurisdiction" (U.S. House, 1984: 1). Clearly, such operations are only a small proportion of total FBI investigations, but the number of and funding for such operations increased significantly during this period.[14]

Webster and the "new" FBI were successful in bringing public attention to the success of the undercover technique, which was most notable in Operation ABSCAM in 1980. Favorable media coverage has probably contributed to an overstatement of the advantages and an understatement of the disadvantages of such operations (Marx, 1982). This is probably also true of the high-tech techniques the "new" FBI has added to its arsenal of proactive investigative methods. While the benefits of the new proactive techniques are somewhat obvious, especially if successful cases are emphasized, the costs and risks of these new investigative technologies are not always so apparent. It is this dark side of the high-tech and proactive FBI that we shall turn to next.

The New FBI Mystique: What Works?

The employment of computer technology and proactive investigative methods in the post-Hoover FBI has contributed to a new FBI mystique, which is enhanced by public faith in technology. The development of these investigative technologies implies that the FBI may be now, or in the near future, on the brink of a high-tech solution to crime. The rapid growth in this aspect of bureau operations has heretofore proceeded without much critical scrutiny. It is difficult to argue with proposals that at face value appear to increase administrative efficiency and coordination. Nevertheless, we need to ask hard questions: Do these techniques work? If they work, at what cost and risk? And what are the policy implications for control of these operations?

The Efficacy of a National Computerized Criminal History

Let us begin with the bureau's recent creation of a national computerized databank of criminal records. The historical rationale for such a databank is that it would provide criminal justice officials with timely information to aid their decision making at critical points in the justice system: arrest, detention, bail, prosecution, sentencing, and so forth. The databank would also serve as an aid to law enforcement in apprehending the highly mobile modern criminal.

As Laudon (1986: 18ff.), one of the foremost authorities and critics of such information systems, notes, this "professional record keeper" vision that promises greater rationality of decisions assumes that such a databank contains perfect, or nearly perfect, information. In fact, one of the great pitfalls of CCH systems at state and federal levels is the quality of data that has been entered into these databanks by literally thousands of different law enforcement agencies. One of the few agencies to seriously examine the issues raised by the advent of computers in government has been the Office of Technology Assessment (OTA) of the U.S. Congress (1982, 1988). In the OTA's first studies of data quality, conducted by Laudon in 1979, it was found that 74.3 percent of records disseminated by the FBI's Identification Division had "some significant quality problems"—most typically no disposition data. Since large numbers of arrests are dismissed or not prosecuted for a variety of reasons, the failure to indicate disposition or outcome of the case has the effect of overstating criminality of the person. Similarly, 54.1 percent of a sample of records in the CCH file of the NCIC computer had "some significant quality problem"—again, mostly lack of disposition data or inaccurate recording of disposition. In the FBI's wanted persons file, 11.2 percent of the warrants were no longer valid, and 23.9 percent were more than three years old (Laudon, 1986: 136–142). While there have been improvements in criminal history records during the 1980s, quality continues to be a problem (U.S. Department of Justice, 1985; U.S. Congress, 1988).

The pervasiveness of such imperfect data in both state and federal CCH information systems seriously undermines the utility of such databanks, not to mention the harm caused to individuals when decisions concerning them are based on incomplete, inaccurate, or ambiguous information. Laudon's (1986: 198–199) research also points to an interesting discrepancy between the FBI (and national representatives of law enforcement) and local and state criminal justice personnel. The FBI has always claimed that such a national computerized databank would have a profound impact on criminal justice decision making and crime investigation. In contrast, interviews with local criminal justice personnel reveal minimal expectations for the value of a national CCH and the view that a local, rather than a national, databank would be more of an aid.[15] This is certainly the position of the SEARCH group, which argues that the national system advocated by the FBI does not meet the needs of the states (U.S. Senate, 1980a: 95).

This lack of consensus on the efficacy of a national CCH, even within the criminal justice community, suggests that there may be other organizational reasons for promoting such an information system—namely, to enhance the organizational power and legitimacy of those agencies in possession of such information systems. Burnham (1983: 11–12) observes that computers, with their enormous ability to collect, store, and distribute information, enhance the power of organizations that possess the technology, particularly their power over individual citizens. We shall return to this issue later.

In congressional hearings during the 1980s, the question of efficacy of a national CCH is seldom raised. While the quality-of-data issue has been an important congressional concern, it is typically related to due process and the privacy rights of individuals. When efficacy was questioned by Congressman Neal Smith, during the 1984 appropriations hearings in relation to the missing persons file of the NCIC, the FBI's response is interesting. Congressman Smith asked, for the record, "How many positive identifications have resulted from the use of this file?" The bureau replied, also for the record, "The FBI does not compile statistics on the number of people located through the use of the files. However, we can show yearly increases in the use of the files" (U.S. House, Appropriations Hearings, 1984: 626). It appears that the efficacy of the missing persons file was taken for granted by the FBI. The measure of utility of the file was simply how often it was used, not the outcome of that use.

Another assumption underlying the claims for a national CCH is that much crime, particularly serious crime, is interstate in nature, involving highly mobile offenders. However, even the FBI's own data contravenes this assumption. In testimony submitted to the Edwards subcommittee in 1985, Webster indicated that only 18 percent of the records in the FBI's NCIC Triple I system involved multistate offenders—that is, offenders having arrest records in more than one state (U.S. House, 1986b: 199). Except in the case of certain serial offenders, who are a minority of violent criminals, it would appear that a vast majority of violent crime is a local phenomenon (Silberman, 1978). The implication is that a national CCH would not be much of an aid in solving these crimes.

Finally, quite aside from the issue of whether such a national databank would work for its intended purpose is the potential for abuse inherent in such a system. One of the foremost potential abuses is the use of the databank for tracking or flagging individuals who have acquired files. Tracking involves the practice of placing flags on the files of designated individuals; when requests or new entries from agencies are made regarding these files, a flag is activated. From 1971 to 1974, the FBI used the NCIC computer for the purpose of tracking some 4,000 political dissidents, which was an unauthorized use of the NCIC records (Gordon and Churchill, 1984: 514). Director Webster acknowledged in 1985 that four types of flags were being employed in the III system for limited purposes but also indicated that there may be some expansion of this use of the NCIC for a classified intelligence purpose he could not publicly divulge (U.S. House, 1986b: 234).[16]

In 1987 NCIC's Advisory Policy Board (APB) considered proposals to broaden the NCIC database to include records of misdemeanors, juvenile offenses, DNA patterns, and some other types of investigative information. The APB did approve tracking files related to drugs, murder, or kidnapping, which according to the OTA was a major departure from past practice. The APB also considered, but rejected, proposals for linking the NCIC with databases operated by the Internal Revenue Service; Social Security Administration; Security and Exchange Commission; Immigration and Naturalization Service; and Bureau of Alcohol, Tobacco, and Firearms (U.S. Congress, 1988: 15–16).

Whatever the efficacy of a national CCH, it exists and, unless carefully regulated, will undoubtedly be expanded for a wider range of purposes, some of which may go beyond the scope intended by the professional record keeper vision of such a national databank—namely, the enhancement of criminal justice decision making (Laudon, 1986: 18).

Profiling and the Prediction Problem

Another component of the FBI's new mystique is its profiling capability. Profiling, like the national CCH, is based on certain assumptions about the nature of crime and criminals. As a response to the problem of violent crime, profiling holds out the promise of solving crimes, serial violent crimes in particular, that local law enforcement has been unable to solve. Herein lies the first of several limitations, acknowledged by FBI profilers: the technique lends itself most readily to certain kinds of violent crime—serial, motiveless, stranger homicides—that unfortunately, from the standpoint of the technique, are not the typical violent crimes in the United States. While the extent of serial violent crime is not exactly known, it is clear, nevertheless, that serial crime is a small percentage of total violent crime—fewer than 18 percent of homicides, according to Unit Chief Alan Burgess of the NCAVC (U.S. House, 1986a: 9).

In addition to being restricted in its application to a narrow range of violent crime, profiling also has the usual prediction problems when it is used to infer characteristics of offenders—whether they are serial murderers, rapists, or child molesters. It is important to recognize that the FBI's profiles are ultimately based on statistical probabilities that a given offender will possess a certain constellation of characteristics, which estimate is based on the characteristics of offenders engaged in similar patterns of crime in the past. Although such prediction methods can be improved, there will always be a problem of false positives and false negatives. In the case of profiling, the prediction error involves attributing erroneous characteristics to unknown offenders.

Making predictions in the social sciences generally has not been very successful. For example, in one recent review of the evidence in a related area, efforts to predict violent individuals, it was found that even the best predictions produced a false positive rate of 60 percent—that is, of every three individuals predicted to be violent, mistakes were made in two of the three predictions (Cohen, 1983: 4). As far as I know, no systematic effort has been made to evaluate the predictive accuracy of profiling, but it is probably not any more successful than predictions in other areas of the social sciences.

The prediction problem in profiling is further compounded by the fact that the characteristics of certain kinds of offenders may change over time. If profiles are based on outdated patterns, this will increase the magnitude of prediction error. This was the theme of a recent article on terrorism, where it was argued that the psychological profile of terrorists in the 1980s is different from that of the 1970s. "To present the profile of left-wing terrorist groups using this 1970 prototype as a guide to current structure and activities would be like teaching someone to start a modern car by discussing the elements of setting the spark, throttle, and choke before turning the crank" (Strentz, 1988: 15).

While the FBI is likely to publicize its successes in profiling, we are not as likely to hear about the missed predictions, although Porter (1983) mentions a Georgia case where the offender turned out to be the exact opposite of the profile. In any case, profiling is not an infallible technique because of the persistence of the prediction problem. The bureau itself recognizes this limitation in the caution that accompanies its profiles when they are sent to local agencies: "Criminal profiling will never take the place of a thorough and well-planned investigation nor will it ever eliminate the seasoned, highly trained, and skilled detective" (Douglas and Burgess, 1986: 13).

The Pitfalls of Undercover Operations

Perhaps the most publicized of the new FBI investigative techniques, and central to its new mystique, is the undercover operation. The public is most familiar with the undercover success stories, beginning with ABSCAM in 1980. Less well known to the public are undercover operations that have not been successful, were plagued with abuses of authority, and actually produced harm to individuals and institutions. Among these less publicized undercover operations involving questionable activities were Frontload, Recoup, Colcor, Corkscrew, Resfix, Greylord, and Iranscam.

The Edwards subcommittee conducted one of the first comprehensive investigations into this new FBI investigative technique, holding twenty-one hearings over four years and issuing a final report in April 1984. Its report is highly critical of bureau undercover operations and discusses the threat such operations pose to public institutions, third parties, and the targets of such investigations.

> The Bureau has not hesitated to interfere with political, judicial, and financial institutions across the nation; they have initiated and continued broad-based investigations on the merest of suspicions of unspecified criminal activity; they have caused innocent third parties to suffer substantial damages; and

there is no assurance that the appropriate individuals are in fact prosecuted or that criminal activity, other than that created or fostered by the undercover activity, is being effectively curtailed (U.S. House, 1984: 75).

The earlier Senate report on undercover activities, which focused primarily on ABSCAM, was more sympathetic to the benefits of undercover work, finding that such operations "have substantially contributed to the detection, investigation, and prosecution of criminal activity." The report went on to argue that some use of the technique was "indispensable," but how many and what safeguards was still a question. The Senate Select Committee was also encouraged by the issuance of Attorney General Guidelines on FBI Undercover Operations on January 5, 1981 (U.S. Senate, 1983a: 11, 23).

The Edwards subcommittee, however, found that these guidelines were not always observed. The subcommittee's investigation revealed "a pattern of widespread deviation from avowed standards, with substantial harm to individuals and public institutions" (U.S. House, 1984: 1). In its inquiry into Operation Corkscrew, where the FBI claimed its safeguards had been followed, the subcommittee concluded that "the safeguards in practice were little more than rhetoric, offering at best limited constraints upon the investigators, and little or no protection to the public" (U.S. House, 1984: 11). Similarly, the ACLU's inquiry into ABSCAM found that "the FBI did not adhere to its own standards in conducting the ABSCAM investigation" (Berman, 1982: 2). In both of these operations, individuals were targeted for investigation without reasonable suspicion that they were involved in an existing pattern of criminal conduct, the first safeguard of the FBI guidelines.

In Operation Corkscrew (1978–1982), the FBI investigation targeted judges in the Cleveland Municipal Court for bribery. Publicity at the early stages of the investigation cast suspicion on the entire Cleveland bench, even though eventually the U.S. attorney found no evidence to prosecute for judicial bribery. Instead, a low-level court employee, a bailiff, was prosecuted for fixing cases; he had also been a middleman in the FBI operation, deceiving the FBI in regard to the involvement of judges in corruption (U.S. House, 1984).

In Operation ABSCAM, twenty-seven public officials were targeted by middlemen for bribe offers. Of the twenty who actually came to such meetings, twelve (or 60 percent) were later convicted (Berman, 1982). Although the Senate Select Committee on undercover activities believed the FBI and the Department of Justice had made progress in improving safeguards on its operations, it nevertheless found deficiencies in the ABSCAM investigation, including (1) problems with the selection and supervision of informants, (2) the fact that initial approval of ABSCAM was virtually unlimited in scope, (3) misconduct by informants, (4) reliance on corrupt middlemen, and (5) lax management and supervision of the operation (U.S. Senate, 1983a: 15–19).

Sometimes the damaging consequences of undercover operations may involve innocent third parties. As of 1984, FBI undercover operations have spawned lawsuits involving over $466 million in damages. In Operation Recoup, for example, which was a 1981 investigation of stolen car racketeering, the bureau set up a bogus used car business in which FBI agents acted as intermediaries in the sale of stolen cars. Those conducting the operation were fully aware that innocent purchasers of these vehicles would eventually lose title to them. By October 1982, more than 250 cars had been confiscated from such innocent purchasers (U.S. House, 1984).

The main result of Operation Frontload, which was an investigation of organized crime influence in the construction industry, was more than $150 million in lawsuits (Kurtz, 1985). The harm produced by this operation was in the unauthorized selling of bogus performance bonds to construction companies by the FBI undercover man. Innocent contractors could not subsequently collect on these bonds.

There is a final concern with undercover operations that is as much a conceptual problem as it is an ethical one: the proactive targeting of offenders. The ethical problem is that individuals may be subject to discriminatory treatment by law enforcement in their selective targeting of resources, thus denying those targeted equal protection of the law. The conceptual problem is that the selective targeting may be based on faulty assumptions. The proactive targeting of offenders is based on what Walker (1989) calls the "conservative crime control theology," which claims that serious crime is highly concentrated in a small hard-core group of offenders variously referred to as chronic offenders or career criminals. If police, prosecutors, and judges could systematically identify, prosecute, and incarcerate this tiny minority of criminals, we would have an effective strategy for reducing crime (Wilson, 1983a).

This theory is so attractively simple that it is difficult to understand why no one thought of it before. Ultimately, this strategy depends on the validity of its assumption about crime being concentrated in a small hard-core group. Currie (1985: 81ff.) mounts what is perhaps the most devastating critique of this assumption, pointing out that this view of the crime problem draws upon research[17] that uses official crime statistics; this has the effect of understating the criminality of the general population, which is not as likely to get arrested or imprisoned, and of overstating the criminality of apprehended offenders. If there are large numbers of low-rate offenders in the community who are likely to escape official attention, this will reduce the impact of a strategy that focuses on the high-rate offenders. By sharply dichotomizing high-rate and low-rate offenders, the conservative "theology" perpetuates the dualistic fallacy that the world can be divided into criminals and law-abiding citizens.

Currie also demonstrates that what at first appears to be a small group, 6 to 7.5 percent of the population, becomes a sizable group when that percentage is extrapolated to the total U.S. population. He estimates that over a six-year period, approximately one million new "chronic offenders" enter the population. In short, by showing that criminality is not as concentrated as "conservative crime control theology" assumes, any strategy based on that assumption is weakened accordingly.

A second problem with the proactive strategy, independent of the size of the hard-core group, is the prediction problem. In anticipating the criminality of the hard-core group, it is necessary to predict future criminality, since we do not know in advance which persons will be highly active career criminals. This is a problem, whether it pertains to predicting dangerousness during pretrial detention, career criminals for selective incapacitation, or high-risk potential offenders in the community for proactive targeting by law enforcement. Each of these strategies will produce its share of false positives and false negatives.

Specifically, in reference to undercover activities, certain assumptions are made as to the efficacy and consequences of undercover work: (1) those arrested are repeat offenders who otherwise would avoid arrest, (2) the kinds of crime targeted will be reduced, and (3) more crime will not be generated (Marx, 1988: 118–119). In Marx's (1988: 128) excellent review of these and other assumptions pertaining to undercover operations, he concludes that "these assumptions are often questionable." In his summary of the limited research evaluating antifencing programs, Marx observes that those arrested are not new to the criminal justice system and that it is not clear whether they would have been arrested by conventional tactics. He also points out that while undercover operations often result in many arrests and much recovered property, they do not appear to have a major impact on reducing crime (Marx, 1988: 118ff.). Langworthy's (1989) recent study of a sting operation further supports this conclusion.

The Faith in Technology

To acknowledge the limitations of the new investigative technologies is not to deny their benefits in terms of crimes solved and increased administrative efficiency. However, in order to strike a balance between the benefits and the costs and risks of the new technologies for policy considerations, we need a complete understanding of both sides of the cost-benefit equation. Marx's (1988) recent work on undercover activities shows that this is no easy task. I have focused on what works, because this tends to demystify the benefits and shows the limitations of these new methods. I have also emphasized the costs and risks (potential or actual), because these are often understated in the publicity surrounding the successful cases. The above assessment of the high-tech proactive strategies currently being advanced raises questions as to whether the benefits outweigh the costs and risks and whether the development of these techniques precludes developments in other areas, given the existence of limited resources. The assessment also casts doubt on the role of technology as a panacea for the crime problem.

Approximately $1 billion has been spent since 1967 on the development of a national CCH (Laudon, 1986: 348). It is fair to ask whether this has been the most cost-effective way to reduce violent crime. What other programs could have been developed to achieve that same goal?

Similarly, although certainly not on the same scale, $2 million was spent to make the FBI's Violent Criminal Apprehension Program (VICAP) operational, giving it an annual operating expense of $200,000 to $300,000. After its first year of operation, Executive Assistant Director John Otto was asked about the success of the program. His response revealed that no crimes had yet been solved as a direct result of VICAP; the successes had been more with profiling and "not as a direct result of the computer so far" (U.S. House, 1986a: 56). The point is not that VICAP,

AI, and other high-tech FBI programs will not produce benefits in due time but that the mystique surrounding these programs will mislead us into thinking that there is a technological solution to the crime problem; this is the element of faith in these new technologies.[18]

About a decade ago, Silberman (1978: 330ff.) observed that for the last half-century we have sought a technological solution to the problems of policing. Some of this technology was aimed at reducing police response time to the crime scene. Then in the 1970s it was discovered that citizens delay reporting crimes to the police and that reducing police response time to zero would not solve this aspect of the problem. In fact, the technology employed to reduce response time—patrol cars—might have contributed to the problem by insulating police from their communities.

It has been further argued that a major long-term unintended consequence of the police professionalism movement itself was to increasingly isolate police from their communities. This is the result of professionalization that attempts to remove police from partisan politics and corruption (Walker, 1977; Kelling and Moore, 1988). It is this very problem, the separation of police from their communities, that inhibits the flow of information from community to police—whether that information be from victims, witnesses, informers, or others. This flow of information is critical to the solution of crimes. Technology may sometimes facilitate this flow; at other times, technology may actually serve as an obstacle to such communication. The central issue in this process, which is not addressed by the new technologies, is the distance, or even alienation, of law enforcement from the communities policed. Ultimately, law enforcement is dependent on those communities for support, cooperation, and legitimacy. The solution to this dimension of the problem is a sociological, not a technological, one. In fact, this awareness has led to experiments in "community policing" and "problem-solving policing" in police departments across the United States during the 1980s (Kelling, 1988).[19]

The aura of technology and science surrounding the new high-tech proactive FBI evokes a confidence—a mystique—in a high-tech solution to crime. This is part of the new glorifying myth of the contemporary bureau. In the long run, given the limitations noted, there will continue to be a disparity between the promise of the new technologies and their efficacy in combating the vast majority of violent crime.

Again, this is not to deny the benefits of some of these efforts in solving particular crimes; rather, it is to point out their limits as a wholesale solution to the crime problem. We place an enormous burden on law enforcement, including the FBI, by expecting them to solve what are essentially institutional or societal problems; the FBI responds with bureaucratic and technological ingenuity that may even give the appearance of dealing with the problem—in this case violent crime. By holding out the promise that proactive methods and the new technologies can prevent or reduce serious crime, we are perhaps perpetuating the illusion that the solution to crime lies primarily within the criminal justice system and that broader issues, such as poverty, inequality, and the problems of the inner cities, need not be addressed.[20]

NOTES

1. The NCIC is a computerized information system that, as of September 1987 contained 19.4 million records in twelve different kinds of files including criminal history information (arrests, dispositions), wanted persons, missing persons, stolen vehicles, stolen boats, stolen securities, and stolen and recovered guns (Dahl, 1988: 1). The information in the NCIC computer is linked through a telecommunications system with some 62,000 federal, state, and local criminal justice agencies nationwide (U.S. House, 1986b: 4).

2. Recommendation 14 of the Rockefeller Commission *Report* (1975: 23) advocates that "a capability should be developed within the FBI, or elsewhere in the Department of Justice, to evaluate, analyze, and coordinate intelligence and counterintelligence collected by the FBI concerning espionage, terrorism, and other related matters of internal security."

Even with COINTELPRO, where there was a disruption program for targeted groups, specific proposals for disruption were submitted from the field offices to FBI headquarters for approval. The proposals themselves did not emanate from Washington as part of a centralized and coordinated plan. As an example of unsystematic intelligence gathering, the use of domestic intelligence informants has been likened to a "vacuum cleaner" operation in which reports are submitted on every aspect of the individual's or group's activity (U.S. Senate, 1976b: 229).

3. FBI officials responded to this criticism by claiming that "evaluating domestic intelligence has never been its responsibility. They stated that as an investigative agency its job is to collect and report the facts" (U.S. Comptroller General, 1976: 146).

4. C-SPAN interview on February 12, 1987, with Dennis Kurre of the Identification Division.

5. The passage of the Privacy Act of 1974, under the sponsorship of Sen. Sam Ervin, represented the height of opposition to the formation of an integrated national information system, forbidding the executive branch from using information gathered in one program to be used in another—that is, computer matching. In a critical compromise that was made in order to secure passage of the act, the Office of Management and Budget (OMB) became the designated agency for enforcing the legislation. "The OMB in subsequent administrations has unfortunately refused to enforce the principles outlined in the Privacy Act. As a result, the development of an integrated, general purpose, national information system is proceeding unabated" (Laudon, 1986: 6). It should also be pointed out that criminal justice records are exempt from the Privacy Act (Laudon, 1986: 315).

6. William Bayse, assistant director of technical services who heads the computerization program, divides computerization into three categories: (1) the bureau's support of local and state agencies, (2) computer services aimed at aiding the bureau's own investigations, and (3) administrative support (Burnham, 1984: A16).

7. As of January 1, 1987, 10,493,088 records were contained in the III file—55 percent of the total records in the NCIC computer (U.S. House, Appropriations Hearings, 1987).

8. As of January 1984, approximately 70 percent of the total criminal fingerprint file had been automated (Laudon, 1986: 87). In a letter from Director Webster to Congressman Don Edwards, dated August 7, 1985, Webster indicated that "on February 7, 1983, these AIDS computerized criminal history records were made available through the NCIC's III to law enforcement agencies making criminal history record requests (U.S. House, 1986b: 228).

9. Within the NCAVC, the Computer Engineering Services Program provides the expertise in computer technology.

10. Profiler is one computer program developed at NCAVC to produce "statistical profiles of temporal, geographic, and behavioral characteristics of criminals based upon their prior behavior in targeting their victims" (U.S. House, 1986a: 52).

11. The FBI has established linkages and contracts with the Defense Advanced Research Products Agency, the Institute for Defense Analysis, and other Department of Defense entities with "state-of-the-art technical expertise to support new initiatives such as AI, rapid prototyping, and teleconferencing" (U.S. House, Appropriations Hearings, 1986: 186). Budget restrictions in FY 1988 have slowed some of these developments (U.S. House, Appropriations Hearings, 1987: 1792).

12. An example of the proactive approach, as it relates to law enforcement administration, appeared in a recent article of the *FBI Law Enforcement Bulletin*. The author, special agent James H. Earle, asserts that "in the past, and even today, law enforcement administrators have tended to play 'administrative catch up.' They have reacted to problems rather than anticipating them.... The twenty-first-century administrator will have to be a forecaster and long-range planner in order to run a professional department" (Earle, 1988: 2).

13. There are a few isolated instances of short-term undercover work done by FBI agents in the 1930s and intelligence work during World War II, but after the war, FBI agents were seldom used in long-term, complex undercover activities—until 1972 (U.S. Senate, 1983a: 36–39).

14. The number of undercover operations increased from 53 in FY 1977 to 316 in FY 1983. Appropriations similarly increased from $1 million in FY 1977 to $12,518,000 in FY 1984. These amounts only include the special costs of such operations (such as informants, lease expenses, and so on) and do not include agent salaries and normal overhead expenses (U.S. House, 1984: 1). The number of undercover operations, particularly in sensitive areas, appears to have leveled off since 1982 (U.S. House, Appropriations Hearings, 1987: 1885).

15. Ironically, as Laudon (1986: 222) observes, the greatest social impact of a national CCH may well be on noncriminal justice users (public and private employers), who would have access to such a databank for employment and screening purposes. The unintended consequences for minorities, who would be disproportionately represented in criminal history records, could be devastating in terms of institutional discrimination.

16. The four types of flags in effect on August 7, 1985, were (1) individuals with outstanding arrest warrants, (2) FBI informants, (3) persons protected under Witness Security Program, and (4) undercover agents. In an August 7, 1985, letter from Director Webster to Congressman Edwards, Webster mentions that "the Department of Justice is now considering a proposal for an off-line use of NCIC

log tapes for a classified purpose." In a follow-up letter to Edwards, dated September 19, 1985, after Edwards expressed concern that the FBI was using NCIC inquiries for operational purposes, Webster offered to provide a briefing to those of Edwards's staff with the necessary security clearances (U.S. House, 1986b: 228–234).

17. Wolfgang and colleagues' (1972) study of delinquent birth cohorts in Philadelphia is one of the influential works. In the original study of those boys born in 1945, 6 percent were categorized as chronic offenders—that is, arrested five or more times during their growing-up years. In the subsequent study of boys born in 1958, 7.5 percent were chronic offenders. A Rand study of prison inmates similarly found a high concentration of self-reported crimes among those inmates incarcerated in three states (Greenwood, 1982).

18. Another example of problems with the FBI's high-tech approach is in its information system on organized criminals. At a cost of $25 million, the Organized Crime Information System (OCIS) is designed to store data on known or suspected organized crime figures. A recent report in the newsletter *CJ—The Americas* (Feb.–Mar. 1988) indicates that the OCIS is apparently not working as planned. At the FBI appropriation hearings for FY 1988, Webster acknowledged that "we are still having trouble getting the information into our system. Presently, only about 50 percent of the information is being processed into OCIS." When asked whether the sixty-four additional personnel requested to support the system would "solve" its data and computer problems, Webster could not give a definitive answer (U.S. House, Appropriations Hearings, 1987: 1875).

19. Although there is some overlap between these two concepts, community policing emphasizes "the creation of an effective working partnership between the community and the police" (Moore and Trojanowicz, 1988: 8). This may take expression in increasing police foot patrols, "storefront" police precincts in local neighborhoods, or citizen watch groups that cooperate with the police. Problem-solving policing also involves working with the community, but it involves attempting to identify the underlying problems that give rise to crime (rather than simply identifying offenders) and "mobilizing the community and governmental agencies to act on the problems" (Moore and Trojanowicz, 1988: 8).

20. The FBI, of course, does not have jurisdiction over the vast majority of violent crimes in the United States; these are local and state responsibilities. The technologies we are discussing, such as profiling and a national CCH, are services the bureau provides to local and state law enforcement agencies.

Part Four
ASSESSMENT OF REFORM

Chapter 11

THE "NEW" FBI APPRAISED

In this book we set out to assess the nature and character of the FBI that emerged in the post-Hoover, post-Watergate period. We traced the roots of the Hoover FBI as it emerged from a relatively obscure federal agency in the 1920s to a superpolice agency in the 1930s. The New Deal expansion of federal authority was the basis for the G-man myth: FBI agents doing battle with the crime menaces of the Depression era—kidnappers, gangsters, and bank robbers. This formative period of the Hoover FBI gave us insight into how the bureau over the next several decades would accumulate bureaucratic power and establish an autonomy unparalleled in the federal government. It remained, however, for World War II and the McCarthy era, when the FBI institutionalized its domestic intelligence authority and operations, to give the bureau a distinctive organizational power base. Domestic intelligence remained a top priority of the bureau until the post-Watergate scandal involving the FBI and the intelligence agencies. At this point, the Hoover FBI, its investigative priorities, and its power and autonomy as an agency began to unravel. This transformation of the Hoover FBI is the focus of this inquiry. Is the "new" FBI genuinely new and different from the "old" Hoover FBI? Did the FBI scandal of the mid-1970s produce substantive reform? Have the abuses of the past been curbed, and is the "new" FBI under public control? It is time to take stock of what we have learned about these questions in the several chapters contained in this volume.

The Failure of the Hoover FBI

A successful inquiry into the transformation of the bureau requires that we penetrate the myths of both the "old" and "new" FBI. The FBI has historically been adept at "selling" itself to the public and at creating a favorable public image. This is no less true today of the "new" FBI than it was of the FBI of the 1930s and 1940s. Publicity related to the capture of a Soviet spy or to the arrest of an organized crime figure highlights current bureau priorities just as the sensational arrest of a kidnapper or bank robber brought public attention to the priorities of the Hoover FBI. To a large extent, the question of FBI reform has played on some of these public images, which neatly contrast "old" and "new" FBIs. In this view, it is the "old" FBI that has been tainted with scandal and abuse and the "new" FBI that has rid itself of the past misdeeds of the Hoover era. Accordingly, the lines of reform are sharply drawn. The task of reform becomes simply a matter of eliminating from the FBI any vestiges of Hoover influence. In a 1979 interview in the *Washington Post* (Babcock, 1979: 2), Director Webster referred to the abuses of the past as "archeology" and "residuals." This was his way of symbolically dissociating the "new" FBI from the scandal-ridden Hoover bureau.

As we saw in our analysis of the public disclosures of the 1970s, this is a bit too facile and oversimplified. The management of public disclosures by the FBI and the Justice Department during the 1970s provided insight into the real nature of what was happening in the FBI. During and immediately after the Watergate investigation (1973–1976), FBI and DOJ strategy of news management was to acknowledge the past abuses of the Hoover era and even to occasionally release documents or make statements confirming those abuses. After 1977 the FBI policy of managing public information became decidedly different. The new policy was to disclose as little as possible, whether it pertains to criminal investigations, informants, or intelligence matters. In fact, Director Webster argued that certain categories of records should be exempt from the Freedom of Information Act.[1] In 1977 the FBI adopted a policy of destroying certain investigative records more than five years old. Webster also suggested that there be a seven-year moratorium on criminal investigative records before they are subject to disclosure (U.S. Senate 1980b: 80). However, since 1978 the FBI has shown little interest, and even reluctance, in commenting on the abuses of the past. During the 1980s the Webster FBI attempted to strike a balance between being accessible to the press yet guarding against too much openness (Werner, 1984).

How can we account for this change of strategy, from apparent openness to relative secrecy, in managing public information in the 1970s? The answer to this question gives us a clue to the real transformation that was occurring in the 1970s. What was taking place was not what the public was led to believe: that the abuses of the Hoover era were being eliminated from the "new" FBI once and for all. The major substantive reform that occurred in the 1970s was a change in the locus of administrative control over the FBI. The FBI and DOJ strategy of acknowledging past abuses in the immediate post-Watergate period was simply a way of discrediting the "old" FBI and of undermining the authority of the old guard Hoover-era veterans still in positions of power in the FBI bureaucracy. The change in public information management by the end of the 1970s, during Webster's tenure, revealed some stability in the bureaucratic power struggle that was taking place. The earlier policy of mildly discrediting the Hooverite old guard and of forcing many of them into early retirement had effectively undermined their position in the "new" FBI. By the late 1970s, the task of creating a new executive structure for the FBI had largely been completed. The U.S. attorney general was again the superior, not just nominally, of the FBI director, and a new dominant coalition was in charge of the FBI bureaucracy. This was the major organizational dynamic of the post-Hoover FBI.

That this transformation, which ensured executive control of the FBI, overshadowed other changes is underscored by the reform response to Hoover-era abuses. Although the public disclosures of FBI violations of the rights of Americans had inspired the reform debate and preceded the mid-1970s scandal, the thrust of reform measures centered on making the FBI more accountable to the executive, especially to the Department of Justice. The organizational abuses that generated outrage during the Church and Pike hearings were never specifically prohibited. One of the key recommendations of the Church report, the establishment of a legislative charter for the FBI, was never implemented. In the legislative charters that were proposed,[2] questionable and abusive practices of the past were not prohibited. Even COINTELPRO-type activities were not explicitly prohibited, and no external checks were provided on the bureau's use of informants or undercover agents.

Although it is certainly true that the FBI operations that produced most of the organizational abuses—domestic intelligence activities—were dramatically reduced after 1973, what is also clear is that the authority for conducting these operations was retained within the executive. The reform measures implemented, such as the Levi Guidelines, were part of the process of institutionalizing discretion for FBI operations within the executive branch of government.

In hindsight, the failure of the Hoover FBI was not what it appeared to the public during the mid-1970s scandal: an agency out of control whose director had permitted official lawlessness. The real failure of the Hoover FBI was that it had operated with an autonomy and independence perhaps unparalleled by a U.S. government agency. The reform issue was not the nature and character of the "old" FBI operations but that they were not conducted as an integral part of the executive branch and the intelligence community. The problem was not COINTELPRO-type activities but domestic intelligence that was useful for anticipating and managing dissent. To put the matter in Weberian terms, what was needed was an FBI based on rational-legal authority rather than charismatic authority (Gerth and Mills, 1958: 295ff.).[3]

Scandal and the Illusion of Reform

In our inquiry into the FBI transformation of the 1970s, we examined the impact of public disclosures and scandal on the post-Watergate FBI. The expectation is that the scandal events would produce substantive reform, what the public and media have recognized as the "new" FBI. As we have noted, the commonplace view of what happened was that the "new" FBI had shed the abuses of the past and that this had come about because of the "big scandal" of the mid-1970s. It was further argued that while the "old" abuses, especially those associated with domestic intelligence, may have declined in the immediate post-Watergate period, the "old" practices have, for the most part, not been specifically prohibited. Furthermore, the authority for conducting such operations was retained largely in the executive branch. The impetus for this scenario was presumed to have originated in the public disclosures of FBI lawlessness.

Once again, what appears plausible does not fit the actual sequence of events of the 1970s. The commonplace view considers public disclosures and scandal the independent variable in the causal chain of events culminating in reform. The problem with this view is that some of the "reform" measures preceded the "big scandal" of 1974–1976, so logically, the scandal events could not have produced those organizational changes. What is missed in all of this is that the mobilization of scandal and promotion of disclosures as news were symptomatic of an underlying policy dispute between major social and political actors. In the present case, the primary conflict centered on controlling the FBI of the 1970s. There was also a policy debate about authority to conduct intelligence activities and about where the discretion for such operations resides. This bureaucratic power struggle involved actors internal and external to the FBI as well as in the executive and legislative branches. The struggle was manifest first in declining FBI organizational power after 1968 and was later expressed by the increase in public disclosures revealing FBI misconduct. The scandal process was part of the conflict previously mentioned: the decade-long struggle to make the FBI a more integral part of the executive branch, especially of the Department of Justice. In this case, the vast majority of the disclosures served to undermine the Hoover old guard and to strengthen the position of those seeking a limited restructuring of the FBI within the executive. The goal of the reformers was to end the operation of the bureau as an independent fiefdom.

It is important to understand that the "new" FBI was a product of these organizational conflicts rather than simply a spin-off of the Watergate scandal. While Hoover was alive, no president had the political courage to make such changes. Richard Nixon was apparently on the brink of asking Hoover to resign but then got "cold feet" (Sullivan with Brown, 1979a: 240; Ehrlichman, 1982: 166–167). Lyndon Johnson had earlier reached an accommodation with the aging director. It was apparently Johnson's contention that it was better to have Hoover "on the inside of the tent pissing out than on the outside of the tent pissing in" (Halperin et al., 1976: 83). Hoover's death in 1972 removed an important obstacle from the path of those who wished to change the bureau. Nixon's disenchantment with FBI intelligence and his failed effort to implement the Huston Plan in 1970 were early signs that the executive desired not just a new FBI director but a bureau more in line with the political and ideological predilections of the governing administration. The Hoover FBI had been so insulated from outside control that its domestic intelligence activities had largely been guided by the personal prejudices and idiosyncracies of the director, whether this took the form of a personal vendetta against Martin Luther King, Jr. (Halperin et al., 1976; Garrow, 1981) or the pursuit of old leftists and communists. Moreover, the intelligence collection techniques the bureau was willing to engage in also seemed limited by Hoover's preoccupation with the FBI image; disclosure of such activities might embarrass the agency that Hoover had spent a lifetime building. Nixon discovered in the late 1960s that the Hoover FBI had become an anachronism. Its intelligence operations were not oriented toward the collection of systematic intelligence that might be useful in anticipating and managing dissent. Instead, the Hoover FBI was largely unprepared to deal with the antiwar movement and New Left of the 1960s. Later, in the mid-1970s, both the GAO (U.S. Comptroller General, 1976) and the Rockefeller Commission (1975) criticized the FBI for not producing "tangible results" and for not having an "evaluation and analysis capability" with respect to domestic intelligence. This awareness of the disparity between FBI image and performance and the autonomy of the "old" FBI provided the impetus for FBI reform during the 1970s. The public disclosures and the "big scandal" were a byproduct of this larger struggle for reform. The concern for the past abuses of the Hoover era were part of the symbolic politics of reform, although, ironically, not the focus of actual organizational change.

The incorporation of the FBI into the Department of Justice, the intelligence community, and the executive represents the culmination of an historical process beginning during World War II. This process entailed the establishment of a permanent intelligence structure, both foreign and domestic, in the federal government (Raskin, 1979; Morgan, 1980); the rise of an "invisible government" (Wise and Ross, 1964); and the increasing concentration of power in the postwar presidency (Halperin et al., 1976). The integration of the FBI into this national security apparatus is a logical outgrowth of this long-term trend.

What Is New About the "New" FBI?

Perhaps the most obvious change in the post-Watergate FBI was the reordering of its top investigative priorities in the wake of massive disclosures and a major scandal in the mid-1970s. In this rethinking of the Hoover FBI, white-collar crime, organized crime, and foreign counterintelligence emerged as the new top priorities.

It is important to not only recognize that these priorities are different from those of the Hoover FBI but to also understand their relevance to the broader political and economic milieu of the "new" FBI. Along with the integration of the FBI into the DOJ and the executive came priorities more closely in line with the political and ideological persuasions of the governing administration. This is more or less explicitly stated at the FBI's annual appropriations hearings: "In keeping with the desires of the President and the Attorney General, foreign counterintelligence, organized crime, terrorism, and white-collar crime continue to be top priorities" (U.S. House, Appropriations Hearings, 1984: 444). While the blatant use of the FBI for political purposes was considered improper in the "old" FBI, as it is in the "new" FBI, the politicization of the bureau has taken on a new meaning. Politics and ideology increasingly shape the priorities and general direction of the "new" FBI, unlike the "old" FBI, where Hoover's idiosyncratic concerns dominated.

This is perhaps nowhere more apparent than in the transformation of organized crime as a top bureau priority in the mid-1970s and in the FBI's subsequent enlistment in the Reagan drug war of the 1980s. In contrast to Hoover's "strange reluctance" in these investigative areas, the pursuit of both organized crime and drug traffickers became one of the key investigative priorities of the "new" FBI. The FBI's National Drug Strategy, redefined in 1986, is aimed at organized criminal groups that are high-level traffickers (U.S. House, Appropriations Hearings, 1987: 1756). The rise of the Mafia threat and the "new" FBI's desire to combat organized crime was predicated on the discovery that organized crime had expanded outside the traditional arena of illegal goods and services. The FBI in the post-Watergate era was enlisted as part of a broader federal effort to contain the influence and penetration of organized crime groups as competitors in the legal marketplace.

Similarly, white-collar crime had received little attention in the "old" FBI. The "discovery" of white-collar crime and public corruption in the immediate post-Watergate era was linked to the federal response to bolster the sagging public confidence and trust in the U.S. political economy. By the early 1980s, the Reagan administration again shifted the emphasis in the white-collar crime program away from public corruption to fraud against government, as white-collar crime was increasingly viewed as a cost-benefit problem, the regulation of which could impact negatively on the economy. In this reordering of priorities—what essentially amounted to the deregulation of white-collar crime—the FBI's white-collar crime program became part of the politics of redistributing income and wealth in the 1980s.

While the erosion of the FBI's internal security apparatus was an important element in the FBI reform of the 1970s, its partial resurrection in the early 1980s was part of the Reagan administration's effort to combat terrorism and, in the view of some critics, to silence individuals and groups opposed to the administration's policies in Central America. When specifically asked in congressional hearings about the FBI's political role in its visits to U.S. citizens returning from Nicaragua, Director Webster denied that the FBI was taking sides for or against the Contras. He insisted that the bureau has a legitimate foreign counterintelligence interest in citizens who might possess "positive intelligence" relating to Nicaragua and national security and that the FBI is not interested in their political beliefs. Webster further argued that the authority for such FBI activities derives from Reagan's executive order on intelligence (E.O. 12333) and that pursuant to that order, the FBI "from time to time receives tasking from the National Security Council and the Director of Central Intelligence" (U.S. House, 1986b: 8–9). While the authority for the FBI's targeting of terrorist groups is couched in seemingly legalistic, neutral terms—legitimate FCI interests and responsibilities, taskings, and so forth—it is not out of the question that such taskings are political in nature. This is a distinct possibility, given the revelations in the subsequent Iran-Contra affair and the released CISPES documents.

In less than a decade, we have moved from an FBI that operated as a relatively independent empire within the federal government to an FBI whose organizational priorities are in close concert with the administration and political forces dominant at the time. But what is new about the post-Watergate FBI is more than just its investigative priorities and its integration into the executive. As we elaborated in the last chapter, the FBI of Kelley and Webster has been refashioned as a high-tech proactive law enforcement agency. The computerization of the FBI brings with it not only increased administrative efficiency but also an aura of science and technology that even surpasses the imagery of the Hoover FBI in its claims for professionalism and scientific law enforcement. The application of computer technology to FBI investigations, bureau management, support to local law enforcement, and even executive decision making convey this new high-tech mystique. This technology, the bureau's new investigative strategy, and the quality-over-quantity approach that has led to proactive investigative methods are at the cutting edge of the "new" FBI.

With the collapse of the G-man myth in the 1970s, the new emerging mystique provides a new basis for FBI organizational power and legitimacy. An FBI that controls the national information system on criminal records, possesses the expertise and technology on the new high-tech methods (such as profiling and artificial intelligence), and excels in its use of the undercover technique can only be enhanced in terms of its bureaucratic power and legitimacy as an agency. This is the FBI's surrogate in the 1980s for the G-men of the Depression era, who battled kidnappers and bank robbers, and of the McCarthy era, who defended us against subversion.

The Dangers of the "New" FBI

Because Hoover has become so strongly identified with the abuses of the past, to a large extent the reform agenda for the FBI has focused on not reproducing the characteristics of the Hoover FBI. The problem of reform becomes a matter of eliminating the vestiges of Hoover influence and of ensuring that old practices, most notably the widespread political surveillance of U.S. citizens, are not restored. This should be an important aspect of FBI reform: to eliminate once and for all the lawlessness of the past. However, in this preoccupation with the Hoover FBI the dangers and potential threat to civil liberties embedded in some of the distinctive features of the post-Watergate FBI are often overlooked.

The resurgence of FBI domestic intelligence operations in the 1980s in the form of terrorism investigations, as epitomized by the CISPES case, once again raises the specter of the Hoover FBI. However, the revival of domestic intelligence is not just a matter of restoring Hoover-style operations; we must also take into account the context of the "new" FBI. Although such operations were dramatically reduced during the 1970s, the quality-over-quantity approach of the bureau led to a more careful targeting of its domestic security and terrorism resources. As the GAO report indicates, even though the volume of domestic intelligence operations was scaled down, there was little change in the sources and techniques used in these investigations (U.S. Comptroller General, 1977: 144). In addition, as domestic security and terrorism operations were increasing in the 1980s, the authority for conducting these activities was broadening under Reagan's executive order on intelligence, the Smith Guidelines, and the foreign counterintelligence guidelines. The "new" FBI, with its high-tech proactive style, is oriented toward managerial efficiency and providing technocratically useful information to an administration that might be bent on "neutralizing and disrupting" dissident groups. The "new" FBI's priorities and operations, as we have seen, are more closely in line with those of the prevailing administration. If the FBI and the Justice Department take the GAO and the Rockefeller Commission criticisms seriously, then future domestic intelligence could be more concerned with systematic intelligence gathering, "tangible results," and an "evaluation and analysis capability." The FBI has, in fact, established a Terrorist Research and Analytical Center (TRAC) precisely "to detect associations between groups and individuals, corroborate information received from sources, establish patterns of activity, identify group leadership, and trace financial and support networks" (Pomerantz, 1987: 16–17). Domestic intelligence under these circumstances could be a more powerful weapon of social control as well as a greater threat to First Amendment political activities than was true under the "old" FBI, which was more concerned with its own organizational image and reputation and whose operations were not part of a centrally coordinated and well-orchestrated plan to suppress radicals and dissenters.[4]

There are, however, dangers in the "new" FBI that go beyond its domestic intelligence function. Some of these dangers are inherent in the bureau's proactive investigative strategy, which relies on the targeting of offenders in anticipation of crime. The undercover operation is the principal mechanism for carrying out such investigations on individuals or groups where there is a reasonable suspicion of involvement in an existing pattern of criminal conduct, whether they be terrorists, white-collar criminals, or organized crime figures. This strategy requires state intervention at a highly intrusive level, below the "reasonable and probable cause" threshold for arrest, and without any external checks and balances on police conduct.

The possibility for abuse is considerable. As noted in the last chapter, the aggressive targeting of potential offenders involves making a prediction as to the future criminality of the targeted individual or group.[5] The prediction error will vary according to the threshold for intervention. Intervention based on probable cause will have less error than that based on reasonable suspicion, simply because a higher level of proof and evidence is required. Although the FBI has operated according to the reasonable suspicion predicate as a basis for opening investigations, according to Webster, this standard is not required by law (U.S. Senate, 1987b: 127–129).

The Edwards subcommittee finding that the FBI has often deviated from its own standards and safeguards is not very reassuring in this respect (U.S. House, 1984: 1). Without external checks and balances on FBI and DOJ decisions for intervention in the form of undercover operations, there is a real possibility that a much wider net will be cast, one that will ensnare innocent members of the community in the effort to detect the crimes of hard-core elements. This problem is compounded by the tendency to pursue an investigative path once there has been a commitment of resources; agents, their supervisors, and even bureau officials could lose face if their commitment of substantial resources to an operation does not produce results (U.S. House, 1984: 9, 21). Presumably, the tendency would be to salvage something from an undercover operation, even when a prediction error has been made. Operation Corkscrew is a good example of this problem.

The specific dangers resulting from such proactive targeting of investigative resources have already been extensively discussed by the Edwards subcommittee (U.S. House, 1984) and more recently by Marx (1988). The dangers involve consequences for those targeted (rightly or wrongly) through coercion and trickery, which may border on entrapment; there may also be consequences of damaged reputations for those targeted. There may be injury to innocent third parties unwittingly brought into the orbit of an undercover operation by middlemen or agents; such injury typically takes the form of financial losses. Finally, undercover operations may unwittingly harm public institutions through targeting of specific individuals, thereby casting doubt on the integrity of those institutions. Such were the implications of ABSCAM for Congress and of Corkscrew for the Cleveland Municipal Court. (No judges were prosecuted in the Corkscrew case.)

In 1987 the Edwards subcommittee conducted follow-up hearings on its 1984 report on undercover operations to determine whether some of the problems it noted then had continued. Although the subcommittee received assurances from FBI Assistant Director Floyd Clarke that the bureau was following the attorney general guidelines and that it had made "enhancements in the area of oversight, training, and the use of the undercover technique" (U.S. House, 1988a: 6), it also received alarming testimony regarding Operation Iranscam—an FBI undercover operation that was conducted at complete variance with the bureau's own guidelines and safeguards.[6]

Iranscam was initiated in March 1985, when Anthony Romano made allegations to the Orlando, Florida, FBI office about a scheme to buy arms for Iran by an arms broker who was trying to fill his arms "shopping list," which included TOW and Sidewinder missiles. Although representing himself as a patriotic citizen who was still upset over the Iranian takeover of the U.S. embassy in 1979, it later turned out that Romano had been a member of the Buffalo Mafia family. This was documented in a 1978 report on organized crime by the attorney general of California; the FBI agents involved in the Iranscam case were also aware of this information. Despite the fact that a foreign government might be involved in the case, an undercover operation was approved at the field level—a violation of FBI oversight procedures. It appears, moreover, that the agents in the case were not even aware of the attorney general guidelines on undercover operations. The operation initially involved Romano playing himself, a Mafia figure, with an FBI agent as his bodyguard. As events unfolded, the undercover operation moved to California, where a third participant was recruited, Emilio Maldonado, who would serve as the West Coast Mafia representative. Astonishingly, Maldonado was even unaware that he was part of an FBI undercover operation; he thought all along that he was participating in a Mafia crime. During the course of the undercover operation, both Romano and Maldonado engaged in "rather violent and threatening acts"—all on FBI tape recordings—against persons they sought to involve in the arms sale scheme. While Romano had initially claimed that there was an ongoing arms sale conspiracy, none of the defendants in the cases had any missiles for sale. It was Romano and Maldonado who were now representing that they were selling missiles, with the covert cooperation of the U.S. government, and then attempting to induce the defendants as co-conspirators in arms dealing—although it was not even clear to the defendants that they were being solicited for a crime. Iranscam resulted in the arrest of seven persons and a six-week trial, with five acquittals and two convictions. The two defendants who were convicted were subsequently granted a new trial after the Iran-Contra affair came to light (U.S. House, 1988a: 45–60).

It is surely not an overstatement that Iranscam was an undercover operation out of control. The operation was poorly supervised and controlled by the bureau. The FBI's own procedures and the attorney general guidelines were violated at every stage. Incredibly, the agents in the case were even unaware of the guidelines. While it is difficult to ascertain whether Iranscam represents a continued "pattern of widespread deviation from avowed standards," as the 1984 report maintained, it seems clear that the guidelines for undercover operations and internal FBI oversight procedures, in effect for several years now, are insufficient to guarantee that undercover operations are conducted under the rule of law.

Finally, the computerization of the FBI has resulted in yet another set of dangers, mostly those associated with the development of a national databank of criminal records. We previously established that the quality of data in both state and federal CCH information systems, due to incomplete, inaccurate, or ambiguous records, undermines the utility of a national CCH for law enforcement purposes. Perhaps only in a utopian society would it be possible to create a national databank where the criminal records are complete, accurate, and unambiguous, since there are so many variables that must be taken into account to arrive at relatively perfect data. There is the problem of thousands of police agencies entering criminal records into the databank. The task of ensuring that this information is entered in a standardized way and that it is accurate is enormous. A second problem arises in providing follow-up data to the initial entry of arrest data. What was the outcome of the arrest? Was the initial charge dismissed or changed? Was there a conviction? Courts are overburdened to begin with, and reporting dispositions is not one of their high priorities. When a disposition is reported, it is reported to the state recordkeepers, who often will not report it to the FBI (U.S. House, 1988b: 3). This issue of record completeness has been one of the most significant problems plaguing crime information systems. Then there is the problem of how the user interprets the recorded data. Since the data is taken out of its local context, problems of interpretation may arise.

One of the dangers inherent in a national CCH stems from the imperfect information in the databank. For example, incorrect data about whether an individual is wanted by the police may lead to a wrongful arrest. Congressional hearings in 1985 produced a number of such cases, including that of Sheila Jackson Stossier. Stossier, who sometimes used Sheila Jackson for her ID, was arrested in 1983 as she got off a plane in New Orleans; she was an Eastern Airlines flight attendant.

In the course of passing through customs, the agent checked her ID against the NCIC computer and found that a Sheila Jackson was wanted in Texas as a parole violator. Stossier was then arrested and jailed for three days until the matter was eventually straightened out (U.S. House, 1986b: 32–33). In this case, the NCIC data were correctly entered; a new problem arises, however, when people having common names or aliases are mistaken for one another. This is a flaw in the wanted persons file; names, unlike fingerprints, do not uniquely identify the person. Furthermore, had the agent using the NCIC computer in this instance properly interpreted Sheila Jackson's records, Stossier's arrest could have been avoided. Had the agent observed, for example, that Stossier obtained her passport after Sheila Jackson's parole violation, he could have realized that he might have a case of mistaken identity, or at least it should have cast doubt on whether these women were one and the same person. Stossier's situation was further complicated by the fact that her arrest may have been entered in the NCIC computer, so that she now also had an official criminal record. It will be no simple task to have her record expunged so that future users of the NCIC do not infer that she has a criminal record.

It is not known how many similar episodes occur nationwide, although many individual cases have been brought to public attention. If we use Laudon's (1986) estimate in his 1979 study for OTA that 11.2 percent of the warrants in the wanted persons file are no longer valid, and as of December 31, 1984, some 219,681 records were in the wanted persons file, on any given day there is a potential for 2,636 wrongful arrests. It is, of course, not likely that all persons in the FBI's wanted persons file would come to official attention on the same day, but nevertheless, this is a conservative estimate, since there are other possible sources of error in the file, such as aging records (23.9 percent were more than three years old).

In addition to problems of input and the quality of information in a national databank, there is the question of access. Who will have access to these records besides criminal justice agencies? Will the records be "matched" with information systems in other government agencies? It is Laudon's (1986) contention that the greatest social impact of a national CCH is not on the criminal justice system but rather on minorities, which are disproportionately represented in criminal history records. Since public and private employers often have access to FBI Identification Division records for hiring and screening purposes, the potential for institutional discrimination is enormous and is exacerbated by the frequent omission of disposition data in the records so that the user will often not know the outcome of an arrest record. A 1987 FBI study of a sample of 4,000 arrest records revealed that approximately half of them did not indicate whether a conviction was obtained (U.S. House, 1988b: 1). The consequence is that the criminality of those persons in the file, particularly minorities, may be overstated, since many arrests are dismissed or do not result in conviction.

Although the FBI has operated since 1974 under the so-called one-year rule, which prohibited the dissemination to noncriminal justice users of arrest records more than one year old that did not show the disposition of arrest, the bureau in 1987 proposed abandoning this rule to provide greater access to arrest records by private employers. In addition to the discrimination problem, this widening of access to FBI criminal history records raises important privacy issues as well as concerns about the presumption of innocence when arrest records are unaccompanied by the disposition. An applicant's record is in all probability tainted when an arrest-only record is provided to a prospective employer (U.S. House, 1988b: 1–4).

As of 1987, the NCIC databank has not been linked with the databanks of other government agencies, such as the IRS or the Social Security Administration, although such computer matching has been considered (U.S. Congress, 1988: 15–16). Should computer matching take place at some future date, the imperfect data in the national CCH could be magnified across other areas of personal life, again disproportionately impacting minorities.

There is a final area of potential abuse to be considered in the use of a national CCH. It is possible that such a depository of criminal records could be used to track individuals in our society for some unauthorized purpose. The NCIC database, which now incorporates both III and AIDS, not only includes records on the most serious criminals but also on a broad cross section of those arrested for any crime. It is estimated that 40 million U.S. citizens could have their criminal histories entered in this national CCH (Gordon and Churchill, 1984). By flagging the files of individuals because of their political beliefs, criticism of foreign policy, perceived dangerousness to the state, and so on, such a databank could be a useful aid in the proactive targeting of such individuals. In the 1985 hearings before the Edwards subcommittee, Director Webster indicated that flagging was not being used for such a purpose and that the FBI did not have a radical file (U.S. House, 1986b). In the early 1970s, the FBI did, however, use the NCIC computer to track some 4,000 political dissidents (Gordon and Churchill, 1984).

At the December 1987 meeting of the NCIC Advisory Policy Board (APB), the concept of using the NCIC to track subjects in drug, kidnapping, and murder investigations was approved for further development (Dahl, 1988: 4). This tracking proposal was part of the FBI's larger program of modernizing the NCIC (NCIC 2000). This use of the NCIC would depart from past practice by tracking persons who are merely suspects in an investigation and who are otherwise not charged with any crime (or subject to arrest). A report prepared by a panel of computer scientists (Computer Professionals for Social Responsibility) criticized the tracking plan as a threat to privacy and constitutional rights (Dahl, 1988). The tracking proposal was eventually rejected by the FBI, as confirmed by Congressman Edwards in a letter from Director Sessions (*New York Times*, Mar. 4, 1989).

Should the "new" FBI expand its current use of flags in the NCIC computer for domestic intelligence purposes, the "new" FBI would not only be reviving Hoover-style policies but also, given the current bureau's much greater sophistication in the use of computer technology, the potential for abuse would exceed anything possible in the Hoover FBI.[7]

The Lessons of Watergate Revisited

While the meaning of Watergate may be subject to a variety of interpretations, there is one central problem that emerges from this scandal of the Nixon administration: the limits of power of the modern presidency. A corollary problem relates to the adequacy of the system of checks and balances on the three branches of government in post–World War II America. More pertinent to our inquiry into the "old" and "new" FBI is whether the reforms of the post-Watergate era have placed the FBI under firm public control, with an adequate system of checks and balances on executive action.

The problem of control under the old regime had been that bureau operations were largely under the authoritarian control of one man who had unusual autonomy within the executive and whose behavior was not subject to meaningful congressional review. This is clearly no longer the case. The "new" FBI, as we have seen, is firmly under executive control, subject to various attorney general guidelines, and its top investigative priorities are strongly influenced by the ideology of the prevailing administration. This raises different problems of FBI accountability than encountered with the Hoover bureau. If the thrust of reform has been to restructure control of the FBI within the executive, this begs the more fundamental issue of controlling the executive itself.[8]

The dangers posed by a resurgence of domestic intelligence activities and the institutionalization of undercover operations in the FBI of the 1980s are heightened by this new context. Such operations are not simply guided by the idiosyncrasies of the bureau director but are the result of policies of the executive. As Shattuck (1983: 69) points out, after we thought we had eliminated the abuses that produced Watergate, a new system has developed that in effect institutionalizes much of the discretion for national security operations within the executive. Perhaps the unnoticed legacy of Watergate is this further consolidation of executive power. In relation to the FBI, while we thought we had reformed the lawlessness of the Hoover FBI, instead we have ensured that such lawlessness, if conducted in the future, would be carried out under the auspices of broader executive authority and not simply as an initiative of the FBI Director.

Marx (1982, 1988) suggests that we are entering a new era of social control that represents a fundamental shift away from the Anglo-American tradition of reactive policing. The new police strategies parallel the management strategies of modern corporations, where demand is not simply anticipated but is also developed and managed through advertising and other types of intervention. "By secretly gathering information and facilitating crime under controlled conditions, the police obtain a degree of control over the 'demand' for police services hardly possible with traditional reactive practices" (Marx, 1982: 190). Both domestic intelligence and undercover operations involve the selective targeting of individuals and groups for investigation and the involvement of police in illegal activities in order to develop the demand, some of which may be police-generated crimes. This process of targeting groups in anticipation of their criminality reached a new height in the summer of 1986 as the FBI introduced its computer program Big Floyd to assist in a labor racketeering case. Big Floyd, and future programs still to be developed, assists by profiling potential types of criminals, whether they are terrorists or drug smugglers. In addition to serving as an aid in the targeting of potential law violators, such expert systems assist agents in making investigative decisions in a case (Schrage, 1986). In time, however, these proactive investigative strategies may come in direct conflict with established constitutional principles. As they seek to identify and target potential offenders, these strategies cast a wide net in the community.

The legal basis for proactive police intervention, which by definition is at an early stage of criminal procedure, raises unsettled legal issues—unlike the law of arrest, where reasonable and probable cause is the well-established predicate for legal intervention. In light of the new high-tech proactive strategies, a wide array of constitutional issues will have to be reconsidered, including: When does a citizen have a "reasonable expectation of privacy"? What is a legal search under the Fourth Amendment?[9] What constitutes entrapment? Is proactive targeting discriminatory? Does it violate equal protection of the law? What should be the legal standard for opening investigations, particularly undercover operations?

The contemporary FBI's sophistication in its use and application of computer technology to enhance its effectiveness, along with the development of proactive investigative strategies, raises one of the basic dilemmas of organizations in modern society. While organizations increase administrative efficiency and coordination in the operations of society, they also tend to concentrate power in the hands of administrators, who possess or have access to expert knowledge or secret information and who control certain technologies (like a national CCH) in their organizational domain. The trend, as Weber saw it (Gerth and Mills, 1958: 232ff.), was for power to pass from the democratically elected officials, "the political masters," to those who manage the administrative structure of government. Clearly, the FBI, as well as numerous other organizations, renders important services and benefits for maintaining a democratic society. This is at the heart of the dilemma. What measures are necessary for making administrative structures such as the FBI accountable to the public? The FBI reforms of the post-Watergate period resolved this dilemma by placing administrative control more broadly within the executive, along with some legislative oversight. The reforms, however, largely beg the question of controlling the executive itself.

This again brings us full circle to the unaddressed issues at the heart of Watergate and the FBI scandal of the mid-1970s, issues that relate to the limits and control of executive authority and what Wise and Ross (1964) call the "invisible government." Until these issues are squarely faced, the major business of Watergate will remain unfinished, and the problem of controlling the "new" FBI will persist.

NOTES

1.   In the 1986 amendments to the Freedom of Information Act (FOIA), law enforcement records became more inaccessible through the broadening of the basis for exemption. Furthermore, under certain circumstances, the existence of FBI records pertaining to foreign intelligence, counterintelligence, or international terrorism does not have to be confirmed or denied. Curiously, the 1986 FOIA amendments were little-noticed riders to the Anti-Drug Abuse Act of 1986 (Buitrago, 1987: 34–36)

2.   The FBI Charter Act of 1979 and the National Intelligence Act of 1980.

3.   Weber identified three types of authority: traditional, charismatic, and rational-legal. Each type of authority makes a different claim to legitimacy in the authority relation. Traditionalism rests on the sanctity of traditions and customs and those who exercise authority under them—that is, patriarchal authority. Char-

ismatic authority rests on the belief in the extraordinary qualities of the individual that may be revealed through miracles, victories, or other successes. This type of authority may involve a cult of personality or hero worship. Finally, rational-legal authority is the type of authority large organizations in modern society rely on. Legitimacy derives from the sanctity of rules, procedures, and laws that govern those organizations. Authority, accordingly, is determined by those same rules: those who occupy designated positions in organizations. According to Weber, the growth of rational-legal authority in society was an important element in the rationalization of modern life (Gerth and Mills, 1958: 51, 295ff.; Scott, 1987: 40ff.).

4.   Apparently, this is still not the case. In his September 16, 1988, testimony before the Edwards subcommittee, Director Sessions observed in his conclusions from the internal CISPES inquiry:

> There was no automatic reminder or "tickler" system in place to ensure timely and appropriate review of incoming information. The field agents collecting information on CISPES could reasonably have assumed that the information would be properly reviewed at FBI Headquarters, but in many cases it was not; it was simply placed in files and left there (Stern, 1988: 7).

5.   The prediction problem applies to the decision to initiate an undercover operation. If the prediction is correct, there will eventually be a basis for arrest. The problem in long-term undercover operations then becomes one of when to make the arrests in order to maximize the investigative benefits of the undercover operation.

6.   This testimony was provided by Alan S. Ross, a lawyer in Miami, Florida, whose client was one of the defendants in the Iranscam case who had been threatened by Romano and Maldonado (two operatives in the FBI undercover operation).

7.   In 1985 the FBI was, in fact, considering using the NCIC for a classified intelligence purpose (U.S. House, 1986b). Refer to note 16 in chapter 10.

8.   The current FBI director, William Sessions, disputes the need for a statutory FBI charter. He claims that the bureau's internal inquiry in the CISPES case is evidence of its ability to police itself without legislative restrictions (Stern, 1988). Critics of the FBI on the CISPES matter conclude just the opposite: the CISPES case illustrates the failure of the post-Watergate attorney general guidelines in themselves to regulate FBI conduct.

9.   On April 3, 1989, in *United States* v. *Sokolow,* the U.S. Supreme Court, in a seven to two decision, gave constitutional support to the profiling technique. In this case, DEA agents briefly detained a passenger at Honolulu International Airport who displayed behavior patterns similar to those in the FBI's drug courier profile. The profile lists various behavior patterns exhibited by typical narcotics carriers on commercial airliners. This profile has been developed by the DEA over the last fifteen years and is based on agent observations and experience. It includes the following behaviors: paying for tickets with cash, using an alias, boarding a long flight without checking luggage, and staying briefly in distant cities known to be sources of narcotics. The behavior patterns included in the profile were interpreted by the court as constituting the reasonable suspicion required for such brief investigative stops—a lower standard than the reasonable and probable cause

needed for an arrest. In this case, the defendant was detained and sniffed by dogs; several pounds of cocaine were found in his shoulder bag. The Supreme Court's decision overturned a U.S. Court of Appeals ruling that had found the detention to be unconstitutional (Greenhouse, 1989).

REFERENCES

Abadinsky, Howard (1981) *Organized Crime*. Newton, Mass.: Allyn & Bacon.

Albanese, Jay (1985) *Organized Crime in America*. Cincinnati, Ohio: Anderson.

Alexander, Jack (1937) "Profiles: The Director." *New Yorker* (Sept. 25, Oct. 2, Oct. 9): 20–25, 21–26, 22–27, respectively.

Babcock, Charles R. (1979) "FBI Chief After 12 Months: Low Profile, Firm Control." *Washington Post* (Mar. 5): 2.

Ball, George W. (1983) "Guest Point of View." *First Principles* 9 (Nov./Dec.): 16.

Becker, H. S. (1963) *Outsiders: Studies in the Sociology of Deviance*. New York: Free Press.

Belknap, Michal (1977a) *Cold War Political Justice*. Westport, Conn.: Greenwood Press.

_____ (1977b) "The Mechanics of Repression: J. Edgar Hoover, The Bureau of Investigation and the Radicals, 1917–1925." *Crime and Social Justice* 7: 49–58.

Bell, Daniel (1964) "Crime as an American Way of Life." In D. Bell, ed., *The End of Ideology*. New York: Free Press.

Berman, Jerry (1985) "Political Surveillance in the Reagan Era." *First Principles* (May/June): 1–3.

_____ (1982) *The Lessons of ABSCAM: A Public Policy Report by ACLU*. Washington, D.C.: American Civil Liberties Union.

Bernstein, B. (1976) "The Road to Watergate and Beyond: The Growth and Abuse of Executive Authority Since 1940." *Law and Contemporary Problems* 40: 58–86.

Blau, Peter M., and Marshall W. Meyer (1971) *Bureaucracy in Modern Society*. 2nd ed. New York: Random House.

Block, Alan A. (1979) "The Snowman Cometh: Coke in Progressive New York." *Criminology* 17 (May): 75–99.

Box, Steven (1983) *Power, Crime, and Mystification*. London: Tavistock.

Brown, L., and C. Brown (1973) *An Unauthorized History of the RCMP*. Toronto: James Lorimer.

Buitrago, Ann-Mari (1988) "CISPES and the FBI—Hoover Returns to Haunt Us." *Our Right to Know* (Winter/Spring): 1–4.

_____ (1987) "FOIA: First Casualty of the War on Drugs." *Our Right to Know* (Spring-Summer): 34–39.

Burnham, David (1984) "From G-Man to Cursor-Man." *New York Times* (Oct. 22): A16.

_____ (1983) *The Rise of the Computer State.* New York: Random House.

_____ (1971) "Agent Who Quit FBI Scores Bureau Investigations, Discipline, and Leadership." *New York Times* (Jan. 23): 27.

Cardman, Denise (1978) "Status Report on Intelligence Legislation." *First Principles* 4 (Nov.): 5–8.

Center for Constitutional Rights (1987) "Testimony Before the Subcommittee on CCR of House Judiciary Committee, Feb. 20, 1987." *Our Right to Know* (Spring/Summer): 8–18.

Chambliss, William (1971) "Vice, Corruption, Bureaucracy, and Power." *Wisconsin Law Review* 4: 1130–1155.

Civil Liberties is a newsletter published by the American Civil Liberties Union.

Clark, Ramsey (1970) *Crime in America.* New York: Pocket Books.

Cohen, Jacqueline (1983) *Incapacitating Criminals: Recent Research Findings.* NIJ (National Institute of Justice) Research in Brief. Washington, D.C.: U.S. Department of Justice.

Coleman, James W. (1987) "Organizational Crime and the Enforcement Bureaucracy: Trends in the 1980s." Paper presented at the American Society of Criminology annual meeting, Montreal, Quebec, Nov. 14.

_____ (1985) *The Criminal Elite.* New York: St. Martin's Press.

Congressional Quarterly (1975) *Watergate: Chronology of a Crisis.* Washington, D.C.: Congressional Quarterly.

Cook, Fred J. (1981) "The Coming Catastrophe." *The Nation* (Apr. 25): 492–500.

_____ (1973) "The Strange Reluctance." In P. Watters and S. Gillers, eds., *Investigating the FBI.* New York: Ballantine.

_____ (1964) *The FBI Nobody Knows.* New York: Macmillan.

_____ (1958) "The FBI." *The Nation* 187 (Oct. 18): 221–280.

Crawford, Kenneth (1937a) "J. Edgar Hoover: Part I." *The Nation* 144 (Feb. 27): 232–234.

_____ (1937b) "J. Edgar Hoover: Part II." *The Nation* 144 (Mar. 6): 262–264.

Cressey, Donald R. (1969) *Theft of the Nation.* New York: Harper & Row.

_____ (1967) "The Functions and Structure of Criminal Syndicates." In the President's Commission on Law Enforcement and the Administration of Justice, *Task Force Report: Organized Crime.* Washington, D.C.: U.S. Government Printing Office.

Crewdson, John (1976a) "FBI Chief Curbs Intelligence Arm." *New York Times* (Aug. 12): 1.

_____ (1976b) "New FBI Inquiry on Funds Ordered." *New York Times* (Mar. 20): 1.

_____ (1973a) "Burglaries Laid to Agents of FBI in 30-Year Period." *New York Times* (Aug. 24): 1.

_____ (1973b) "FBI Warns Staff on Leaking Data." *New York Times* (Aug. 26): 1.

Cullen, Francis T., William J. Maakestad, and Gray Cavender (1987) *Corporate Crime Under Attack: The Ford Pinto Case and Beyond.* Cincinnati, Ohio: Anderson.

Currie, Elliott (1985) *Confronting Crime: An American Challenge.* New York: Pantheon Books.

Dahl, Mary Karen (1988) *The National Crime Information Center: A Case Study in National Databases.* Palo Alto, Calif.: Computer Professionals for Social Responsibility.

Demaris, Ovid (1975) *The Director: An Oral Biography of J. Edgar Hoover.* New York: *Harper's* Magazine Press.

_____ (1974) *Dirty Business.* New York: *Harper's* Magazine Press.

Depue, Roger L. (1986) "An American Response to an Era of Violence." *FBI Law Enforcement Bulletin* 55 (Dec.): 2–5.

Donner, Frank (1982) "Rounding Up the Usual Suspects." *The Nation* (Aug. 7–14): 109–116.

_____ (1980) *The Age of Surveillance.* New York: Knopf.

Douglas, John, and Alan Burgess (1986) "Criminal Profiling: A Viable Investigative Tool Against Violent Crime." *FBI Law Enforcement Bulletin* 55 (Dec.): 9–13.

Dreier, P. (1982) "The Position of the Press in the U.S. Power Structure." *Social Problems* 29 (Feb.): 298–310.

Earle, James H. (1988) "Law Enforcement Administration: Yesterday, Today, Tomorrow." *FBI Law Enforcement Bulletin* 57 (Apr.): 2–7.

Edwards, Don (1980) "Spying on Ourselves." *Congressional Record* (Feb. 25): E800.

Ehrlichman, John (1982) *Witness to Power: The Nixon Years.* New York: Simon & Schuster.

Elliff, John T. (1979) *The Reform of FBI Intelligence Operations.* Princteon, N.J.: Princeton University Press.

Engler, R. (1977) *The Brotherhood of Oil.* Chicago: University of Chicago Press.

Enter, Jack E. (1987) "Psychological Profiling and the Predator Criminal: A New Form of Criminological Inquiry?" Paper presented at the American Society of Criminology annual meeting, Montreal, Canada, Nov. 12.

Ermann, M. David, and Richard J. Lundman (1987) *Corporate and Governmental Deviance.* 3rd ed. New York: Oxford University Press.

Fain, Tyrus G., ed. (1977) *The Intelligence Community: History, Organization, and Issues.* New York: Bowker.

Felt, W. Mark (1979) *The FBI Pyramid.* New York: Putnam.

First Principles is a periodical published by the Center for National Security Studies in Washington, D.C.

Gallup, George (1979) *The Gallup Opinion Index.* Princeton, N.J.: The Gallup Poll.

Gans, Herbert J. (1979) *Deciding What's News: A Study of CBS Evening News, NBC Nightly News, Newsweek, and Time.* New York: Pantheon Books.

Garrow, David (1981) *The FBI and Martin Luther King, Jr.* New York: Norton.

Gerth, H. H., and C. Wright Mills, trans. (1958) *From Max Weber: Essays in Sociology.* New York: Oxford University Press.

Gettleman, Marvin E., and David Mermelstein, eds. (1967) *The Great Society Reader: The Failure of American Liberalism.* New York: Vintage Books.

Gordon, Diana R., and Mae Churchill (1984) "'Triple I' Will Be Tracking Us." *The Nation* (Apr. 28): 497, 513–515.

Green, Mark, and Norman Waitzman (1979) "A Challenge to Murray Weidenbaum." *New York Times* (Oct. 28): B18.

Greenhouse, Linda (1989) "High Court Backs Airport Detention Based on Behavior." *New York Times* (Apr. 4): A1, B10.

Greenwood, Peter W. (1982) *Selective Incapacitation.* Santa Monica, Calif.: Rand.

Halperin, Morton H. (1980) "Authorizing Abuse." *New York Times* (Feb. 24): sec. 4, p. 19.

_____ (1979) "The CIA/FBI Campaign for New FOIA Amendments." *First Principles* 4 (Jan.): 16.

Halperin, Morton, J. Berman, R. Borosage, and C. Marwick (1976) *The Lawless State.* New York: Penguin Books.

Hawkins, Gordon (1969) "God and the Mafia." *The Public Interest* 14 (Winter): 24–38, 40–51.

Hazelwood, Robert (1987) "An Introduction to the Serial Rapist: Research by the FBI." *FBI Law Enforcement Bulletin* 56 (Sept.): 16–24.

Henderson, Neil (1985) "Time to Revise the Clayton Act?" *The Washington Post National Weekly* (Mar. 18): 2.

Hofstadter, Richard (1955) *The Age of Reform.* New York: Vintage Books.

Hopkins, Elaine (1988) "A Matter of Conscience for a G-Man." *Progressive* 52 (Jan.): 14.

Horrock, Nicholas (1978) "Gray and Two Ex-FBI Aides Indicted on Conspiracy in Search for Radicals." *New York Times* (Apr. 11): 1.

_____ (1975) "Levi Details Wide Scope of Hoover's Secret Files." *New York Times* (Feb. 28): 1.

Howlett, James, Kenneth Hanfland, and Robert Ressler (1986) "The Violent Criminal Apprehension Program." *FBI Law Enforcement Bulletin* 55 (Dec.): 14–22.

Icove, David (1986) "Automated Crime Profiling." *FBI Law Enforcement Bulletin* 55 (Dec.): 27–30.

Inciardi, James (1975) *Careers in Crime.* Skokie, Ill.: Rand McNally.

Isaacson, Walter (1981) "Let the Buyers Beware." *Time* (Sept. 21): 22–23.

Isikoff, Michael (1984) "The FTC Throws Away the Old Monopoly Board." *The Washington Post National Weekly* (July 2): 33.

Kefauver, Estes (1951) *Crime in America.* New York: Doubleday.

Keller, William W. (1989) *The Liberals and J. Edgar Hoover: Rise and Fall of a Domestic Intelligence State.* Princeton, N.J.: Princeton University Press.

Kelley, Clarence (1974) "Message from the Director: 'White-collar' Crime—A Serious Problem." *FBI Law Enforcement Bulletin* 43 (Sept.): 1.

Kelley, Clarence M., and James K. Davis (1987) *Kelley: The Story of an FBI Director.* Kansas City, Mo.: Andrews, McMeel, and Parker.

Kelling, George L. (1988) *Police and Communities: The Quiet Revolution.* NIJ Perspectives on Policing. Washington, D.C.: U.S. Department of Justice.

Kelling, George L., and Mark H. Moore (1988) *The Evolving Strategy of Policing.* NIJ Perspectives on Policing. Washington, D.C.: U.S. Department of Justice.

Kurtz, Howard (1987) "One That Got Away?" *Washington Post National Weekly* (July 13).

_____ (1986a) "Dulling It Up: A Hearing on White-Collar Crime Lives Down to Its Billing." *Washington Post National Weekly* (Mar. 17): 14.

_____ (1986b) "Joe Biden, The Talk of the Town." *The Washington Post National Weekly* (Oct. 27): 13.

_____ (1985) "This 'Sting' Really Hurt." *Washington Post National Weekly* (Aug. 19).

Kwitny, Jonathan (1978) "FBI Agents Rap Policy of Burning Files, Link It to Public-Access Acts." *Wall Street Journal* (Sept. 27): 1, 21.

Langworthy, Robert H. (1989) "Do Stings Control Crime? An Evaluation of a Police Fencing Operation." *Justice Quarterly* 6 (Mar.): 27–45.

Lardner, George, Jr. (1980) "Charter Would Let FBI Disrupt Some Domestic Groups." *Washington Post* (Mar. 19): 1, 12.

Laudon, Kenneth (1986) *The Dossier Society.* New York: Columbia University Press.

Lindesmith, Alfred (1965) *The Addict and the Law.* New York: Vintage Books.

Lipset, S. M., and W. Schneider (1978) "How's Business: What the Public Thinks." *Public Opinion* 1 (July/Aug.): 41–47.

Lowenthal, Max (1950) *The Federal Bureau of Investigation.* Westport, Conn.: Greenwood Press.

McLellan, Howard (1936) "Shoot to Kill?" *Harpers Magazine* (Jan.): 236–244.

Marro, Anthony (1978) "Pattern of FBI Petty Corruption Related in Justice Agency Report." *New York Times* (Jan. 11): 8.

Marx, Gary T. (1988) *Undercover: Police Surveillance in America.* Berkeley: University of California Press.

_____ (1985) "I'll Be Watching You." *Dissent* (Winter): 26–34.

_____ (1982) "Who Really Gets Stung? Some Issues Raised by the New Police Undercover Work." *Crime and Delinquency* 28 (Apr.): 165–193.

_____ (1974) "Thoughts on a Neglected Category of Social Movement Participant: The Agent Provocateur and the Informant." *American Journal of Sociology* 80 (Sept.): 402–442.

Mayer, Milton S. (1935) "Myth of the 'G-Men'" *Forum* (Sept): 144–148.

Merton, Robert K. (1938) "Social Structure and Anomie." *American Sociological Review* 3 (Oct.): 672–682.

Messick, H. (1972) *John Edgar Hoover.* New York: McKay.

Molotch, H., and M. Lester (1975) "Accidental News: The Great Oil Spill as Local Occurrence and National Event." *American Journal of Sociology* 81 (Sept.): 235–239.

_____ (1974) "News as Purposive Behavior: On the Strategic Use of Routine Events, Accidents, and Scandals." *American Sociological Review* 39 (Feb.): 101–112.

_____ (1973) "Accidents, Scandals, and Routines: Resources for Insurgent Methodology." *Insurgent Sociologist* 3 (Summer): 1–11.

Moore, Mark H., and Robert C. Trojanowicz (1988) *Corporate Strategies for Policing.* NIJ Perspectives on Policing. Washington, D.C.: U.S. Department of Justice.

Morgan, Richard E. (1980) *Domestic Intelligence: Monitoring Dissent in America.* Austin: University of Texas Press.

Murray, Robert (1955) *Red Scare: A Study of National Hysteria, 1919–1920.* New York: McGraw-Hill.

Nash, Jay R. (1972) *Citizen Hoover.* Chicago: Nelson-Hall.

National Advisory Committee on Criminal Justice Standards and Goals (1976) *Disorders and Terrorism.* Washington, D.C.: U.S. Government Printing Office.

Nixon, Richard (1979) *The Memoirs of Richard Nixon.* Vol. 2. New York: Warner Books.

_____ (1978) *The Memoirs of Richard Nixon.* Vol. 1. New York: Grosset & Dunlap.

O'Reilly, Kenneth (1988) "The FBI and the Civil Rights Movement During the Kennedy Years—From the Freedom Rides to Albany." *Journal of Southern History* 54 (May): 201–232.

_____ (1982) "A New Deal for the FBI: The Roosevelt Administration, Crime Control, and National Security." *Journal of American History* 69 (Dec.): 638–658.

Packer, Herbert L. (1968) *The Limits of the Criminal Sanction.* Stanford, Calif.: Stanford University Press.

Palmer, R. R. (1962) *A History of the Modern World.* New York: Knopf.

Pear, Robert (1980a) "Extensive Study Asked on FBI Use of Informers." *New York Times* (Mar. 23): 21.

_____ (1980b) "The 'New' FBI Is Exorcising the Ghost of J. Edgar Hoover." *New York Times* (Mar. 16): sec. 4, p. 5.

Pearce, Frank (1981) "Organized Crime and Class Politics." In David Greenberg, ed. *Crime and Capitalism.* Palo Alto, Calif.: Mayfield.

Perkus, Cathy, ed. (1975) *COINTELPRO: The FBI's Secret War on Political Freedom.* New York: Monad Press.

Peterzell, Jay (1981a) "The Intelligence Transition." *First Principles* 6 (Jan.): 1–3.

_____ (1981b) "Unleashing the Dogs of McCarthyism." *The Nation* (Jan. 17): 50–52.

Pincus, Walter (1973) "The Bureau's Budget: A Source of Power." In P. Watters and S. Gillers, eds., *Investigating the FBI.* New York: Ballantine Books.

Pomerantz, Steven (1987) "The FBI and Terrorism." *FBI Law Enforcement Bulletin* 56 (Oct.): 14–17.

Porter, Bruce (1983) "Mind Hunters." *Psychology Today* (Apr.): 44–52.

Poveda, Tony G. (1985) "The Effect of Scandal on Organizational Deviance: The Case of the FBI." *Justice Quarterly* 2 (June): 237–258.

_____ (1982) "The Rise and Fall of FBI Domestic Intelligence Operations." *Contemporary Crises* 6: 103–118.

_____ (1981) "Scandal and Reform in the FBI." In J. Fyfe, ed., *Contemporary Issues in Law Enforcement*. Newbury Park, Calif.: Sage.

Powers, Richard G. (1987) *Secrecy and Power: The Life of J. Edgar Hoover*. New York: Free Press.

_____ (1983) *G-Men: Hoover's FBI in American Popular Culture*. Carbondale: Southern Illinois University Press.

Powers, Thomas (1979) "Inside the Department of Dirty Tricks." *The Atlantic* 244 (Aug.): 33–64.

President's Commission on Law Enforcement and the Administration of Justice (1967a) *The Challenge of Crime in a Free Society*. Washington, D.C.: U.S. Government Printing Office.

_____ (1967b) *Task Force Report: Organized Crime*. Washington, D.C.: U.S. Government Printing Office.

_____ (1967c) *Task Force Report: Science and Technology*. Washington, D.C.: U.S. Government Printing Office.

President's Commission on Organized Crime (1986a) *The Edge: Organized Crime, Business, and Labor Unions*. Washington, D.C., U.S. Government Printing Office.

_____ (1986b) *The Impact: Organized Crime Today*. Washington, D.C.: U.S. Government Printing Office.

_____ (1983) *Hearings on Organized Crime: The Federal Law Enforcement Perspective*. Washington, D.C.: U.S. Government Printing Office.

Preston, W. (1963) *Aliens and Dissenters: Federal Suppression of Radicals, 1903–1933*. New York: Harper & Row.

Raines, Howell (1980a) "Cover-Up Seen in 60s Klan Attacks." *New York Times* (Feb. 17): 1, 16.

_____ (1980b) "Federal Report Says Hoover Barred Trial for Klansmen in 1963 Bombing." *New York Times* (Feb. 18): 1.

_____ (1978) "Inquiries Link Informer for FBI to Major Klan Terrorism in '60s." *New York Times* (July 17): 1.

Raskin, Marcus (1979) *The Politics of National Security*. New Brunswick, N.J.: Transaction Books.

Reiman, J. (1979) *The Rich Get Richer and the Poor Get Prison*. New York: Wiley.

Reuter, Peter (1983) *Disorganized Crime: Illegal Markets and the Mafia*. Cambridge, Mass.: MIT Press.

Revell, Oliver B. (1987) "Terrorism Today." *FBI Law Enforcement Bulletin* 56 (Oct.): 1–4.

Rhodes, Robert (1984) *Organized Crime: Crime Control and Civil Liberties*. New York: Random House.

Rockefeller Commission (1975) *Report to the President by the Commission on CIA Activities Within the United States*. Washington, D.C.: U.S. Government Printing Office.

Rubenstein, J., and P. Reuter (1978) "Fact, Fancy, and Organized Crime." *Public Interest* 53 (Fall): 45–67.

Ryter, Mark (1978a) "COINTELPRO: Corrupting American Institutions." *First Principles* 3 (May): 1–5.

_____ (1978b) "COINTELPRO: FBI Lawbreaking and Violence." *First Principles* 3 (June): 1–6.

Schrage, Michael (1986) "The New Cop on the Beat." *Washington Post National Weekly* (Aug. 4): 6.

Scott, W. Richard (1987) *Organizations: Rational, Natural and Open Systems.* 2nd ed. Englewood Cliffs, N.J.: Prentice-Hall.

Seagle, William (1934) "The American National Police: The Dangers of Federal Crime Control." *Harpers Magazine* 169 (Nov.): 751–761.

Shattuck, John (1983) "National Security a Decade after Watergate." *Democracy* (Winter): 56–71.

Shattuck, John, and Sally Berman (1977) "A Bill to Stop Government Spying." *Civil Liberties* (May): 1, 3.

Shattuck, John, Jerry Berman, and Morton Halperin (1982) "The Executive Order on Intelligence Activities." *First Principles* 7 (Jan.): 7–10.

Sheehan, Neil, Hedrick Smith, E. W. Kenworthy, and Fox Butterfield (1971) *The Pentagon Papers.* New York: Bantam Books.

Shenon, Philip (1988a) "FBI Chief Disciplines Six for Surveillance Activities." *New York Times* (Sept. 15): 20.

_____ (1988b) "FBI Papers Show Wide Surveillance of Reagan Critics." *New York Times* (Jan. 28): 1, 18.

Sherman, Lawrence (1978) *Scandal and Reform: Controlling Police Corruption.* Berkeley: University of California Press.

Sherrill, Robert (1973) "The Selling of the FBI." In P. Watters and S. Gillers, eds., *Investigating the FBI.* New York: Ballantine Books.

Silberman, Charles (1978) *Criminal Violence, Criminal Justice.* New York: Random House.

Simon, David, and D. S. Eitzen (1986) *Elite Deviance.* Boston: Allyn & Bacon.

Simon, David, and S. Swart (1984) "The Justice Department Focuses on White-Collar Crime: Promises and Pitfalls." *Crime and Delinquency* 30 (Jan.): 107–119.

Skolnick, Jerome H. (1966) *Justice Without Trial.* New York: Wiley.

_____ (1969) *The Politics of Protest.* New York: Ballantine Books.

Smith, Dwight C. (1975) *The Mafia Mystique.* New York: Basic Books.

Solberg, Carl (1976) *Oil Power.* New York: New American Library.

Stern, Gary (1988) "Probing Dissent: A Review of the FBI's 27-month Investigation of CISPES." *First Principles* 13 (Dec.): 6–8.

Strentz, Thomas (1988) "A Terrorist Psychosocial Profile: Past and Present." *FBI Law Enforcement Bulletin* 57 (Apr.): 13–19.

Sullivan, William C., with Bill Brown (1979a) *The Bureau: My Thirty Years in Hoover's FBI.* New York: Norton.

_____ (1979b) "Life with a Tyrant." *Washington Post Magazine* (Sept. 23): 14–21.

Sussman, Barry (1986) "It May Be Morning in America, But It's Midnight in the Polls." *Washington Post National Weekly* (Sept. 22): 37.

Sutherland, Edwin H. (1945) "Is 'White-Collar Crime' Crime?" *American Sociological Review.* 10 (Apr.): 132–139.

Tappan, Paul W. (1947) "Who Is the Criminal?" *American Sociological Review.* 10 (Feb.): 96–102.

Taylor, C. L., and M. C. Hudson (1972) *World Handbook of Political and Social Indicators.* New Haven, Conn.: Yale University Press.

Taylor, Robert E. (1984) "White-Collar Crime Getting Less Attention." *Wall Street Journal* (Feb. 1): 27.

Theoharis, Athan G., ed. (1982) *Beyond the Hiss Case: The FBI, Congress and the Cold War.* Philadelphia: Temple University Press.

_____ (1978) *Spying on Americans.* Philadelphia: Temple University Press.

_____ (1971) *The Seeds of Repression: Harry S. Truman and the Origins of McCarthyism.* Chicago: Quadrangle Books.

Theoharis, Athan G., and John Stuart Cox (1988) *The Boss: J. Edgar Hoover and the Great American Inquisition.* Philadelphia: Temple University Press.

Turner, W. (1970) *Hoover's FBI: The Men and the Myth.* Los Angeles: Sherbourne Press.

Ungar, Sanford J. (1975) *FBI.* Boston: Little, Brown.

U.S. Attorney General (1935, 1938, 1950–1957, 1968–1981) *Annual Report of Attorney General of United States.* Washington, D.C.: U.S. Government Printing Office.

U.S. Bureau of the Budget (1935–1986) *The Budget of the U.S. Government.* Washington, D.C.: U.S. Government Printing Office.

U.S. Comptroller General (1977) *FBI Domestic Intelligence Operations: An Uncertain Future.* Washington, D.C.: U.S. Government Printing Office.

_____ (1976) *FBI Domestic Intelligence Operations—Their Purpose and Scope: Issues That Need to Be Resolved.* Washington, D.C.: U.S. Government Printing Office.

U.S. Congress, Office of Technology Assessment (1988) *Criminal Justice, New Technologies, and the Constitution.* Washington, D.C.: U.S. Government Printing Office.

_____ (1982) *An Assessment of Alternatives for a National Computerized Criminal History System: Summary.* Washington, D.C.: U.S. Government Printing Office.

U.S. Department of Justice, Bureau of Justice Statistics (1987) "Federal Offenses and Offenders: White-Collar Crime." BJS Special Report. Washington, D.C.

_____ (1986) "Tracking Offenders: White-Collar Crime." BJS Special Report. Washington, D.C.

_____ (1985) *Data Quality of Criminal History Records.* Washington, D.C.: U.S. Government Printing Office.

_____ (1980) *National Priorities for the Investigation and Prosecution of White-Collar Crime.* Washington, D.C.: U.S. Government Printing Office.

U.S. House of Representatives (1972–1988) *Hearings Before a Subcommittee of the Committee of Appropriations* (appropriations for FY 1973–1989, Department of Justice). Washington, D.C.: U.S. Government Printing Office.

_____ (1988a) *Hearing Before the Subcommittee on Civil and Constitutional Rights on FBI Undercover Operations.* 100th Cong., 2nd sess. (Mar. 25, 1987). Washington, D.C.: U.S. Government Printing Office.

_____ (1988b) *Hearings Before the Subcommittee on Civil and Constitutional Rights on Dissemination of FBI Arrest Records.* 100th Cong., 1st sess. (Oct. 14 and 21, 1987). Washington, D.C.: U.S. Government Printing Office.

_____ (1987a) *Oversight Hearing on FBI Domestic Security Guidelines Before the Subcommittee on Civil and Constitutional Rights of the Committee on the Judiciary.* 98th Cong., 1st sess. (Apr. 27, 1983). Washington, D.C.: U.S. Government Printing Office.

_____ (1987b) *Oversight Hearings on Terrorism Before the Subcommittee on Civil and Constitutional Rights of the Committee on the Judiciary.* 99th Cong., 1st and 2nd sess. (Aug. 26, 1985 and Feb. 29, May 14, and May 15, 1986). Washington, D.C.: U.S. Government Printing Office.

_____ (1986a) *Hearings Before the Committee on Government Operations on the Federal Role in Investigation of Serial Violent Crime.* 99th Cong., 2nd sess. (Apr. 9 and May 21). Washington, D.C.: U.S. Government Printing Office.

_____ (1986b) *Hearings Before the Subcommittee on Civil and Constitutional Rights of the Committee on the Judiciary on FBI Authorization Request for FY 1986.* 99th Cong., 1st sess. (Apr. 17, 1985). Washington, D.C.: U.S. Government Printing Office.

_____ (1985). *Hearings Before a Subcommittee of the Committee on Government Operations on the Freedom of Information Reform Act.* 98th Cong., 2nd sess. (Aug. 9, 1984). Washington, D.C.: U.S. Government Printing Office.

_____ (1984). Subcommittee on Civil and Constitutional Rights of the Committee on the Judiciary, *Report of Subcommittee on FBI Undercover Operations.* 98th Cong., 2nd sess. Washington, D.C.: U.S. Government Printing Office.

_____ (1983) *Hearings Before the Subcommittee on Civil and Constitutional Rights of the Committee on the Judiciary.* Washington, D.C.: U.S. Government Printing Office.

_____ (1981) *Hearings Before the Subcommittee on Oversight and Investigations of the Committee on Energy and Commerce.* 97th Cong., 1st sess. (Mar. 12 and Apr. 2 and 3). Washington, D.C.: U.S. Government Printing Office.

_____ (1980a) *Hearings on FBI Oversight Before the Subcommittee on Civil and Constitutional Rights of the Committee on the Judiciary.* 96th Cong., 1st and 2nd sess. (Mar. 8, 1979 and Mar. 1980). Washington, D.C.: U.S. Government Printing Office.

_____ (1980b) *Joint Hearings Before the Subcommittee on Energy and Power of the Committee on Interstate and Foreign Commerce and the Subcommittee on Crime of the Committee on the Judiciary.* 96th Cong., 1st sess. (May 30 and June 4, 1979). Washington, D.C.: U.S. Government Printing Office.

_____ (1980c) *Oversight Hearings on Federal Capabilities in Crisis Management and Terrorism Before the Subcommittee on Civil and Constitutional Rights of the Committee on the Judiciary.* 96th Cong., 1st sess. (May 19). Washington, D.C.: U.S. Government Printing Office.

_____ (1979) *Hearings Before the Subcommittee on Crime of the Committee on the Judiciary.* 95th Cong., 2nd sess. (June 21, July 12 and 19, and Dec. 1, 1978). Washington, D.C.: U.S. Government Printing Office.

_____ (1975a) *Hearings Before the Subcommittee on Civil and Constitutional Rights of the Committee on the Judiciary.* 94th Cong., 1st sess. (Feb. 27). Washington, D.C.: U.S. Government Printing Office.

_____ (1975b) *Hearings of the Select Committee on Intelligence.* 94th Cong., 1st sess. (Aug. to Dec.). Washington, D.C.: U.S. Government Printing Office.

_____ (1975c) *Hearings on FBI Counterintelligence Programs Before the Subcommittee on Civil and Constitutional Rights of the Committee on the Judiciary.* 93rd Cong., 1st sess. (Nov. 20, 1974). Washington, D.C.: U.S. Government Printing Office.

U.S. Senate (1988) *Hearings Before the Permanent Subcommittee on Investigations on the Status of Organized Crime.* C-SPAN (Apr. 11). Washington, D.C.: The Cable Satellite Public Affairs Network.

_____ (1987a) *Hearings Before the Committee on the Judiciary on Oversight of the Problem of White-Collar Crime,* parts 1–3. 99th Cong., 2nd sess. (Feb. 27 and May 8, 1986). Washington, D.C.: U.S. Government Printing Office.

_____ (1987b) *Hearings on Nomination of William Webster for CIA Director Before the Select Committee on Intelligence.* 100th Cong., 1st sess. (Apr. 8). Washington, D.C.: U.S. Government Printing Office.

_____ (1984) *Report of the Chairman of the Subcommittee on Security and Terrorism: Impact of Attorney General's Guidelines for Domestic Security Investigations (the Levi Guidelines).* (Nov. 1983). Washington, D.C.: U.S. Government Printing Office.

_____ (1983a) *Final Report of the Select Committee to Study Undercover Activities of Components of the Department of Justice.* 97th Cong., 2nd sess. Washington, D.C.: U.S. Government Printing Office.

_____ (1983b) *Hearings on Domestic Security Guidelines Before the Subcommittee on Security and Terrorism of the Committee on the Judiciary.* 98th Cong., 1st sess. (Mar. 25). Washington, D.C.: U.S. Government Printing Office.

_____ (1982a) *Hearings on Domestic Security (Levi) Guidelines Before the Subcommittee on Security and Terrorism of the Committee on the Judiciary.* 97th Cong., 2nd sess. (June and Aug.). Washington, D.C.: U.S. Government Printing Office.

_____ (1982b) *Hearings on FBI Oversight Before the Subcommittee on Security and Terrorism of the Committee on the Judiciary.* 97th Cong., 2nd sess. (Feb. 4). Washington, D.C.: U.S. Government Printing Office.

_____ (1981) *Hearings Before a Subcommittee of the Committee on Appro-

priations (Department of Justice). 97th Cong., 1st sess. (Mar. 18). Washington, D.C.: U.S. Government Printing Office.

_____ (1980a) *Hearings Before the Committee on the Judiciary on FBI Charter Act of 1979*. 96th Cong., 1st sess. Washington, D.C.: U.S. Government Printing Office.

_____ (1980b) *Hearings Before the Select Committee on Intelligence on the National Intelligence Act of 1980*. 96th Cong., 2nd sess. Washington, D.C.: U.S. Government Printing Office.

_____ (1978) *Hearings Before the Subcommittee on Administrative Practice and Procedure of the Committee on the Judiciary on FBI Statutory Charter*. 95th Cong., 2nd sess. (June to Sept.). Washington, D.C.: U.S. Government Printing Office.

_____ (1976a) *Final Report of the Select Committee to Study Governmental Operations with Respect to Intelligence Activities*. 94th Cong., 2nd sess., Book I. Washington, D.C.: U.S. Government Printing Office.

_____ (1976b) *Final Report of the Select Committee to Study Governmental Operations with Respect to Intelligence Activities*. 94th Cong., 2nd sess. (Apr. 23), Book III. Washington, D.C.: U.S. Government Printing Office.

_____ (1975) *Hearings Before the Select Committee to Study Government Operations with Respect to Intelligence Activities*, 94th Cong., 1st sess., Vol. 6. Washington, D.C.: U.S. Government Printing Office.

_____ (1974). *Hearing Before the Subcommittee on FBI Oversight of the Committee on the Judiciary on Ten-Year Term for FBI Director*. 93rd Cong., 2nd sess. (Mar.). Washington, D.C.: U.S. Government Printing Office.

_____ (1973) *Hearings Before the Committee on the Judiciary on Nomination of L. Patrick Gray to be FBI Director*. 93rd Cong., 1st sess. (Feb. and Mar.). Washington, D.C.: U.S. Government Printing Office.

Walker, Samuel (1989) *Sense and Nonsense About Crime,* 2nd ed., Pacific Grove, Calif.: Brooks/Cole.

_____ (1980) *Popular Justice: A History of American Criminal Justice*. New York: Oxford University Press.

_____ (1977) *A Critical History of Police Reform: The Emergence of Professionalism*. Lexington, Mass.: Heath.

Watters, Pat, and Stephen Gillers, eds. (1973) *Investigating the FBI*. New York: Ballantine Books.

Webster, William H. (1980) "An Examination of FBI Theory and Methodology Regarding White-Collar Crime Investigation and Prevention." *American Criminal Law Review* (Winter): 275–286.

Wecter, Dixon (1971) *The Age of the Great Depression*. Chicago: Quadrangle Books.

Welch, Neil J., and David W. Marston (1984) *Inside Hoover's FBI*. New York: Doubleday.

Werner, Leslie Maitland (1984) "Dealing with the Press: It's One Up and One Out." *New York Times* (Jan. 20): B8.

Whitehead, Donald F. (1956) *The FBI Story: A Report to the People*. New York: Random House.

Wicker, Tom (1973) "A Battle Congress Could Win." *New York Times* (Apr. 5): 45.

Wilensky, Harold L. (1967) *Organizational Intelligence: Knowledge and Policy in Government and Industry.* New York: Basic Books.

Wilson, James Q. (1983a) *Crime and Public Policy.* San Francisco: ICS Press.

_____ (1983b) *Thinking About Crime.* New York: Random House.

_____ (1980) "The Changing FBI: The Road to ABSCAM." *Public Interest* (Spring): 3–14.

Wines, Michael (1989) "FBI Rejects Plan to Widen Computer's Data on Suspects." *New York Times* (Mar. 4): 6.

Wise, David (1976) *The American Police State.* New York: Random House.

Wise, David, and Thomas B. Ross (1964) *The Invisible Government.* New York: Random House.

Wolfe, Alan (1979) *The Rise and Fall of the "Soviet Threat": Domestic Sources of the Cold War Consensus.* Washington, D.C.: Institute for Policy Studies.

Wolfgang, Marvin, Robert Figlio, and Thorsten Sellin (1972) *Delinquency in a Birth Cohort.* Chicago: University of Chicago Press.

Woodiwiss, Michael (1988) *Crime, Crusades, and Corruption: Prohibitions in the United States, 1900–1987.* Totowa, N.J.: Barnes & Noble.

Wright, J. Patrick (1979) *On a Clear Day You Can See General Motors.* New York: Avon Books.

Index

About the Author

Tony G. Poveda is associate professor of sociology at the State University of New York at Plattsburgh. He is the author of numerous journal articles and professional papers, including many relating to the FBI, organizational deviance, delinquency, the fear of crime, and criminological theory. He has been the coordinator of the criminal justice program as well as chair of the sociology department during his nineteen years at SUNY at Plattsburgh.

Dr. Poveda received his doctorate in criminology (D.Crim.) in 1970 from the School of Criminology at the University of California at Berkeley. His initial interests in criminology ranged from criminalistics to delinquency and criminological theory. In the past decade, the crimes of large organizations and various criminal justice policy issues have occupied his attention. His research on the FBI stems from this larger concern with organizational deviance: how is it possible for perfectly legitimate organizations, corporate and governmental, to institutionalize illegal activities in their everyday operations? The occasional disclosure of such practices makes them appear episodic rather than routine and systemic. Dr. Poveda's nine years of research and writing on the FBI converge on this very point: to show how much of FBI organizational behavior is linked to patterns in history and social structure rather than simply an aberration of Hoover's personality or an isolated episode of organizational misconduct unrelated to broader social and historical forces. This research has clear policy implications for the control of organizational misconduct in society, including the control of law enforcement.